BOSWELL THE BIOGRAPHER

April 29th 1793

Geo Dance

Emery Walker Ph. sc.

James Boswell
from a drawing by George Dance R.A.

BOSWELL

THE BIOGRAPHER

BY

GEORGE MALLORY

WITH A PORTRAIT BY GEORGE DANCE, R.A.

LONDON

SMITH, ELDER & CO., 15 WATERLOO PLACE

1912

PREFACE

THE responsibility for upwards of 300 pages in print is a burden which my unaccustomed conscience cannot easily bear, and by accepting it I lose for ever the unassailable dignity of private criticism. In these circumstances I approach my readers in an apologetic frame of mind. I shall not apologise for writing a dull book by explaining in what manner it is interesting. I had thought of doing something of the sort, but at the present moment that course presents insuperable difficulties. An explanation, if not apology, is however necessary ; for this volume is in one sense a compromise. It is less than a biography and more than an essay. It aims at being not a complete Life of Boswell, but an explanation of his character. This purpose may not seem to require so long a treatment as mine. Certainly it would have been easier to say, and easier to read, all that I have said about Boswell's psychology in far fewer words. But my design was to prove my case. Boswell has been so much a subject of controversy that, were I merely to state my views, I should convince, if anyone is to be convinced by me, only those who

had observed the same facts as myself—the facts
upon which those views are based. By bringing
forward the evidence without stint I have hoped to
establish my opinions on a firmer base.

A list of the books to which I have referred is
printed at the beginning of this volume. I am naturally
indebted to the researches of Dr. G. Birkbeck Hill,
to the three biographers of Boswell—Dr. Rogers (in
'Boswelliana'), Mr. Percy Fitzgerald, and Mr. W. K.
Leask—and to the brilliant study by Carlyle. I must
also mention three essays which have been particularly
illuminating—that by W. E. Henley in 'Views and
Reviews,' by Lionel Johnson in 'Post Liminium,'
and by Mr. Birrell in his edition of Boswell's 'Life of
Johnson.'

I am grateful especially to Mr. A. C. Benson, whose
encouragement promoted this enterprise, to Mr. G. L.
Strachey for many valuable suggestions, and to Mr.
E. H. Marsh for correcting my proofs, which was no
mean labour.

GEORGE MALLORY.

CHARTERHOUSE :
July 25, 1912.

BIBLIOGRAPHY

[This is a list of books bearing directly upon Boswell which have been used for this volume.]

Birrell, A., Introduction to his edition of Boswell's
    Life of Johnson .   .   .   .   .   . London, 1906
Boswell, James :
    Elegy on the Death of an Amiable Young Lady .   . 1761
    Ode to Tragedy   1761
    Collection of Original Poems, contributions to   .   . 1762
    The Cub at Newmarket   1762
    Critical Strictures on Mallet's Elvira, by A. Erskine and
        J. Boswell   1763
    Correspondence with the Hon. Andrew Erskine .   . 1763
    Dorando, a Spanish Tale 1767
    Essence of the Douglas Cause 1767
    Account of Corsica, &c., 2nd edition .   .   . 1768
        (1st edition was published 1768)
    British Essays in favour of the Brave Corsicans .   . 1769
    The Hypochondriack in the London Magazine, Oct. 1777
                                             to Dec. 1779
    Letter to the People of Scotland on the Present State of
        the Nation 1783
    Journal of a Tour to the Hebrides.   Ed. G. Birkbeck Hill 1887
        (1st edition 1785)
    Letter to the People of Scotland against the attempt to
        diminish the number of the Lords of Session .   . 1785
    No Abolition of Slavery, or the Universal Empire of Love 1791
    Life of Johnson.   Ed. Right Hon. John Wilson Croker . 1866
    Life of Samuel Johnson.   Ed. G. Birkbeck Hill.   6 vols.
                                          Oxford, 1887[1]
        (1st edition 1791)
    Letters to Temple, reprint .   .   .   . London, 1908[1]
    —— Life of, see Rogers, Fitzgerald, and Leask.
Boswelliana, the Commonplace Book of James Boswell,
                  London, Grampian Club, 1876

[1] All references are to this edition.

Burke, Edmund, Correspondence . . . London, 1824
Burney, Miss, *see* D'Arblay.

Campbell, Rev. Dr. Thomas, Diary . . . London, 1854
Carlyle, Miscellanies . . . . . London, 1872
Chatham, Earl of, Correspondence. 4 vols. . . London, 1838
Collection of Original Poems . . . Edinburgh, 1763
Croker, Right Hon. John Wilson, Correspondence
   and Diaries. 3 vols. . . . . . London, 1884

D'Arblay, Diary of Madame. Ed. Austin Dobson.
   6 vols. . . . . London, 1904
—— Memoirs of Dr. Burney. 3 vols. . . . London, 1832

Edinburgh, Traditions of 1869
Eldon, Lord Chancellor, Life of, by Horace Twiss.
   3 vols. . . . . London, 1844

Fitzgerald, Percy, Life of Boswell . . . London, 1891
Forbes, Sir William, Life of James Beattie . London, 1806

Gentleman's Magazine
Goldsmith, Life by James Prior. 2 vols. . . London, 1837
Gray, Life by Mason. 2 vols. . . . . London, 1807

Hawkins, Sir John, Life of Johnson . . . London, 1787
—— Lætitia Matilda, Memoirs. 2 vols. . . London, 1824
Henley, W. E., Views and Reviews . . . London, 1902
Hill, Dr. George Birkbeck, Life of Johnson. 6 vols. Oxford, 1887
—— Dr. Johnson, his Friends and Critics . . London, 1878
   See also Johnson Club Papers.
Holcroft, Thomas, Memoirs. 3 vols. . . London, 1816
Hume, David, Correspondence . . . . London, 1846

Ireland, S. W. H., The Confessions of W. H.
   Ireland . . . . London, 1805

Johnson, Dr. Samuel, Dictionary . . . London, 1755
—— Lives of the Poets . . . . . London, 1781
—— Journey to the Western Islands . . . London, 1775
Johnson, Lionel, Post Liminium, Critical Essays . London, 1911
Johnson Club Papers, by various hands . . London, 1899

Leask, W. K., James Boswell, Famous Scots Series. Edinburgh, 1896
London Magazine

Macaulay, Critical and Historical Essays. 3 vols. London, 1843
Malone, Life of, Prior . . . . . London, 1860
More, Hannah, Memoirs of. 4 vols. . . . London, 1834

BIBLIOGRAPHY ix

Nichols, John, Literary Anecdotes of the XVIIIth
    Century. 9 vols. . . . . .London, 1812–15
—— Literary History of the XVIIIth Century.
    8 vols. . . . . . . London, 1817–58

Piozzi, Mrs., Autobiography. 2 vols. . . London, 1861
—— Johnson's Letters to. 2 vols. . . . London, 1788
—— Anecdotes of the late Samuel Johnson,
    2nd edition . . . . London, 1789

Raleigh, Sir Walter, Six Essays on Johnson . Oxford, 1910
Reynolds, Sir Joshua, Life by Leslie and Taylor.
    2 vols. . . . . London, 1865
Rogers, Rev. Charles, Memoir of Boswell, in Bos-
    welliana . . . . . .

Taylor, John, Records of My Life . . . London, 1832
Trevelyan, Sir G. O., Life of Fox . . . London, 1912

Walpole, Horace, Letters. 9 vols. . . . London, 1861

BOSWELL THE BIOGRAPHER

CHAPTER I

BOSWELL'S 'Life of Johnson' is, as we all know, a
unique biography ; it has no rival. Its unchallenged
supremacy has a special significance from the position
which Johnson himself retains in literature. For
as it must be admitted that his work has been but
little read since his own day, and that by far his
greatest performance, the compiling of a dictionary,
has in its nature nothing of an artistic appeal, it may
well be supposed that the literary men of this age
find more to stir the imagination in the lives of the
great figures of the nineteenth century, in the romance
of Byron, Shelley, Keats, and at a later date of the Pre-
Raphaelite group, in the peculiar simplicity of Words-
worth, the splendour of Tennyson, and the fervid
passion of Browning. And yet we have for Johnson
a more intimate place which is all his own.

It is because we know him better. Subsequent
biographers, Lockhart, Froude, Trevelyan—to mention

a few of the more successful—have like Boswell written
good biographies : we know much that is interesting
about Scott, Carlyle, and Macaulay. But what we
know of Johnson is more vivid, real, and true; it is
the man himself. Boswell is therefore the first of
biographers. He is first beyond the jealousy of a
rival and above the common earth of imitators—as
Homer is first in epic poetry, as Molière and Racine,
Shakespeare and Milton are all first where they most
excel. And he is first only for this reason, that we
know most intimately the man who was portrayed
by him.

But if the mere extent of our knowledge of Johnson
determines the greatness of Boswell, there is yet
some particular appeal besides, some special charm
that wins us in Boswell's ' Johnson.' When we
come to think of the nature of Boswell's value for
so many people, we shall find that it depends not
altogether upon the completeness of his method or
his capacity for giving expression to it, but also upon
an interest which exists apart from any structural or
artistic quality. The ' Life of Johnson ' is one of
those rare books which have by nature a certain
universality. It exists not for one but for every
generation. It is not for the cultured alone nor for
the uncultured, nor yet, if he exists, for the normal
person. It is everybody's book. And this is a fact
which requires explanation.

It would be easy if we were merely seeking to distinguish that which has a special value or quality from what is merely commonplace, if we simply wished to determine the peculiar flavour and virtue of the work, to find a number of reasons why the book we are speaking of should have a special value among biographies. The careful art of the writer, the vividness of the scenes he depicts, his unrivalled humour, the mere form of what he presents, including as it does all that he meant by biography, the interest we feel in the distinguished men who play, as it were, the minor parts of the drama—all these are responsible in their several degrees for the pleasure we derive from Boswell's ' Johnson.'

But to account for its universality we must look elsewhere—to the simple human interest felt by everyone in two such characters as Johnson and Boswell. A biography may be written about an interesting man by a dull one or about a dull man by an interesting one ; and interest in either may be satisfied by reading it : even when both the men are dull some pleasure may be obtained from a biography by one who is interested in the psychological phenomenon of dullness. The ' Life of Johnson ' may be read with pleasure, and even with something more than pleasure, because both Johnson and his biographer are supremely interesting men. There may be some of Boswell's readers who have pleasure from his *magnum opus*, for the treatment,

as it is technically called ; but it is the subject, or
rather one might say the two subjects, since there
is in it so much also of autobiography, that attract
the greater number of them.   And there must be
many to whom—of these two historic people, Johnson
and Boswell—the more interesting because he was more
interested in himself, the more attractive because we can
see in him more of ourselves, is Boswell the biographer.

.   .   .   .   .

In presenting the literary portrait of a man there
can be no greater error than to indulge in controversy.
It is an error which one may make very readily, for
we have all at heart the love of battle ; moreover, it
is easy to contradict another, and difficult to give a
whole picture of one's own.   And in the case of Boswell
there is matter for controversy particularly obvious
and particularly inviting. Distinguished men have
formed entirely different conceptions of his character
and used the pen with more energy than wisdom to
support their views.   It seems clear now that Boswell
has been widely misunderstood.

We are confronted at the outset by a sort of popular
paradox. Not only Lord Macaulay, but most of Boswell's contemporaries and most of his editors, have
thought of him as nothing more than a fool—they have
supposed with the poet Gray, ' Any fool may write
a most valuable book by chance.'   No one has ever
denied that the ' Life ' is a good book.   No one after

his own generation, till Carlyle, ever denied that Boswell was a bad man, just the mean, snivelling creature imagined by Macaulay.

Modern criticism has done much to raise the besmirched name of the biographer, but has managed at the same time to envelop his character in a sort of generous obscurity. 'Boswell,' Professor Raleigh has boldly exclaimed, 'was a genius.' The Boswellian student will probably agree : but in agreeing we must be cautious not to confuse our ideas about Boswell's character ; to say that a man is a genius is not to say that he is unaccountable for his actions, or even of necessity to imply that he is mad. The genius is often more complex than other men, but not more incomprehensible. It is possible, if we like, to look behind the veil that is drawn between humanity and a particular human being. We can see in a genius not less than in others the meaning of all the names which we use to describe life, of love and sympathy, greed and egoism, hate, fear, joy, and the rest ; of all the qualities that form for better or for worse what we call character, what it is to be kind or cruel, vain or modest, false or true. Nor, when we say that Boswell is a genius, do we preclude the possibility of his being a fool. Boswell was indeed a fool, as is easy enough to show ; but he was not, as was long supposed, a stupid fool.

We do, however, mean something by the term

genius ; and it is something of the inward life.   The
soul of man is composed of combustible matter, and
the violence and quality of its conflagration depend
upon the proportions in which the ingredients are mixed.
In certain cases an abnormal quantity of one substance
or another produces an extraordinary result ; and when
this result can be classified neither as criminal nor lunatic
it is called by the more approved name of genius.

Two questions therefore are to be asked especially
with regard to a genius : First, in what way was the
conflagration peculiar ? Secondly, what were the sub-
stances present in abnormal quantity which caused
the peculiarity ?

It is intended that these two questions shall be
answered with regard to Boswell in the course of this
general inquiry concerning his psychology.   It is held
that Boswell was a genius ; it must be explained in
what his genius consisted, and how, in the end, this
abnormal essence dominated the whole man and
inspired the great work of his life.

.   .   .   .   .

James Boswell was born in Edinburgh on October
29th, 1740.   He came of an old Scottish stock, and his
ancestors, if not eminent, were at least distinguished
men and proud of being the Lairds of Auchinleck.

Of his mother we know but little ; she was,
however, a woman of ' almost unexampled piety and
goodness.'

Lord Auchinleck, his father, figures occasionally in the various authorities for Boswell's 'Life,' and we can get a very good picture of him. Scott gives the following account :

Old Lord Auchinleck was an able lawyer, a good scholar, after the manner of Scotland, and highly valued his own advantages as a man of good estate and ancient family ; and, moreover, he was a strict Presbyterian and Whig of the old Scottish cast. This did not prevent his being a terribly proud aristocrat, and great was the contempt he entertained and expressed for his son James, for the nature of his friendships and the character of the personages of whom he was *engoué* one after another. ' There's nae hope for Jamie, mon,' he said to a friend. ' Jamie is gaen clean gyte. . . . Whose tail do you think he has pinned himself to now, mon ? ' Here the old judge summoned up a sneer of most sovereign contempt. ' A *dominie*, mon—an auld dominie ; he keeped a schule and cau'd it an acaadamy.'

The Laird, as is evident from the account in the ' Tour to the Hebrides ' of Johnson's visit to Boswell's home, held his opinions with that conviction which admits of no discussion. A story of him is related by Scott that when challenged by Johnson to explain the utility of Cromwell's career, he very curtly remarked : ' God, Doctor, he gart kings ken they had a lith [1] in their neck.'

Boswell seems to have summed up the situation at

[1] Joint.

home when he wrote in the *London Magazine* for
1781 :

> I knew a father who was a violent Whig and
> used to attack his son for being a Tory, upbraiding
> him with being deficient in noble sentiments of liberty,
> while at the same time he made this son live under
> his roof in such bondage as he was not only afraid
> to stir from home without leave like a child, but durst
> scarcely open his mouth in his father's presence.
> This was sad living.

The problem of youth is one of selection. Not
many of us accept for ourselves the whole of our inheritance. Of the influences of our early years there
are some which we reject ; and the judgments which
we make about the problems that affected us when
young, differ as a rule from those about other questions
which come upon us only in maturer years. In
youth we must either love or hate—there is no indifference ; and so in youth very often are formed the
prejudices of a lifetime. Thus it was with Boswell.
It was inevitable that the inflexible, hard-headed old
judge, and the gay, clever son, should agree very ill.
The latter contrived to be in many ways the exact
antithesis of his father, and he had the courage of his
opinions. It is remarkable, when we think of the
violence of the old Whig's political views, that in 1745
Boswell ' wore a white cockade and prayed for King
James.' The advances of an uncle it is true were
able to purchase his political sympathies, and for the

sum of one shilling Boswell became a Whig. But it is more decorous, at the age of five, to side with one's father without the persuasion of a silver bribe, especially upon a question of so great importance as the choice of a sovereign. For his tutor, Mr. Dunn, James seems to have retained no startling degree of affection or even of respect ; for it was he who ' discovered a narrowness of information concerning the dignitaries of the Church of England. He talked before Dr. Johnson of fat bishops and drowsy deans, and in short seemed to believe the illiberal and profane scoffings of professed satirists or vulgar railers ' ; and so brought upon himself the admirable rebuke : ' Sir, you know no more of our Church than a Hottentot.'

In the uncongenial atmosphere of home Boswell learnt, no doubt, to dislike instruction and to mistrust what he was told about the way to live, about manners in the old use of the word. There is, however, the trace of a pious mother's influence in the respect which Boswell always showed for religion and for principles. To know what he thought right or wrong was always of importance to him, however slight the relation to his practice of these moral decisions. It is possible indeed that he could never have been better than a tyro in the art of living : but the close-fettered days of this unfortunate childhood must be partly responsible for the fact.

When the term of his education at home was accomplished, Boswell very properly went to school at Edinburgh. We have reason to complain, if we may complain at all, that we can know nothing of Boswell's school life. It is idle to conjecture what it was like. We may only suppose that school was to him a place of comparative freedom, and that to his schoolfellows his presence there was a valuable source of merriment, and perhaps also an occasion of maliciousness.

From school Boswell went by a natural sequence to Edinburgh University : he was barely seventeen years old when the change took place. It was at Edinburgh University, at Hunter's Greek class, that Boswell met his lifelong friend William Temple.

Temple is distinguished as the grandfather of an archbishop. Beyond this his life has no considerable distinction ; and beyond the fact that he was Boswell's friend it has no peculiar interest. His eminence in the immediate affairs of this world may be rightly judged from the unembellished statement that, after his ordination in 1766, he remained a country parson, first at Mamhead, near Exeter, and later at St. Gluvias, in Cornwall, for his entire life. It is a curiously undecorated career for one who obtained so large a measure not merely of Boswell's friendship, but of his admiration.

A sad mischance has denied us at least the gratifica-

tion of curiosity by hiding from our view, and perhaps
destroying, the letters of Temple to Boswell ; those
qualities which attracted the youthful biographer,
and completely won his confidence, are no doubt
exposed therein ; but we may not see. Boswell's
own letters however reveal something of his correspondent's character. Temple in the first place—
and this perhaps is the most important fact—was
literary. He was evidently a far better scholar than
Boswell, and knew more about books. He was a
writer too in a small way. He published several
unpretentious volumes. They have no particular
interest that demands our attention, but one of them,
' An Essay on the Clergy, &c.,' ' by some divine mischance,' as Mr. Seccombe puts it, ' materially aided
his prospects.' Temple's ability seems rather to have
been that of a critic. In the letters that he wrote to
Boswell he pronounced his views about books and
authors : Boswell esteemed his opinions highly, and
there was a proposal, apparently fruitless, that these
passages should be collected into a book. It would
be wrong to assume from Boswell's optimistic remarks
that Temple was really capable of writing anything
valuable. But his opinion was in one instance at
least supported by eminent men of letters. Boswell
quoted in a periodical an appreciation of Gray which
Temple wrote at the time of that poet's death ; Mason
thought this so good that he inserted it in his ' Life

of Gray '; and Dr. Johnson afterwards included the same passage in the ' Lives of the Poets.'

Temple, as we see, is not entitled to the fame of Letters; but it is important to realise, since he was the greatest friend both of the young and the old Boswell, that though he had not the qualities that deserve success, and had not the good fortune that may bring it by chance, he had, however, a certain distinction.

There are other reasons for Boswell's preference. If neither Temple nor Boswell was a successful man, yet they both desired success in a quite extraordinary degree, and in the early days of their friendship at Edinburgh this was a strong link. They perceived, no doubt, that they were unlike the majority of students, and concluded they were better than the rest. They looked forward to brilliant careers and elegant fame, to the respect of princes and the friendship of the ingenious. Boswell lived for the greater part of his life in a palace of boyish dreams where Wishes became Destiny, and it is fair to suppose that Temple at the Scottish University shared this luxury of anticipation. He, too, could look back to the Edinburgh days and consider if he were becoming ' the great man, as we used to say.' And in later life the link held firm; for neither of them was ' the great man ' in the sense that he intended. If they were companions in hopeful optimism when young, they were equally

companions at a maturer age in the discontent and
despair of unrealised ambition.

It might be supposed that any friend of Boswell
would play the part of the strong man. He might
not have the capacity of Dr. Johnson for sweeping
away cobwebs and for discouraging complaint, but
one would expect to find him upon the same platform.
Temple, however, did not take this attitude. On the
contrary it was Boswell who encouraged Temple.
Not once but many times we find in the letters that
Temple has told the tale of his evil fortune in tones of
despondency, and Boswell tries to present the circumstances in a more favourable light. Boswell perhaps
did not do this very well. Neither the cheerfulness
of optimism nor the consolation of philosophy is
sufficient for the occasion; and it may be doubted
whether the philosophy advocated by Boswell was
anything more than an affectation of indifference.
But it does him credit that he should have made the
attempt to console, and at the same time displays
the weakness of Temple's character. Certainly this
was not the kind of man to exert a strong influence.
Boswell seems to have regarded him in the light of a
father confessor with whom a certain ceremony is
to be performed, and is reproved and forgiven by a
natural sequence, which adds nothing but pleasure
to the agreeable duty of confession. Temple expos-
tulates in the *rôle* of parson when the conduct of

his friend is particularly damnable ; it is possible there shall be a 'blaze hereafter,' and one must at least be on the safe side.   So Boswell no doubt understood it.   The mild reproofs of his clerical friend never for a moment deterred him either from doing or from telling of his deed.   He came to expect and even to like them.   ' Admonish me, but forgive me,' he says after a particularly detailed account of his amours ; and at a later date, in an expression which seems to epitomise the relations of the pastor and his erring sheep, ' Your soft admonitions,' he writes, ' would at any time calm the tempests of my soul.'

It is clear that Boswell had no moral respect for Temple ; it was not in search of guidance that he told stories of his profligacy, but simply because he liked to tell them.   Boswell, as his friend remarked, mounted the hobby-horse of his own temperament ; this was his perennial and unfailing interest, and the irrepressible delight which he had in his own feelings and performances found an outlet in the ' Letters to Temple ' and in many amusing passages in the ' Life of Johnson.'

Boswell no doubt was capable of self-revelation without encouragement, and it is difficult for this reason to tell how much sympathy he had from his friend.   Temple wanted to hear from Boswell ; he asked him to write, and praised his letters.   But his mild disapproval was probably genuine.   When he

accuses Boswell of neglecting a friend or of unkindness
to his father, he must have thought himself a more
considerate man. He was not like Boswell, a tippler,
and seems to have been really distressed by the other's
intemperate habits. In a manuscript diary, reports
Mr. Seccombe, he describes Boswell, no doubt in a
moment of irritation, as ' irregular in conduct and
manners, selfish, indelicate, no sensibility or feeling
for others.' And yet Temple himself was not above
a gross fault ; he talks of a ' dear infidel,' and Boswell
exclaims that he is exceeded by his friend. Boswell
no doubt made the most of any lapse on Temple's
part from the path of rectitude ; he would like to feel
that he had the support of a respectable companion.
His conscience was by no means complacent, and it
would become more tranquil if one whom he respected
were in the same boat with himself. It is conceivable
that Temple encouraged Boswell's confidence with the
object of controlling him as much as he could ; his
advice certainly was always that he should get well
married instead of carrying on a number of flirtations.
But it is difficult to believe, if we read the letters
carefully, that Temple ever appeared to be shocked
by Boswell's confessions ; and to the latter no doubt
that was an encouragement.

In brief, we may describe Temple as a refined and
well-intentioned creature, but hardly wise and not
courageous. His marriage was so much a failure that

he sought at one time a colonial chaplaincy with the object of living apart from his wife. He was discontented with his lot and inclined rather to complain acrimoniously than to make the best of it. He had apparently no staunch qualities to influence a friend ; and this friend needed a firm monitor.

.   .   .   .   .

The date of the first of Boswell's letters to Temple is July 1758. In 1763 he met Johnson. In the five years between these dates we see Boswell in a number of characteristic lights. The period from eighteen to twenty-three is commonly held to mark a special change and development in a man's character. In Boswell's, however, we do not see this very strongly. As he grew up he did fewer, no doubt, of the wild things of youth. But he seems hardly to have become older in the ordinary way, until towards the close of his life. He was always to the world the gay, good-humoured, sociable being, with a strong vein of fatuous buffoonery, that we see in these early years. A great difficulty in rightly understanding Boswell's life lies in this fact. It seems impossible at times to realise that this was a serious man ; he appears to find the world and himself such a preposterous joke. And yet if he saw to the full the humour of living, he felt too very keenly that it was an important matter, that there were real standards. No one has valued more the opinion of others about himself, and no one

has experienced more miserably the bitterness of
disappointed ambition. It must be our duty, then,
to mark, with all the follies and frivolities which express the youth he retained so long, a more serious
nature within, which showed itself also from time to
time to the outer world.

The course of Boswell's life during this period of
five years may be briefly followed in chronological
order. In 1758 he was at Edinburgh University, and
it is from there that his first letter to Temple is dated.
The summer vacation was spent on the Northern
Circuit with his father and Sir David Dalrymple,
afterwards also a Scottish judge with the title of Lord
Hailes. In November 1759, he entered Adam Smith's
class for Moral Philosophy in Glasgow University.
In 1760 he paid his first visit to London, and in the
spring of 1761 returned to Edinburgh, where he resided
until the close of 1762 ; he then went for the second
time to London. It was upon this second visit that
he met Dr. Johnson.

It is characteristic of these years that he did not
quite know what he was or what he wanted. He was
posing now in one guise and now in another, wondering
the while what his serious purpose might be. At
Edinburgh University he seems to have wished to
appear an intellectual cynic. He writes to Temple :

Don't be surprised if your grave, sedate, philosophic
friend, who used to carry it so high, and talk with such
composed indifference of the beauteous sex, and whom

c

you used to admonish not to turn an old man too soon
—don't be thunderstruck if this same fellow should
all at once *subito furore obreptus* commence Don
Quixote for his adorable Dulcinea.

The inference is clear ; the *subito furore obreptus*
type of conduct is a great change from a sedate
indifference.

He often adopted the *rôle* of the wise counsellor.
His letters to Temple are full of excellent advice. It
is always hard to be quite certain that Boswell is
serious, but it is probable that he was sincere enough
in this. He was ready always with sympathy and
kind actions for his friend, and we may conjecture
that besides wishing to appear wise beyond his years
he thought that Temple could best be served by the
commonplace advice of the old to the young.

But it is pre-eminently as the promising young
littérateur that we see Boswell in these years. He
became acquainted with many interesting people, who
were attracted, no doubt, by a clever young man, fond
of literature and appearing less ignorant than most
young men. Lord Hailes, Lord Kames, and Dr.
Robertson were numbered among his friends. Even
Hume took notice of him : ' We talk a great deal of
genius, fine learning, improving in our style, &c., but
I am afraid solid learning is much wore out. Mr.
Hume, I think, is a very proper person for a young
man to cultivate an acquaintance with.' Boswell
was not eighteen when he wrote these words. They

suggest an amusing picture of a clever and conceited young genius. He was admitted in 1761 to the Select Society, a distinguished group of men who represented the best learning of Edinburgh—a high compliment this, both to his brains and to his social qualities.

Among Boswell's friends of the aristocracy of letters were several younger men. Charles Dilly, the publisher, who was afterwards host at the famous dinner when Dr. Johnson met Jack Wilkes, was a native of Edinburgh; and George Dempster, who became M.P. for the burghs of Fife and Forfar in 1762, was, like Boswell, a member of the Select Society; it was he who afterwards appeared as the disciple of Hume and Rousseau, and of whom Johnson said, ' I have not met with any man for a long time who has given me such general displeasure.'

A greater friend than either of these, and one who had far more influence in forming the literary tastes of Boswell, was the Honourable Andrew Erskine. This lively young gentleman was both soldier and writer. His interest in literature was not of a very creative order : he edited, however, in 1760 and 1761, two volumes of a ' Collection of Original Poems by the Rev. Mr. Blacklock and other Scotch Gentlemen,' to which both he and Boswell contributed; in 1764, he published a farce in two acts, and in 1773 he issued a poem of twenty-two quarto pages intended ' to expose the false taste for florid description which prevails in modern poetry.' He appears to have had considerable discrimination ; he was an early admirer of the poet Burns, and Burns, in a letter to a friend, praises some of Erskine's songs ; an eminent publisher describes him as having ' an excellent taste in the fine arts.' Such a man may well have had influence with Boswell, and the two became associated in several small literary ventures.

The early tastes and tendencies of Boswell in literary matters are connected with several influences of a different nature. There was always a strong instinct of rebellion in Boswell, and with him it found expression in sympathy for those whom the world rejected. Some of his friends among those who sought favour of the Muses were therefore less successful and less respectable than the distinguished members of the Select Society, the learned and the grave.

Several of these friends were connected in various ways with the stage. Acting was not supported as an art in Edinburgh, nor countenanced as a profession, at the time when Boswell was an undergraduate at the University. But he came in contact with a Mr. Love who, it would seem, was the first to encourage his sympathy with the drama. Mr. Love had been connected at one time with Drury Lane Theatre ; fortune cannot have favoured him greatly, since he left London for Edinburgh ; and there after fruitless attempts to practise private theatricals he became a teacher of elocution. It was in this last capacity that Boswell met him.

The lessons of Mr. Love were apparently of some
use to Boswell ; for Dr. Johnson said in commendation
of his English accent, ' Sir, your pronunciation is
not offensive ' ; and Miss Burney too speaks approv-
ingly. Mr. Love became the great friend of Boswell
after Temple had proceeded to the University of
Cambridge. He is mentioned in the first of the
' Letters to Temple ' as the only other confidant of
Boswell in a matter of the heart ; and in the next
letter he is called his ' second-best friend.' Boswell
says of him : ' He has not only good taste, genius
and learning, but a good heart.' He must in any case
have been a man of singular virtue, for it was he who
persuaded Boswell to keep a diary. ' I went along
with my father to the Northern Circuit and was so
happy as to be in the same chaise as Sir David Dalrymple the whole way. I kept an exact journal,
at the particular desire of my friend Mr. Love, and
sent it to him in sheets every post.' So was the habit
of ' memorandising ' begun. Boswell was destined
no doubt to form that habit ; it was the most vital
factor in his method of biography ; and it was besides
a complete expression in itself of that inner secret
which, by a magic touch, was to marshal the soul of
a glorious man before the eyes of us all. The wheel
of Fate might have turned ever so little differently
for Boswell and altered the whole course of his mortal
existence ; but if it were still to be Boswell, there

must still have been the tablets; and his title to immortality would have been secured by these alone. And yet, though the tablets are Boswell's by indubitable birthright, we may allow ourselves a pious exclamation at the name of Mr. Love.

When Boswell went to Glasgow he made friends with another actor in depressed circumstances. ' The merchants of Glasgow,' Dr. Rogers tells us, ' tolerated theatrical representations, obtaining on their boards such talent as their provincial situation could afford.' Boswell evidently took an interest in the Glasgow theatre. One of those who sought a livelihood there was a certain Francis Gentleman, a native of Ireland, and originally an officer in the army. ' This amiable gentleman sold his commission in the hope of obtaining fame and opulence as a dramatic author.' He obtained neither, and became an actor; and so he qualified to be the friend of Boswell, who entertained him, and ' encouraged him to publish an edition of Southern's " Tragedy of Oroonoco." ' To Boswell it must have been a double pleasure to play the patron and to read the dedication of the volume addressed to himself. Mr. Gentleman thought well of the man who had befriended him, and the dedication ends thus :

> But where, with honest pleasure, she can find
> Sense, taste, religion, and good nature joined,
> There gladly will she raise her feeble voice
> Nor fear to tell that Boswell is her choice.

On his return to Edinburgh Boswell became more
than ever concerned with the ill-favoured art of the
drama. ' The popular prejudice against theatricals,'
says Dr. Rogers, ' was a sufficient cause for our author
falling into the opposite extreme ; he threw his whole
energies into a movement which led, six years afterwards, to a theatre being licensed in the capital.'

He became associated in this movement with a
Mr. David Ross, the most important save Garrick
of his actor friends. Ross, too, was acquainted with
misfortune, yet not without earning some kind of
celebrity. When he made his first appearance at
Drury Lane, ' he was approved by a polite and distinguishing audience, who seemed to congratulate themselves on seeing an actor whom they imagined capable
of restoring to the stage the long-lost character
of the real fine gentleman ' ; and his first success
was followed by a considerable measure of popularity
at Covent Garden. He must have been a good actor,
for Garrick is said to have been jealous of his reputation. It was the ' fine gentleman ' we may suppose
that Boswell particularly admired. ' Poor Ross ! '
he exclaims at the time of his death ; ' he was an unfortunate man in some respects ; but he was a true
bon-vivant, a most social man, and never was without
good eating and drinking and hearty companions.'
These qualities were no doubt to Boswell the highest
recommendation. And he seems besides to have found

the society of actors in general especially congenial. In his own character there was much of the actor : he was so often conscious of a part to be played ! And he had a way of occupying the stage when conversing in company. He may have found, too, that actors appreciated best his lively social qualities.

Ross, though irregular habits, as we are told, may have interfered with his advancement, was evidently a man of some talents and some enthusiasm, and eventually he succeeded in starting a theatre in Edinburgh. He had some respect, it would appear, for Boswell's talents ; for on the occasion of his first performance in the capital of Scotland, he requested Boswell to write a prologue which the actor himself was to recite. Boswell can hardly have seen much of Ross in later years, but the friendship between them was preserved, and Boswell was chief mourner at the actor's funeral in 1790.

One other friend of Boswell's in these early years must be mentioned here. Actors may have had particular qualities which made them attractive to him, but Boswell in any case had always a sympathy with misfortune which was mere good-nature ; he had at the same time an interest in the shady walks of life, in human nature exhibited under stress of adverse circumstances, and in an added poignancy to the performance of intellect when spurred by poverty. These feelings may account for his friendship with

Mr. Derrick the poet. Derrick, like Love and Gentleman and Ross, was somewhat of a failure. He had
been apprenticed to a linendraper, and deserted the
concerns of trade to seek his fortune as an actor ;
when Boswell met him as a man of thirty-six he aspired
to be a poet. His verses must have been remarkably
poor ; Boswell refers to some of them as ' infamously
bad.' Dr. Johnson, who knew him slightly, ' reproved
his muse and condemned his levity.' But he was
a writer, and that meant a great deal to Boswell ;
the mark of his profession was a sign of grace. The
Doctor was probably right when he said : ' It is to
his being a writer that he owes anything he has. Sir,
had not Derrick been a writer, he would have been
sweeping the crosses in the streets, and asking half-
pence from everybody that passed.' Derrick no
doubt was a gay companion, and Boswell evidently
liked him, though not excessively. He was of some
importance, too, in the youth of Boswell, for he was his
first tutor in the ways of London, and these were not
entirely good ways.

.   .   .   .   .

It was as a poet that Boswell was to make his *début*
in literary performance. Besides his contributions
to the collections edited by Erskine, he published in
1761 two longer poems, ' An Elegy on the Death of an
Amiable Young Lady ' and ' An Ode to Tragedy.'
The latter was apparently a serious attempt at poetry ;

but it serves only to demonstrate that poetry was quite beyond Boswell's grasp.   His productions were typical of the eighteenth century.   He had no imagination teeming with beautiful images, such as came to a later generation ; the graces and conceits of the Elizabethans, and the appeal of Nature, were alike unknown to him ; and he never acquired the technical skill which was the merit of the best poets of the age. The ' Ode ' is neither better nor worse than might be expected from a wholly misdirected literary talent ; it could have been written by almost anyone who had read a certain quantity of English verse.

The ' Elegy ' also was intended to express a serious vein.   It would be an error to suppose that Boswell meant to be satirical ; but he evidently saw that he might be laughed at as extravagant, and published it without alteration, introducing some prefatory letters to ridicule its sentimentality.

In 1762 he published, apparently at his own expense, ' The Cub at Newmarket, a tale.'   This, as he states in the preface, is the story told in doggerel verse of his visit to the Jockey Club at Newmarket. He had been taken there when in London by Lord Eglinton, and was discovered in the coffee-room while in the act of composing.   The Cub at Newmarket is, of course, himself.   Lord Eglinton afterwards introduced him to the Duke of York, to whom Boswell, not unwillingly we may suppose, read out his poem.   It

must have been a triumphant moment for the young
author, and he felt obliged to preserve the memory of
it by asking and obtaining leave to dedicate the poem
to his Royal Highness—he desired, as he explains
in the preface, ' to let the world know that this same
Cub has been laughed at by the Duke of York, has
been read to his Royal Highness by the genius himself, and warmed by the immediate beams of his kind
indulgence.' The humorous poem is not remarkably
funny ; one stanza which describes himself is perhaps
worthy to be quoted :

> He was not of the iron Race,
> Which sometimes Caledonia grace,
> Though he to combat could advance—
> Plumpness shone in his countenance ;
> And Belly prominent declar'd
> That he for Beef and Pudding car'd ;
> He had a large and pond'rous head,
> That seemed to be composed of lead ;
> From which hung down such stiff, lank hair,
> As might the crows in Autumn scare.

But besides being a somewhat light-headed poet,
Boswell was anxious to appear as the ' young Buck.'
' The Epistle of a London Buck to his Friend ' is the
title of one of his publications in the ' Collection of
Original Poems.' There is also a confused story of a
club he formed in Edinburgh called the ' Soaping Club,'
which existed apparently for Bacchanalian purposes ;
Boswell was the king of the Soapers and wrote some
verses about himself :

Boswell is pleasant and gay,
For frolic by nature designed ;
He heedlessly rattles away
When the company is to his mind.
'This maxim,' he says, ' you may see,
We never can have corn without chaff ' ;
So not a bent sixpence cares he,
Whether *with* him, or *at* him you laugh.

Boswell does women adore,
And never once means to deceive,
He 's in love with at least half a score ;
If they 're serious he smiles in his sleeve.
He has all the bright fancy of youth,
With the judgment of forty and five ;
In short, to declare the plain truth,
There is no better fellow alive.'

Stories about ' frolic ' (to use Boswell's word) are not as a rule very laughable, and we are perhaps too apt to consider them as merely childish and contemptible when they fail to amuse us. The exact atmosphere of the moment which accounts for its merriment is forgotten too often and seldom reproduced, and we are left cold after a recital of such behaviour as we may suppose the Club of Soapers to have indulged in. In Boswell's character there was a large vein of buffoonery which is apt when recounted by anyone but himself to appear stupid enough. But in reality it seems to have contained a true sense of the incongruous, and had at least the success of making people laugh. What an incomparable moment that must have been when Boswell, as one of the audience at Drury Lane theatre, took upon himself to imitate the lowing of a cow ! ' I was so successful in this boyish frolic,' he relates, ' that the universal cry of the galleries was : " Encore the cow ! Encore the cow ! " '

There is nothing very brilliant about Boswell's comic verses, but it is curious that those we have quoted should represent the facts so closely :

> So not a bent sixpence cares he
> Whether *with* him or *at* him you laugh ;

these lines express exactly the social principle which Boswell adopted. He had no objection to men laughing at his oddities so long as they laughed good-humouredly.

He wished to find gaiety in every company, and it is just to say that he brought more than his share of mirth regardless of dignity.

There are many other instances of these self-portraits, anonymous sometimes, but easily to be recognised. We can hardly do better than illustrate Boswell's life by his own words about himself, because upon this subject he found it necessary, when he had anything to say, to say it truthfully. In another early literary venture, the correspondence between Erskine and Boswell, which these two young gentlemen published, there is a letter of Boswell's containing an account of the author of the ' Ode to Tragedy,' which he had published anonymously ; he thus describes himself :

The author of the ' Ode to Tragedy,' is a most excellent man : he is of an ancient family in the West of Scotland, upon which he values himself not a little. At his nativity there appeared omens of his future greatness ; his parts are bright, and his education has been good ; he has travelled in postchaises miles without number ; he is fond of seeing much of the world ; he eats of every good dish, especially apple-pie ; he drinks old hock ; he has a very fine temper ; he is somewhat of a humourist, and a little tinctured with pride ; he has a good, manly countenance, and he owns himself to be amorous ; he has infinite vivacity, yet is observed at times to have a melancholy cast ; he is rather fat than lean, rather short than tall, rather young than old ; his shoes are neatly made, and he never wears spectacles.

The ' Letters between the Honourable Andrew Erskine and James Boswell, Esq.' are the most re-markable in some ways of these early literary ventures. The letters were evidently written from the first with a view to publication. They are completely frivolous, but attempt to be satirical and amusing. Boswell and Erskine wish to appear as two young men of society who are budding poets and have brilliant wit. They hoped; perhaps, to take the world by storm like the Admirable Crichton and his friend Aldus. The result, if far from brilliant, is certainly clever and amusing.

The *rôle* which Boswell played in this theatrical performance may be illustrated by some passages of his own letters. He was before everything else the knight of chivalry—a chivalry which was occupied exclusively with an excess of romantic attachment and an adoring worship of female charm. Boswell in real life was extravagant enough, we may suppose, in his homage to women ; but his performance can have hardly reached the standard set up in the letters to Erskine :

Lady B—— entreats me to come and pass the Christmas holidays with her. Guess, O guess ! what transport I felt at reading that ; I did not know how to contain my elevation of spirits. I thought myself one of the greatest geniuses in Europe ; I thought I could write all sorts of books and work at all handi-craft trades ; I imagined that I had fourscore millions of money out at interest, and, that I should actually be chosen Pope at the next election.

It is conceivable of course that Boswell imagined that he had the fourscore millions ; there is evidence which might suggest a misconception of this kind. And it is even possible that he entertained at some time the dream of becoming Pope. But that at all events is not meant to appear. It is meant as the froth of youthful gallantry. There is no deception. We are not expected to suppose that Boswell was like this : we are expected merely to be amused at the pose.

He represents himself also as the *bon-vivant*. There are allusions to splendid feasts and there is an ' Ode to Gluttony.' The poet is always very much to the fore, and his behaviour is supposed to be

marked occasionally by a vein of seriousness, which is
to suggest the anxious cogitation of the philosopher :

> We had a splendid ball. . . . I exhibited my exist-
> ence in a minuet, and as I was dressed in a full
> chocolate suit and wore my most solemn counten-
> ance, I looked, as you used to tell me, like the fifth
> act of a deep tragedy.

Perhaps the most significant passages in these
letters are where Boswell plays the cynic :

> A light heart may bid defiance to fortune. And
> yet, Erskine, I must tell you that I have been a little
> pensive of late, amorously pensive, and disposed to
> read Shenstone's ' Pastoral on Absence,' the tendency of
> which I greatly admire. A man who is in love is like
> a man who has got the toothache : he feels in most
> acute pain, while nobody pities him. In that situation
> I am at present, but well do I know that I will not be
> long so. So much for inconstancy !

Boswell represented himself in the letters to Erskine
very much as he affected to be in real life—the gay
young wit with a serious background, the jolly good
fellow and at the same time the budding genius, and
finally, the cynical philosopher, such as he alludes to
in the first letter to Temple. The whole picture is
exaggerated and laughed at : yet we feel very often
that the laughter has a hollow ring. It is the laughter
in reality of one who wishes to protect himself from
ridicule by jesting at his own expense. The real

Boswell peeps through in many places. The remark about Shenstone's 'Pastoral on Absence' might equally well have been made in all seriousness to Temple.

In another letter he says :

Allow me a few more words. I live here in a remote corner of an old ruinous house, where my ancestors have been very jovial. What a solemn idea rushes on my mind ! They are all gone : I must follow. Well, and what then ? I must shift about to another subject. The best I can think of is a sound sleep : so good-night !

The sentiment about his dead ancestors is a flash of the true Boswell as bright and real as anything in Pepys' Diary. The pleasure which the thought gave him and the pleasure he had in imparting it to another cannot be concealed by the forced levity of the ending.

The friendship of Boswell with Erskine was responsible for yet another publication ; these two with George Dempster collaborated to criticise some dramatic performances in 'Critical Strictures on Mallet's " Elvira." ' This brochure [1] would seem to have been written in the same flippant manner as the 'Letters.' Mr. Mallet's 'Elvira' came in for plenty of abuse, but there was no serious attempt at literary criticism. And yet this publication must rank with

---

[1] I have not seen a copy ; *v.* Fitzgerald, *Life of Boswell* i. 37–38, and *Life of Garrick.*

D

the letters as the most important exhibition of Boswell's talents up to the age of twenty-three.

.   .   .   .   .

In London no doubt Boswell enjoyed himself very well, and Edinburgh seemed a dull town by comparison. In May, 1761, Boswell writes :

A young fellow whose happiness was always centred in London, who had at last got there, and had begun to taste its delights, who had got his mind filled with the most gay ideas,—getting into the Guards, being about the court, enjoying the happiness of the *beau monde*, and the company of men of genius, in short everything that he could wish,—consider this poor fellow hauled away to the town of Edinburgh, obliged to conform to every Scotch custom or be laughed at— ' Will you hae some jeel ? oh fie ! oh fie ! '—his flighty imagination quite cramped, and he obliged to study Corpus Juris Civilis, and live in his father's strict family ; is there any wonder, Sir, that the unlucky dog should be somewhat fretful ?

This passage from a letter to Temple explains very well the attitude of Boswell towards the world at the age of twenty-one. He is the gay, frank, talkative, amusing, sociable young man, frivolous if you like and a little unrestrained in his affections, extravagant one would rather say in that matter as in others, but quite without malice.

The profession to which for a time he aspired was that of a soldier. In the Guards, no doubt, he would be able to enjoy just that kind of life which attracted him, the ' happiness of the *beau monde*,' with no thought of what is supposed to be the serious business of soldiering, and probably a decided preference for the gay, smart costume. But for the army he was clearly unsuited. ' I like your son,' said the Duke of Argyll to his father ; ' that boy must not be shot at for three-and-sixpence a day.' It was resolved accordingly that he should study law.

We hear so much in the letters to Temple of Boswell's amusements that it is easy to lose sight altogether of a less frivolous side to his life. It is safe at least to conjecture that he read a good many books at this time ; in the *rôle* of a young *littérateur* he would naturally keep up with the books that were coming out ; we know that he read Johnson and Hume and Harris, and, from the knowledge of literature that he always showed, we may infer that he read much else besides.

The law studies he took seriously at this time.

I can assure you [he writes to Temple] the study of law here is a most laborious task. In return for yours, I shall give you an account of my studies. From nine to ten I attend the law class ; from ten to eleven study at home, and from one to two attend a College upon Roman Antiquities. The afternoons and evenings I likewise spend in study ; I never walk except on Saturdays.

This is hard work for one at a University ! And especially for one of Boswell's temperament. There is no great amount of diligence associated as a rule with the youth of either the literary or the very sociable character.

The truth is that Boswell was very far from being idle ; he had great energy, and often applied himself to something which interested him with fervent industry ; he was irregular no doubt, as are very many people who work in this way.

An indication of the channel into which his industry was to be turned is provided by that journal (and what pains it must have cost !), which he began to keep while travelling with Lord Hailes and his father ; and at the same time he was made aware of the existence of Dr. Johnson as a great writer in London, began to read his works, and also no doubt to feel, as he afterwards said, that ' highest reverence for their author, which had grown up with my fancy into a kind of mysterious veneration, by figuring to myself a state of solemn elevated abstraction, in which I supposed him to live in the immense metropolis of London.'

Boswell also seems to have been deeply interested in religion even during these early years. While at Glasgow University his views underwent a violent revolution, most distressing to his parents, and he became for a short time a Roman Catholic. There is no reason to suppose that Boswell was in any way frivolous when he took this decisive step. He clearly hated the Presbyterianism of his youth and was probably in search of some creed to take its place. He cannot, however, have gained much credit from this episode, since it was mixed up in some way with an elopement with a Roman Catholic lady.

It is probable that Boswell was in earnest both about the young lady and about his religion. But since, in order to be entirely respectable, it is often necessary to give a hypocritical consistency to our fickle inclinations, we are not thought to be serious if we do not affect to be constant. We can assume, in the case of most people, from a sort of faith they hold in the durability of sentiment, and a desire which they have to prove by a time test the depth of their emotion, that the feelings which do not appear to endure are trivial and shallow. In Boswell's case we cannot make this assumption ; though he affected much, he yet had real and vivid feelings ; but since they could never be wholly dissociated from the pleasure which they gave him, they were both various and contradictory ; he could be grave and sedate at one moment and gay and boyish the next, yet really feeling something both of the gravity and the gaiety of living ; he could be almost in the same breath either the romantic lover or the indifferent cynic, and yet feel something both of the romance of love and of the aloofness which has tasted often enough the joys and sorrows of life ; he forgot more quickly than most men, but did not care very often—while it was part of his inconsistency that he did sometimes care—to conceal the fundamental elasticity of his nature.

This volatility of Boswell, exhibited especially in his sexual inconstancy, was in itself but a phase of an innate and irrepressible candour which, in spite of a lifelong desire and struggle for respectability, showed itself very often to his friend Temple in the ' Letters,' and not infrequently also to the general public.

In all that he wrote we find passages of amazing frankness about matters which most men would prefer to conceal. He was absurdly vain, he was childishly sanguine, he was often both foolish and ridiculous, and he tells us all about it as a matter that should interest us as well as him. ' Why,' he says, ' " out of the abundance of the heart " should I not speak ? ' The light of truth led him into strange paths. He was a formalist and yet he was sometimes known to fail in formalism through an aversion to insincerity ; when his enemy Baretti came, by chance, into the room where he was being entertained by a friend, Boswell refused to greet him ; he could even be flagrantly rude in company.

To be entirely respectable and conventional, to be the man of the world, the gentleman of society, that is what Boswell wanted most in life ; and that he never could become, because there was in his nature a further consciousness, which was not to be subdued,

and which determined, by reason of the curious inconsistency so produced, his whole capacity for interesting
mankind, for fame, for greatness.

And so beside the sentimentality, the self-deception,
the respectability, which he so often exhibited, we see
the germ of self-knowledge, of honesty, of truth, which
developed and was ultimately expressed, almost by
chance as it seems, in a supreme biography : for it
is the candour of Boswell far more than any other
single factor, the natural instinct to record what he
observed both of himself and of others, the honesty
in observing and the truthfulness which he had as an
artist in recording, that distinguishes his literary work.
Herein lay the essence of his genius. The story of
Boswell's life is the story of a struggle between
influences and ambitions which led him towards the
commonplace, and the rare qualities grafted deeply
within him, which bore him steadily in an opposite
direction. The triumph of the latter involved no
doubt the unhappiness of Boswell, but it also involved
the production of a great work of art ; and this
achievement has won for its author a unique place
among distinguished men ; he is famous beyond any
fame that he dreamed of attaining and failed to
attain.

CHAPTER II

' THE accident,' says Professor Raleigh,[1] ' which gave Boswell to Johnson and Johnson to Boswell is one of the most extraordinary pieces of good fortune in literary history.' The event of their meeting took place on May 16th, 1763, and if in one sense it was clearly, as the word is commonly used, an accident, it was equally the result of a strong wish and intention, if not of deliberate design, on Boswell's part. He had long known of Johnson, and as early as 1760 had hoped for an introduction from ' Mr. Derrick, the poet,' ' an honour,' he says, ' of which I was very ambitious.' This honour bestowed eventually upon a vain and extravagant youth (a circumstance which must be highly esteemed among the good gifts of the Lady Fortune to humanity) was to be attained through a humble agent. Among those of Boswell's friends who were not of the higher strata in society was one Tom Davies. He was at this time a bookseller, but as he had been formerly an actor and then dramatic critic, there was something uncommon and adventurous

[1] *Samuel Johnson*, by Walter Raleigh, 1907.

about his career. He had in fact in some degree the equivalent of what has been known at a later date as Bohemianism. It seems particularly appropriate that Boswell should have forgotten the pride of birth to meet so, in humble circumstances, the object of his devotion. The scene which took place in Tom Davies' back-parlour has the essence of true comedy. Two of the actors are light-heartedly unconscious that the moment has the least importance ; the third is painfully and anxiously aware that it is important to him, and naturally unaware that it can have a value to anyone else. And it has, too, that dramatic quality of great events taking place by accident, as it seems, among incongruous circumstances. It is a scene which must kindle always, for one who feels a serious value in humour, an emotion beyond mere pleasure.

The comedy opens by Tom Davies announcing the eventful news in farcical manner.

At last, on Monday the 16th of May, when I was sitting in Mr. Davies's back-parlour, after having drunk tea with him and Mrs. Davies, Johnson un-expectedly came into the shop ; and Mr. Davies having perceived him, through the glass-door in the room in which we were sitting, advancing towards us,—he announced his aweful approach to me, somewhat in the manner of an actor in the part of Horatio, when he addresses Hamlet on the appearance of his father's ghost, ' Look, my Lord, it comes . . .'

Boswell, who at once became nervous, had only time

to give a warning to Davies, and the latter maliciously said the one thing he had been asked not to say. ' Mr. Davies mentioned my name, and respectfully introduced me to him. I was much agitated; and recollecting his prejudice against the Scotch, of which I had heard much, I said to Davies, "Don't tell where I come from."—"From Scotland," cried Davies roguishly.' This was apparently a disastrous beginning, and something must be done to retrieve the position. '"Mr. Johnson," said I, "I do indeed come from Scotland, but I cannot help it."' It was rash indeed to originate the conversation and not less typical of Boswell for that. But a more pleasing remark could hardly be imagined, at once courteous and frank and full of humour.[1] Johnson no doubt appreciated it very well, and the more because he was able to find an excellent repartee. For the moment, however, Boswell seemed to be involved in fresh calamity. ' This speech was somewhat unlucky; for with that quickness of wit for which he was so remarkable, he seized the expression, "come from Scotland," which I used in the sense of being of that country; and, as if I had said that I had come away from it, or left it,

---

[1] This remark we may suppose was deliberately misinterpreted by some of Boswell's contemporaries and he finds it necessary to introduce a defence of it : ' I am willing to believe that I meant this as light pleasantry to soothe and conciliate him, and not as humiliating abasement at the expense of my country.' It was of course an apology for coming from Scotland, but an absurd apology of which he saw the absurdity, as though a man were to apologise for being six feet high.

retorted, " That, Sir, I find, is what a great many of your countrymen cannot help." ' Boswell for the moment was completely crushed : ' This stroke stunned me a good deal,' and he now found himself left out of the conversation, in which situation he felt that he was unlikely to make a very favourable impression. ' He then addressed himself to Davies : " What do you think of Garrick ? He has refused me an order for the play for Miss Williams, because he knows that the house will be full, and that an order would be worth three shillings." ' No opportunity must be missed, and youth is prompted by enthusiasm. ' Eager to take any opening to get into conversation with him, I ventured to say, " O, Sir, I cannot think Mr. Garrick would grudge such a trifle to you ! " ' If this was bold it was at least both genuine and polite, and the reproof was severe though Boswell admits its justice. ' " Sir," (said he, with a stern look) " I have known David Garrick longer than you have done : and I know no right you have to talk to me on the subject." ' ' Perhaps ' Boswell continues, ' I deserved this check ; for it was rather presumptuous in me, an entire stranger, to express any doubt of the justice of his animadversion upon his old acquaintance and pupil. I now felt myself much mortified, and began to think that the hope which I had long indulged of obtaining his acquaintance was blasted. And, in truth, had not my ardour been uncommonly strong, and my resolution uncommonly persevering, so rough a reception might have deterred me for ever from making any further attempts. Fortunately, however, I remained upon the field not wholly discomfited ; and was soon rewarded by hearing some of his conversation.'

Eventually, when he went away, Davies made some encouraging remarks : ' Tom Davies followed me to the door ; and when I complained to him a little of the hard blows which the great man had given me, he kindly took upon him to console me by saying, " Don't be uneasy. I can see he likes you very well ! " ' The evidence that Johnson liked him very well was not very convincing, we may suppose, to Boswell. But he called upon Johnson a week later.

In the account of Boswell's first visit to Dr. Johnson's house there is one instructive passage :

He told me that he generally went abroad at four in the afternoon, and seldom came home till ten in the morning. I took the liberty to ask if he did not think it wrong to live thus, and not make more use of his great talents. He owned it was a bad habit. On reviewing, at the distance of many years, my journal of this period, I wonder how, at my first visit, I ventured to talk to him so freely, and that he bore it with so much indulgence.

Clearly Boswell was good at saying what he thought —the remark about Garrick and the question as to the morality of Johnson's habits, so early in their acquaintance, show this ; he is himself amazed, at a

later date, 'how I ventured to talk so freely.' It is
this candour, in fact, which particularly attracted
Johnson. His fame for brilliant argument and
crushing repartee, and his unbending dogmatic
manner in conversation, prevented very often the
course of free and fearless expression in his presence.
The young, too, from their supposed ignorance, have
still something of the privilege of childhood in saying
what they think without offending. It is refreshing
to older men to hear the frank opinions of youth ;
and it was very characteristic of Johnson that he
liked people to speak quite openly upon serious
subjects, so long as they were sincere.

It is easy enough indeed to see why the two became
friends. Boswell was attractive to Johnson in more
ways than one. His outspokenness was happily
blended with more gentle softening qualities, which
made it modest and appealing rather than over-
confident and repelling. He expressed, by his ' light
pleasantry to soothe and conciliate him '—and also,
we may suppose, by something respectful in his
manner—a frank admiration for Johnson. And though
some may say that this attitude—flattery one might
almost call it (for it is something very near to that)—
is repulsive to them, there are very few people in
practice who, when it is managed with sufficient
dexterity, do not find in it something peculiarly
pleasant. Johnson certainly liked to have admirers,

and it was Boswell's nature to admire—but not in a mean or servile fashion. He managed, one may suppose, to make Johnson feel pleased with himself, but without lying and without compromising his own opinions. We may see the attitude which he adopted from his own words upon the subject of flattery :

[1] But there may be honest as well as dishonest flattery. There may be flattery from a sincere admiration, and a desire to please. It is benevolent to indulge this : and a man of good disposition may find frequent opportunities for it, by directly or obliquely bringing under the view of those with whom he associates, such circumstances in their situations and characters as are agreeable.

There is nothing unpleasant about this attitude : on the contrary it is a very desirable civility.

It must be remembered, too, that Boswell with all his good-humoured gaiety and pleasant social qualities could be, and often wanted to be, serious. And the conversation of Johnson was very often, at least during the latter end of his life, of a serious nature. Morality, human beings, literature, these were his great subjects ; religion and politics were discussed, but less often. Boswell was interested in the same things ; if with him more than with most men his own case was the mainspring of all interests, this made him not less, but rather more, attentive to all questions dealing with right and wrong and the motives of men ; and

[1] *London Magazine*, vol. li., p. 359.

in literature, as we shall have occasion to show later, he had a strong natural interest.

But there is another reason which made him an extremely suitable companion for Johnson. What Johnson loved best in conversation was to ' buffet ' his adversary ; this mode of proceeding has, however, the obvious disadvantage that it prevents people talking, and also may possibly offend them, a result which Johnson himself held to be inexpedient. Boswell, fortunately, was little affected in either way. Nothing, it is evident, could prevent him talking, and it took a great deal to offend or even to hurt him. He was so divinely good-humoured ! For the moment, sometimes, he might be annoyed ; but it very soon blew over, and there was no malice in his nature to irritate a wound. The consequence of this was that Johnson was often rude, which pleased him, and sometimes went too far, which made him really sorry, so that his kind-hearted nature liked the object of his brutality the better for having injured it.

Of the attraction of Dr. Johnson for Boswell we need hardly speak. The little that has been said already about Boswell's strange personality and desires is almost sufficient explanation. We must not think that he attached himself to Johnson with any particular object. ' To suppose,' said Malone '(as some of his detractors have suggested), that he attached himself to Dr. Johnson for the purpose of writing his life, is to know nothing of the author and nothing of human nature.' Malone, who knew Boswell very well at the end of his life, was probably a good judge ; and it is not difficult to account for Johnson's attraction for Boswell without making a supposition of this kind. Apart from the unique position which he had among literary men, Johnson was a very striking figure and a very lovable man, and one who would readily appeal to the imagination of the young ; the honour of receiving the attentions of Johnson would be pleasant in every way ; and Boswell's character was eminently capable of devotion.

The friendship which grew up between these two men, who were so different, was not wholly without the shadow of romance. The relations between them were of the kind that parents would wish to exist between father and son. A great deal of affection on both sides there certainly was. The journey together which they took to Harwich on the occasion of Boswell's departure for the Continent [1] is significant enough of Johnson's feelings, and Boswell's account of their parting may speak for his :

My revered friend walked down with me to the beach, where we embraced and parted with tenderness and engaged to correspond by letters. I said, ' I hope, Sir, you will not forget me in my absence.' Johnson, ' Nay, Sir, it is more likely you should forget me, than that I should forget you.' As the vessel put out to sea I kept my eyes upon him for a considerable time, while he remained rolling his majestic frame in his usual

[1] In August 1763.

manner : and at last I perceived him walk back into the town, and he disappeared.

There is a note of regret in the paragraph, which, as anyone can see, is perfectly genuine.

But Boswell's attitude was much more complicated than one of mere affection. The friendship was of that complementary order where each person contributes something which the other lacks, so that they have a natural need each of the other. Johnson liked Boswell for his youth and freshness ; Boswell worshipped Johnson for his strength.[1] Worship ! it was no less than that ; he admitted it, he was proud of it. His own mind was of the indecisive kind which sees many things and finds it difficult to choose among them ; he turned very readily to the strong, definite view of life, the expression of an intelligence not smaller, as convinced people are often fundamentally smaller, but clearly larger than his own ; Johnson's overwhelming personality was able to support their common prejudices, usually by argument, but, if not so, by sheer force of conviction. It was not so much that Boswell approved of everything in Johnson's mind as that he could depend upon finding there a certain attitude expressive, as he thought, of his own better self, or of what he would like to have become had he been able to forgo a part of his own nature.

.   .   .   .   .

[1] *Life of Johnson*, iii., 331.

E

Dr. Johnson, if he was by far the most important, was by no means the only great man who was to become Boswell's friend. The paternal graciousness admitted of two years to be spent on the Continent, years that were to be devoted to diligent study in the University of Utrecht. Boswell turned them to the best advantage. The parting was propitious; his friend of the past few months accompanied him to the quay-side and Boswell was launched for the Continent by the great literary dictator. That the excellent advice of the moralist and the command of a father were neglected made little difference to the success of the lively young man. Utrecht was frankly a dull place, and there were several gay spots to be visited. Boswell fulfilled his destiny by amusing the best society, and made acquaintances among distinguished men. The capital of Prussia was visited, and the English ambassador Sir Andrew Mitchell was assailed and surrendered. The courts of Saxe-Gotha and Baden were the sphere of the young Scotsman's wit. Philosophers were among his honoured objects of attachment. The youthful Bozzy called upon Voltaire at Ferney, and became almost the friend of Rousseau. Lord Mount Stuart desired him for a travelling companion. The greatest achievement, perhaps, and the most characteristic was the capture of the notorious Wilkes; and intimacy with him was not unfitting, for the two were much alike in their irresponsible levity.

But all this was no more than the tinkling of a cymbal before the booming of an heroic drum. Boswell determined to visit the Island of Corsica.

Corsica was at this time the scene of a romantic struggle. Tired of the heavy yoke of the Genoese republic, the islanders were in a state of rebellion and were fighting under the flag of Liberty. Their leader was an admirable figurehead, one General Paoli, a zealous and disinterested patriot, a capable soldier and a wise politician. The Byronic furore of a later date for an oppressed people would have found a suitable object in the Corsicans and their national idol. For the mind of Boswell in search of the heroic they had a special appeal. A letter of introduction to Paoli was solicited from Rousseau, and with this the light-hearted young man stepped bravely forth with the bravery of ignorance, to be the first Englishman of his generation to visit those distant and uncivilised shores.

The event was properly considered to be worthy of notice in the English Press, and the requisite information as to Mr. Boswell's movements was supplied from time to time by the pen of Mr. Boswell himself.

The visit of Boswell to Corsica was a complete success. He travelled in the *rôle* of explorer, but was treated as an unknown political force. Men of many wiles sought behind an ingenuous and good-natured simplicity a deeper significance when there was none such to be found; Paoli, who hoped for

E 2

English assistance, was glad to treat with especial favour the one English subject whom he had the opportunity of knowing.   And Boswell, if he disclaimed an embassy, was not unwilling to be seen with an escort of Corsicans as he rode upon the general's horse, and to be entertained with diplomatic courtesy.

His own social qualities were perhaps of even greater service to him.   He exercised to the full his invaluable talent for bringing good cheer to his companions.   In the journal which he afterwards published, the ' Tour to Corsica,' there is an admirable account of an evening spent with the Corsican peasants which shows what an acceptable guest the good-humoured and lively Boswell must have been.

The Corsican peasants and soldiers were quite free and easy with me.   Numbers of them used to come and see me of a morning, and just go out and in as they pleased.   I did everything in my power to make them fond of the British, and bid them hope for an alliance with us.   They asked me a thousand questions about my country, all which I cheerfully answered as well as I could.   One day they would needs hear me play upon my German flute.   To have told my honest natural visitants, " Really, gentlemen, I play very ill,' and put on such airs as we do in our genteel companies, would have been highly ridiculous. I therefore immediately complied with their request. I gave them one or two Italian airs, and then some of our beautiful old Scotch tunes, ' Gilderoy,' ' The Lass of Patie's Mill,' ' Corn Riggs are Bonny.'   The pathetick simplicity and pastoral gaiety of the Scots

musick will always please those who have the genuine
feelings of nature. The Corsicans were charmed
with the specimens I gave them, though I may now
say that they were very indifferently performed.

My good friends insisted also to have an English
song from me. I endeavoured to please them in this
too, and was very lucky in that which occurred to me.
I sung them, ' Hearts of oak are our ships, Hearts of
oak are our men.' I translated it into Italian for
them, and never did I see men so delighted with a
song as the Corsicans were with ' Hearts of Oak.'
' Cuori di querco,' cried they, ' bravo Inglese.' It
was quite a joyous riot. I fancied myself to be a
recruiting sea-officer. I fancied all my chorus of
Corsicans aboard the British fleet.[1]

There is a natural good fellowship or social instinct,
a splendid enjoyment in the company of others, revealed in this story : it is a quality that pleases everybody. To Paoli he was agreeable besides for other
reasons. He had a real enthusiasm and taste for
literature, which the intellectual world understood and
appreciated readily enough. Hume writes of Boswell's
return from Paris, in the company of Thérèse Le
Vasseur. He calls him, ' a young gentleman, very
good-humoured, very agreeable, and very mad ' ; and
afterwards refers to his literary tastes : ' He has such
a rage for literature that I dread some event fatal to
our friend's honour. You remember the story of
Terentia, who was first married to Cicero, then to

[1] *Tour to Corsica*, pp. 320–1.

Sallust, and at last, in her old age, married a young nobleman, who imagined that she must possess some secret which would convey to him eloquence and genius.'[1]

There is a certain extravagance suggested by this which is very characteristic of Boswell.   He produced almost the expectation that he would do something odd. This in itself is not to every one an attractive quality ; but it is one which combined with others may bring an added charm.   Boswell had great generosity of a certain kind which was more than sufficient to excuse anything that might be tiresome about him ; he had an unabashed admiration and real respect for great men.   He was also able and was not unwilling to capture the hearts of men by repeating things that would please them ; as he relates that he did upon his visit to Voltaire, by repeating the dictum of Johnson about Frederick the Great : ' He writes just as you might suppose Voltaire's footboy to do, who has been his amanuensis. He has such parts as the valet might have, and about as much of the colouring of his style as might be got by tran-scribing his works.'   ' When I was at Ferney,' Boswell records, ' I repeated this to Voltaire, in order to recon-cile him somewhat to Johnson, whom he, in affecting the English mode of expression, had previously characterised as ' a superstitious dog ' ; but after

[1] *Private Correspondence of David Hume*, 1820.

hearing such a criticism on Frederick the Great, with whom he was then on bad terms, he exclaimed, ' An honest fellow ! '

With such pleasant qualities Boswell won the esteem of the General of the Corsicans. Paoli not only treated him with the courtesy due to a distinguished and possibly a useful stranger but entertained him with the spontaneous enjoyment of friendship.

The intimate relations which sprang up between Boswell and Paoli were, as we may judge from Boswell's own account, very similar to those already in existence between himself and Johnson.

The taste for the heroic may be satisfied easily. Even about the scamp Wilkes in exile there was a glamour which appealed to the imaginative young Bozzy. But for the real Boswellian admiration something more was required—the portentous possession of the ' solid virtues.' The probity of Paoli could never be in question. He appears to have been a simple character with a noble disinterestedness and the honesty of the Mediterranean sun. His interest was Corsica, and, if we may believe Boswell, there was hardly a thought of self in the matter. In this he was perhaps not different from the greater part of his countrymen ; but he had besides enthusiasm a wise moderation and self-control, a knowledge of men and a military ability which gave him an authority of the most absolute kind over the Corsicans. His power rested solely upon the weight of his personal influence. It was an impressive figure no doubt—a man to be admired ; and Boswell was good at admiring : but a man also to be loved, direct, kind-hearted and sympathetic. He had too what we should scarcely expect in the patriot general—a wide knowledge of literature and considerable culture. General Paoli was in fact entirely suitable to be Boswellised, more suitable it might almost seem than Doctor Sam himself ; but the latter was a man of far greater intelligence.

The opinions of Boswell in any case are clear enough, and we may read a few specimens from the ' Tour in Corsica.'

The contemplation of such a character really existing was of more service to me than all I had been able to draw from books, from conversation or from the exertions of my own mind. I had often enough formed the idea of a man continually such as I could conceive in my best moments. But this idea appeared like the ideas we are taught in the schools to form of things which may exist, but do not ; of seas of milk, and ships of amber. But I saw my highest idea realised in Paoli. It was impossible for me, speculate as I pleased, to have a little opinion of human nature in him.

One morning, I remember, I came in upon him without ceremony, while he was dressing. I was glad to have an opportunity of seeing him in those teasing moments, when, according to the Duke of Roche-foucault, no man is a hero to his valet de chambre. The lively nobleman who has a malicious pleasure in endeavouring to divest human nature of its dignity, by exhibiting partial views, and exaggerating faults, would

have owned that Paoli was every moment of his life
a hero.

Here is a candid unpretending hero-worship. If
it eludes the virtue of moderation it escapes the vice
of mediocrity. In this is its capacity for greatness.
For the moment there is nothing very great about it,
but it has a most desirable effect for good in Boswell:

Never was I so thoroughly sensible of my own
defects as while I was in Corsica. I felt how small
were my abilities, and how little I knew.

The example made for a genuine modesty in the
admirer (though it is doubtful if Boswell was ever
suspected of being modest); the Boswell who was
' ambitious to be the companion of Paoli ' was willing
to deserve the honour of that companionship:

From having known intimately so exalted a character
my sentiments of human nature were raised, while,
by a sort of contagion, I felt an honest ardour to distinguish myself, and be useful, as far as my situation
and abilities would allow ; and I was, for the rest of
my life, set free from a slavish timidity in the presence
of great men, for where shall I find a man greater than
Paoli ?

The expedition to Corsica was, as we have said, a
complete success. To visit the island, to observe the
manners of the heroic peasants, and to become the
friend of Paoli were admirable undertakings at that
time, and under those circumstances. But it was in
England that Boswell was to triumph. He was
launched upon society with the *éclat* of an interesting

personage ; he returned from his adventures over seas
to exact without reluctance the homage due to a
brave traveller.

The early fame of Boswell came not from Johnson,
but from Paoli and Corsica. It is a fact worth re-
marking, because Boswell's connection with Johnson
is so much the more important for us, that we are apt
to forget that he can have had another title to renown.
He was 'Corsica' Boswell and 'Paoli' Boswell, as Dr.
Birkbeck Hill remarks, long before he became famous
as ' Johnson ' Boswell.

Boswell himself fully appreciated the situation.
He felt that he had accomplished something of which
he could be justly proud. He knew himself to be
in the public eye. ' No apology shall be made,' he
writes in the preface to his book, ' for presenting the
world with " An Account of Corsica." It has been
for some time expected from me ; and I own that the
ardour of publick opinion has both encouraged and
intimidated me.' Johnson wrote him a letter which
he quoted without permission in the ' Tour to Corsica '
—' Come home and expect such a welcome as is due
to him whom a wise and noble curiosity has led where
perhaps no native of this country ever was before.'
He said no doubt what he really felt.

When Boswell returned to England in 1766 he
became therefore, quite naturally, the champion of
Corsican liberty. But this was only one phase of the

fame to which he aspired; there was still, and there was always, the desire to shine in the great and elevated sphere of literature, and the opportunity had now arrived to write a book of universal interest.

It was in 1768 that the first literary work of any magnitude which Boswell produced, ' An Account of Corsica, the journal of a tour to that island; and memoirs of Pascal Paoli,' was published. The title explains exactly the scope of the book. The account of Corsica is historical; the journal is in its method much like other books of travel, except for the biographical part which deals with Paoli. Of the historical part of the book there is nothing particular to be said: it is, as Johnson remarked, ' like other histories.' ' Your History,' he told him, ' was copied from books; your Journal rose out of your own experience and observation.' The chief interest of the book is that it is the earliest example of Boswell's biographical method. The memoirs that we have here of Paoli aim at giving a picture of a man in much the same way as does the ' Life of Johnson.' The question as to what exactly was Boswell's method will be discussed later; but we are reminded here that the man who preserved the conversations of Paoli and ' came in upon him without ceremony while he was dressing,' in order to see how he conducted himself before his *valet de chambre*, was becoming an adept in his own peculiar art.

A great charm of the Journal, also prophetic of
the future, lies in the perfect frankness with which
Boswell discusses his own feelings. ' We retired to
another room to drink coffee. My timidity wore off.
I no longer anxiously thought of myself ; my whole
attention was employed in listening to the illustrious
commander of a nation.' Or again, ' I enjoyed a
luxury of noble sentiment. Paoli became more
affable with me. I made myself known to him. I
forgot the great distance between us and had every
day some hours of private conversation with him.'
Boswell realised that a Journal is delightful only if
it is quite informal. We have a pleasing sense of in-
consequent freedom when we read in the Journal
several pages quoted from the ' First Book of the
Maccabees.' But it is not irrelevant to Boswell's
purpose. It occurred to his thoughts; and that is
a sufficient justification, whether it seem ludicrous
or incongruous or ponderous, for its inclusion.
There is no scene in the ' Tour in Corsica ' which
comes up to the best in the ' Life of Johnson,'
but there are several descriptions, such as that
quoted above, when Boswell played the pipe and
sang ' Hearts of Oak,' which are really artistic and
pleasing.

The book, at all events, had the effect of amusing
people and it gave them an interest in Corsica too.
Boswell had good accounts of it on all sides. ' My

book,' he writes to Temple, ' has amazing celebrity: [1] Lord Lyttelton, Mr. Walpole, Mrs. Macaulay, Mr. Garrick, have all written me noble letters about it.' The sale must have been very rapid. The dedication to the first edition is dated October 29, 1767, and the preface to the third edition on the same day of October, his birthday, in the following year. In this preface he explains that he has acquired that literary fame which he desired :

May I be permitted to say that the success of this book has exceeded my warmest hopes. When I first ventured to send it into the world, I fairly owned an ardent desire for literary fame. I have obtained my desire ; and whatever clouds may overcast my days, I can now walk here among the rocks and woods of my ancestors, with an agreeable consciousness that I have done something worthy.

There is nothing deserving particular remark in an author's desire for literary fame. But it is re-markable that a man should proclaim it to the world as Boswell did. The common ideal of an artist sup-poses that his work should be, in the first place, the expression of his own personality ; an expression be-cause to him it is necessary to reproduce in some form what he sees and feels : it is for himself and himself

---

[1] It is an interesting fact that it was translated into German, Dutch, Italian, and French (*Gentleman's Magazine*, June 1795— Letter from J. B. R.) The *Life*, I believe, has never been translated. The same correspondent says, ' It was received with extraordinary approbation.'

alone, and the world without is allowed to share, partly that the artist may earn a living, partly perhaps that he may have some justification for his self-absorption; and in greater part no doubt, in some cases more than in others, but in every case a little, that he may win the applause that we all like at bottom. None of these reasons, and, least of all, the desire for fame, is held to be a motive for producing art. There may be various impulses with varying circumstances; but there can be but one motive.

The ambition which Boswell had, and which he expressed so freely, is peculiar in some ways for the end desired, but it is not essentially different from that of other artists.

He who publishes a book, affecting not to be an ' authour,[1] and professing an indifference for literary fame, may possibly impose upon many people such an idea of his consequence as he wishes may be received. For my part, I should be proud to be known as an authour and I have an ardent ambition for literary fame ; for of all possessions I should imagine literary fame to be the most valuable. A man who has been able to furnish a book which has been approved by the world, has established himself as a respectable character in distant society, without any danger of having that character lessened by the observation of his weaknesses. To preserve an uniform dignity among those who see us every day is hardly possible ; and to aim at it must put us under the fetters of a perpetual

---

[1] For Boswell's views on spelling see this same preface.

restraint. The authour of an approved book may
allow his natural disposition an easy play, and yet
indulge the pride of superiour genius when he considers
that, by those who know him only as an authour, he
never ceases to be respected. Such an authour, when
in his hours of discontent, may have the consolation
to think that his writings are at that very time giving
pleasure to numbers ; and such an authour may cherish
the hope of being remembered after death, which has
been a great object to the noblest minds in all ages.

The nature of the desire for fame which he had is
revealed to us by Boswell in this curious passage.
It does not compromise his character as an artist.[1]
He wished to obtain the public esteem, to have the
reputation of an ingenious and worthy man ; and
literature was considered as a means to this end. But
we cannot argue that he must therefore have pandered
to the public taste : he wrote, as he proclaimed at a
later date in a contribution to a periodical, ' from the
primary motive of pleasing himself.' This ambition
is not in its nature an attitude towards art but towards
the world. In all his writings, even in the frivolous
publications of his youth, Boswell has expressed his
own person in a peculiar degree. We must not suppose,
when we see an eagerness for literary fame, which, from
the frankness of his expression, may appear extravagant,

[1] Mr. Malone, speaking of the *Life*, said, ' That in this work he
had not both fame and profit in view, would be idle to assert ; but
to suppose that these were his principal objects is to know nothing
of the author, and nothing of human nature.' *Gentleman's Magazine*,
June 1795.

that he lacked a literary conscience, for he had an excellent one ; nor indeed that it mattered at all to him whether opinion in general should care about his book, except in so far as it approved of him, of the real Boswell, which it could not but find there.

Boswell's ideal of the literary man's position is well expressed in one of the letters to Temple :

> Temple, I wish to be at last an uniform, pretty man. I am astonishingly so already, but I wish to be a man who deserves Miss B . . . I am always for fixing some period for my perfection as far as possible. Let it be when my account of Corsica is published ; I shall then have a character which I must support. I will swear, like an ancient disciple of Pythagoras, to observe silence ; I will be grave and reserved, though cheerful and communicative of what is *verum atque decens.* One great fault of mine is talking at random ; I will guard against it.

It is amusing to think of Boswell in this *rôle.* Already we may see the great contest in his life between natural candour and commonplace ambition— the charm of the ' Tour to Corsica ' was the charm of candour, and it was dangerous to dreams of future greatness in the sphere of public affairs. Boswell understood that to gain respect he must be more serious. But this he never was able to be ; it was his nature to be extravagant. He had a mind which in some respects was wholly unconventional, and though he tried sometimes, he could never entirely repress his feelings : the consequence was that though there were many things about which he cared very much, it was never possible to take him quite seriously ; if a man plays the buffoon sometimes we are in danger of being fooled if we give him credit for being in earnest ; and so, if we are to preserve our *amour propre*, which is what everybody wants to do, we must laugh at a buffoon whatever he does.

A most notable piece of Boswell's buffoonery was in connection with the Shakespeare Jubilee at Stratford-on-Avon in 1769. He attended this festival dressed as an armed Corsican chief. This perhaps was not particularly odd ; the form of rejoicing which the company indulged in was a ' Mask.' It is dangerous even so, and hardly decent, to blow the personal trumpet so loudly. Boswell, however, was not content merely with the public advertisement of his connexion with Corsica ; he wrote to the *London Magazine* [1] an elaborate unsigned account of himself and his costume : it was entitled ' Account of the Armed Corsican Chief at the Masquerade at Shakespeare's Jubilee, with a fine whole-length portrait of James Boswell, Esq., in the dress of an armed Corsican chief, as he appeared at the Jubilee Mask.' There is no need to give here the text of this document : it has been quoted at length a number of times, and it suffices to say that there can be no possble doubt that Boswell wrote it and

[1] September 1769.

that he wrote it to exhibit himself in a favourable light. The incident is characteristic of Boswell. It is not the mad whim that may occur once in a lifetime, the event which stands as it were by itself apart from the man ; it is not an experiment miscarried, that has taken him away from his usual self and so must remain unexplained or be put to the long account of genius : rather it is the sort of oddity that we come to expect of Boswell.

Frolics of this kind naturally deprived Boswell of the respect which he desired for himself as a man of letters. The ' Tour to Corsica ' was an admirable beginning to a literary career ; he had then the chance of founding the reputation he wanted as a person of weight, a man whose judgment must be accounted of some importance by the world at large. His writings about Corsica had been widely read and his views had found general sympathy. Moreover the popular poetess, Mrs. Barbauld, had paid homage in verse to his fame as an explorer. But by such behaviour as this at Stratford these hopes were frustrated. And to him, though perhaps not to us, this was the tragedy of his life.

CHAPTER III

THE portion of Boswell's career which we have been relating up to this point gives rise by natural sequence to the discussion of one or two interesting questions about his personality. We must know the part played in the main theme by his peculiar qualities. We must notice how they seem to assist or to impede his particular faculty for biography.

Allusion has already been made to the reasons for which Boswell was attracted by two great men, Dr. Johnson and General Paoli. We must see now in general the reason of that intimacy which he took care to cultivate with a large number of distinguished men.

Boswell, there can be no doubt, liked men in some way because they were distinguished. We must remember that the judgments of the world were always very real standards to him. If a man were great, he must be somehow good; and to be the friend of such a man, that was good too. It is not that Boswell judged of characters wholly by success. We may see that as he grew older he judged them more and more by the Johnsonian morality. He grew less tolerant of heresy under the influence of his moral guide.   Hence the dislike of Gibbon :—' He is an ugly, affected, disgusting fellow, and poisons our Literary Club to me.' Johnson probably shared this feeling and un-doubtedly shared the reasons for it, which Boswell expresses in Johnsonian phrases : ' I think it is right that as fast as infidel wasps or venomous insects, whether creeping or flying, are hatched, they should be crushed.' This was said in reference to Gibbon's book ; the sentiments were extended to Adam Smith. ' Murphy says that he has read thirty pages of Smith's " Wealth," but says that he shall read no more : Smith too is now of our Club.   It has lost its select merit.'   Personal antipathy in the one case and ignor-ance of economics in the other need not surprise us. But it comes as a shock, nevertheless, to discover Boswell's views upon the two men who were, in-tellectually, the most distinguished of his contem-poraries.   The Doctor's prejudices may have much to do with it.   Boswell records a similar judgment in the ' Tour to the Hebrides ' :   ' Infidelity in a Highland gentleman appeared to me peculiarly offensive.   I was sorry for him as he had otherwise a good character.'

And yet he was probably always as he was in the early years far more tolerant than Johnson.   There is an instructive passage also in the ' Tour to the Hebrides ' about Hume. Johnson was talking about Hume's infidelity :   ' He added something much too rough, both as to Mr. Hume's head and heart, which I suppress. Violence is, in my opinion, not suitable to the Christian cause.   Besides I always lived on good terms with Mr. Hume, though I have frankly told him I was not clear that it was right in me to keep company with him.' That he did not condemn the infidel Hume, shows that Boswell's prejudices were weaker, at least, than friendship.   Boswell, besides, throughout his life gave a very high value to mere intellectual power.   He complained of 'dull provinciality' in Scotland, because the people of Edinburgh were less intelligent than the Londoners.   His love of London was founded upon the need he felt of conversing with clever people ; and this need became in him with maturity, not weaker, as in most cases, but stronger.

In these early years Boswell was glad to make a friend of any particularly intelligent person, and his acquaintances included characters widely differing— Hume and Rousseau, Johnson and Lord Hailes, Wilkes and Paoli.   Boswell clearly had pleasure in the society of them all ; he did not, like Johnson, condemn them to a place beyond the range of his acquaintance ;   these men were specimens of human nature worthy to be studied ; he saw some good in all of them.   There is a characteristic passage in the ' Life ' about the meeting of Johnson and Wilkes which illustrates the attitude :

My desire of being acquainted with celebrated men

of every description had made me, much about the same time, obtain an introduction to Dr. Samuel Johnson and to John Wilkes, Esq. Two men more different could perhaps not be selected out of all mankind. They have even attacked one another with some asperity in their writings ; yet I lived in habits of friendship with both. I could fully relish the excellence of each ; for I have ever delighted in that intellectual chymistry which can separate good qualities from evil in the same person.

He looked upon men much as we look upon works of art, distinguishing that which, as art, has merit, and crediting with a certain value every design or idea which has been executed well, but attaching ourselves more particularly to a few rare objects which have some special significance or appeal for our own nature. Johnson and Paoli had this appeal for Boswell. Wilkes and Hume attracted him more because they were interesting individuals for whom, though he really disapproved of them, he might retain some slight affection because they were representative men. He might dislike the things they represented, but like them in spite of this : like them, one might almost say, for representing something.

With Hume, for instance, he had a considerable friendship at one time. He was of course, an individual to be studied ; to Temple, Boswell related his conversations much as he recorded those of Johnson and Paoli. But he did not see him merely because he was interested; he liked him too: 'David is really amiable; I always regret to him his unlucky principles and he smiles at my faith.' It is probable that as he grew older Boswell grew less tolerant. He was always somewhat of an experimentalist, interested in various sides of life and fitting one or another to his own case; but though he became with maturity more definitely attached to the conventional Christianity, to 'belief,' as he termed it, as opposed to 'infidelity,' and less tolerant of the people who held different views, he never hated a man for being a Whig or an atheist as Johnson did.

Interest and affection: these, then, are real motives with Boswell for seeking as he did the company of distinguished men. The question, however, of a further motive—of the snobbishness in Boswell's nature—still remains.

Boswell himself was well aware of a certain 'propensity in his disposition,' of a particular pleasure from the society of the great and a desire which he had to form friendships among them; he knew too that his behaviour was condemned by many of his contemporaries. In the 'Tour to the Hebrides'[1] he has given his own account and explanation of his conduct:

My fellow-traveller and I talked of going to Sweden; and, while we were settling our plan, I expressed a

[1] *Tour to the Hebrides*, September 17.

pleasure in the prospect of seeing the king.   Johnson :
' I doubt, Sir, if he would speak to us.'   Colonel McLeod
said, ' I am sure Mr. Boswell would speak to *him*.'
But, seeing me a little disconcerted by his remark, he
politely added, ' and with great propriety.'   Here let
me offer a short defence of that propensity in my disposition, to which this gentleman alluded.   It has
procured me much happiness.   I hope it does not
deserve so hard a name as either forwardness or impudence.   If I know myself, it is nothing more than
an eagerness to enjoy the society of men distinguished
either by their rank or their talents, and a diligence
to attain what I desire.   If a man is praised for seeking
knowledge, though mountains and seas are in his way,
may he not be pardoned, whose ardour, in pursuit of
the same object, leads him to encounter difficulties
as great, though of a different kind ?

This defence is characteristic of the manner in which
Boswell consistently treated the world.   ' Curiosity,'
said Mrs. Thrale, ' carried Boswell farther than it ever
carried any mortal breathing.   He cared not what he
provoked so as he said what *such a one* would say or do.'[1]
But the basis of social conventions is a desire to consider the feelings of others.   A person's ' forwardness '
and ' impudence ' are judged not so much by his own
sentiments as by the effect he produces upon other
people.   Boswell pressed an acquaintanceship entirely
because he thought it might be good for himself ; he
never considered the views of the acquaintance :
' It has procured me much happiness.'   He did not

[1] *Autobiography, Letters, &c., of Mrs. Piozzi*, ii, 124.

understand the consequences of this attitude. He was an intellectual parasite upon society, determined at any cost to feed upon the good qualities of others, taking where he would, without caring if he gave. It may possibly be well for the individual that he should consider himself alone; but society, just because it is society, must object to the egoist. This Boswell never was able to understand. His own point of view was concerned with what he could get from others ; and though he was by nature in many ways excellent as the member of a community, he had no conception of himself in this capacity. He cared a great deal about his importance, but very little about his value. He took systematically, he gave at random. Interest in human beings simply for his own sake because it pleased him [1] : that is one prime motive which impelled him to seek the acquaintance of distinguished men.

Boswell, besides this, was essentially a snob. To have pleasure in the company of distinguished men, not only from a sense of the good qualities they have, but from a feeling that their greatness adds to one's position in the esteem of mankind, that is to be a snob. Boswell had this feeling ; he freely admitted it. ' Now, Temple,' he writes, ' can I help indulging my vanity ? Sir David Dalrymple says to me in his

---

[1] Perhaps the best evidence of all for this quality is Boswell's habit of attending executions (mentioned several times in the *Life* and also in the *Life of Reynolds*, by Leslie and Taylor), and his acquaintance with Mrs. Rudd, a notorious criminal.

last letter, " It gives me much pleasure to think that you have obtained the friendship of Mr. Samuel Johnson. . . ." ' And again :

I am really the great man now. I have had David Hume, in the forenoon, and Mr. Johnson, in the afternoon, of the same day, visiting me. Sir John Pringle, Dr. Franklin, and some more company dined with me to-day ; and Mr. Johnson and General Oglethorpe one day, Mr. Garrick alone another, and David Hume and some more literati another, dine with me next week. I give admirable dinners and good claret ; and the moment I go abroad again, which will be in a day or two, I set up my chariot. This is enjoying the fruit of my labours, and appearing like the friend of Paoli. By the bye, the Earl of Pembroke and Captain Meadows are just setting out for Corsica, and I have the honour of introducing them by a letter to the General. David Hume came on purpose, the other day, to tell me that the Duke of Bedford was very fond of my book, and had recommended it to the Duchess.

' The great man ' because he kept the company of great men—that is what he says, and it is snobbish. His enjoyment of ' the society of men distinguished by their rank or their talents ' depended partly upon that. He considered this to be a legitimate way of acquiring fame.

The absurdity of Boswell's behaviour in this respect seems all the more ridiculous from the fact that it was unnecessary. When he returned from Corsica he had obtained, as we remarked above, a position of

considerable distinction for a young man.   He had
only to wait discreetly and carefully and he was certain
to obtain the patronage of the great.   But he courted
them, on the contrary, with unheard-of fervour.   The
climax was reached in a letter to Chatham, with whom
he had an opportunity of corresponding about Corsica.
He writes from the pinnacle of pomposity to descend
to the pit of adulation : ' I only wish that circumstances
were such that your Lordship could have an opportunity of showing the interest you take in the fate of
a people who well deserve the favour of so illustrious
a patron of liberty as your Lordship.'   He proceeds
by quoting, as the mediator between the General
and Lord Chatham, a letter from Paoli.   There is then
an immortal passage in which the underlying egoism,
too little concealed, is yoked with a flattery which
could scarcely be tolerated in Olympia :

Your Lordship applauds my ' generous warmth
for so striking a character as the able chief.'   Indeed,
my Lord, I have the happiness of being capable to
contemplate with supreme delight those distinguished
spirits by whom God is sometimes pleased to honour
humanity ; and as I have no personal favour to ask
of your Lordship, I will tell you with the confidence
of one who does not fear to be thought a flatterer,
that your character, my Lord, has filled many of my
best hours with that noble admiration which a disinterested soul can enjoy in the bower of philosophy.

Then follows an account of Boswell's plan for his

book about Corsica ; and finally his personal vanity leaps over every barrier.

As for myself, to please a worthy and respected father, one of our Scotch judges, I studied law, and am now fairly entered to the bar. I begin to like it. I can labour hard ; I feel myself coming forward, and I hope to be useful to my country. Could your Lordship find time to honour me now and then with a letter ? I have been told how favourably your Lordship has spoken of me. To correspond with a Paoli and a Chatham is enough to keep a young man ever ardent in the pursuit of virtuous fame.

This letter illustrates much of Boswell's attitude towards the great, and it will be necessary to refer to it again in that connection ; it shows, at least, how earnestly Boswell desired the friendship of the great man, and what a thrill of pleasure those letters from Chatham must have given him.

However much we may dislike this propensity of Boswell's disposition, while admitting that it is unpleasant in itself, although we would not and could not have Boswell without it, there is no reason to see in much of it a blacker vice than merely the ignorance of how to behave. And it was connected as we have shown with feelings not entirely selfish. But of the flagrant self-advertisement to which we have referred above no such agreeable things may be said. It is condemnable without compensation as an obtrusive egoism and foolish vanity. It must be written down frankly on the debit side of Boswell's peculiar genius, and it was as much opposed to the proper exercise of his biographical talents as to his more practical career.

.   .   .   .   .

We are forced to wonder, and it is important that we should decide, whether in spite of his immoderate self-centredness Boswell was capable of acting without considering his own advantage in the interest of others. Had he, in the first place, any real care for the cause of Corsican liberty ?

It is often far from easy to discover what Boswell's feelings were, because the balance between sentiment and expression was with him very ill-adjusted. By prolonged study of the Boswellian extravagances we may come to perceive, as we think, how much Boswell really felt ; but even so it is hardly possible to explain any valid reason for judgments of this nature. Boswell was often guilty of extravagance ; but it would be as false to believe that he felt none of the zeal he talks about so easily, as to believe that he felt as much as he says. He undoubtedly exaggerated, but he probably never made an absolute misstatement.

There is a passage of great enthusiasm for the Corsicans in a letter to Johnson : [1] ' Shall they not rise in the great cause of liberty, and break the galling

[1] *Life of Johnson*, ii, 59. This letter is an admirable instance of Boswell's affected manner of expressing real feelings.

yoke ? And shall not every liberal soul be warm
for them ? ' Boswell's heart must have been warm
when he wrote that : but we are unfortunately still
left in doubt by an anti-climax : ' No ! while I live,
Corsica and the cause of the brave islanders shall ever
employ much of my attention, shall ever interest
me in the sincerest manner.' The letter in which
these quotations occur is dated April 26, 1768 ; it
is possible that Boswell's ardour had begun to cool
by that time and that the cause of liberty, though it
might ' employ much of his attention ' was less vital
to him than he imagined. The ' Tour to Corsica,'
however, gives an impression of genuine interest and
sympathy with the Corsicans. Boswell seems to have
liked very well these simple folk, who appreciated more
readily than his countrymen the natural gaiety and
good humour of his spirits.[1] How different is his attitude in the ' Tour to the Hebrides ' towards the Scots !
We must remember too that Boswell, whatever may
have been his motives, did much in England and
Scotland to help the Corsicans. Besides publishing
his book, which was of value to their cause, he raised
a subscription and sent out £700 worth of ordnance.[2]
He also collected and published a volume of ' British
Essays in favour of the Brave Corsicans,' some of
which he himself wrote.

[1] *Life of Johnson*, ii, 3, note 1.
[2] *Letters to Temple*, p. 126.

Boswell had in fact a real generosity of character ; he hated anything mean, and expressed himself as anxious to cure his own ' narrowness.' He could be kind to his friends and was willing to lend money. He was interested as a lawyer in the decisions of the courts and readily bestowed his sympathy. On behalf of a certain Dr. Dodd, a divine who was under sentence of death for forgery, he wrote to Dr. Johnson : ' If for ten righteous men the Almighty would have spared Sodom, shall not a thousand acts of goodness done by Dr. Dodd counterbalance one crime ? ' And Dr. Johnson afterwards used his pen in Dr. Dodd's service. On another occasion he appealed for his friend's assistance in the case of a Scotch schoolmaster—a client of Boswell's, who had been ' deprived of his office for being somewhat severe in the chastisement of his scholars ' : Boswell in his letter to Johnson seems to have at heart both the interests of the school-master and the principle of corporal punishment. For his friend Temple he more than once went out of his way to obtain some favour. He treated his tenants with the greatest consideration, and even made special provisions in his will for their future welfare.[1] But Boswell was not one of those who continually exercise these amiable qualities. It is probable indeed that, had he tried, he would have met with more rebuffs than encouragement. To be flagrantly kind with

[1] *Boswelliana*, p. 186.

any success requires a good deal of cunning, and of
that useful quality Boswell had extremely little :
he was likely to appear in any good work more meddle-
some than great-hearted. But if with him care for
the happiness of others was not the first consideration, he was at bottom a sympathetic, kind-hearted
man, and capable of generous actions.

It is very important that we should bear this in
mind about Boswell. Those who are gifted with
powers of expression are often in one sense primarily
egoists—more so than other men because they are apt
to become more completely absorbed—and Boswell, as
we have shown, was not without his portion of egoism ;
but there may be a place in the lives of such men for
unselfish feelings, and if we may think that Boswell
had his due share of them we may judge less harshly
in him the egoism which we cannot admire.

.   .   .   .   .

Boswell, as we have seen, had already at the age
of twenty-seven made a bid for renown. He was
anxious to shine in more lights than one. It was not
mere social success or literary fame that he wanted :
he had an ardent desire to be successful in his profession.
The sphere of employment which had been chosen for
him by his father with his own sanction was the
Scotch Bar, to which he was formally ' called ' in 1766.[1]
His work seems to have engrossed at once a great

[1] *Life of Johnson*, ii, 20.

deal of his time. He writes on March 4th, 1767, to Temple:

> I am surprised at myself, I already speak with so much ease and boldness, and have already the language of the bar so much at command. I have now cleared eighty guineas. My clerk comes to me every morning at six, and I have dictated to him forty folio pages in one day. It is impossible to give you an idea of my present life. I send you one of my law papers, and a copy of my thesis. I am doing nobly ; but I have not leisure for learning. I can hardly ever answer the letters of my friends.

This is the letter of a man who finds himself engrossed as well as busy. The truth is that Boswell was extremely anxious to make a mark in his profession. Here, as always, he must win approval ; he must become a person to be considered. To this end he succeeded in mixing himself up with the Douglas Cause, a case concerned with a Scotch title which was commanding much attention in the summer of 1767. He seems to have acted as a voluntary counsel to Mr. Douglas the plaintiff, and was most diligent, even perhaps to excess, in his interest. In connection with this trial, two small publications appeared from Boswell's hand. The first of them, ' The Essence of the Douglas Cause,' is a *précis* of the whole affair, well arranged and clearly expressed ; it was written with a view to aiding Boswell's own side in the case,[1] in

[1] Fitzgerald's *Life of Boswell*, i, 111.

reply to a pleading from the other side, ' Considerations on the Douglas Cause.' The labour of compiling this summary must have been very great. Boswell tells us in the introduction that he was present during the whole deliberation of the Cause before the Court of Session and took very full notes. It shows, as Mr. Fitzgerald has remarked, how industrious Boswell could be when his enthusiasm was aroused.

The other publication, ' Dorando : A Spanish Tale ' [1] affects to be a story about a trial in Spain, but reproduces the characters in the Douglas case. Under this thin veil approbation and criticism are distributed to the two parties, and the cause decided. The publication of ' Dorando,' [2] extracts of which appeared in several of the Scotch newspapers and were held by some of the Scotch judges to be contempt of court, was wholly characteristic of Boswell. Whether or no it would be possible to find in his conduct anything which amounted to a breach of etiquette, it is clear that a publication of this sort might well injure his position at the Bar. It is true that the author's name did not appear, but it was not to be supposed that it would always remain a secret, and the precaution was probably taken with a view to being on the right side rather of the law than of the lawyers. Boswell, with all his wish to win the esteem

---

[1] Boswell's authorship proved by *Letters to Temple*, p. 89.
[2] Fitzgerald's *Life of Boswell*, i, 113.

of men, never understood how easily the opposite is earned and how harshly a tiny cosmos will punish an offence against itself. And when the humorous side of things struck him forcibly he was unable to repress his feelings.

Boswell's behaviour during the Douglas Cause is said to have been decidedly extravagant. His father was heard to say that ' James had taken a tout on a new horn,' [1] and a story got about which, though it may have been false, must have had some relation to the common conception of Boswell, that when he heard that the House of Lords had reversed the decision of the Court of Session, he placed himself at the head of an uproarious mob who broke his father's windows.

There are other indications than the Douglas Cause to show that Boswell was anxious to be successful in his legal career. It is not to be thought that he always displayed the energy which he showed at this time. But he clearly took the trouble, on several occasions recorded in the ' Life,' to prepare the best arguments he could to support his case ; and if we must suppose that he was as anxious as he represents himself to be that justice should be done, it is still quite evident that he hoped to gain some advantage to himself from the assistance which he solicited and obtained from Johnson, and was glad that the right should triumph, in part no doubt because it was

---

[1] Fitzgerald's *Life of Boswell*, i, 116.

supported by James Boswell.   In fact it is probable that
Johnson's assistance was of little value.   As Boswell
says on one occasion, having presented the written
arguments of Johnson without success, ' their Lordships
in general, though they were pleased to call this, " a
well-drawn paper," preferred the former very inferior
petition which I had written ; thus confirming the
truth of an observation made to me by one of their
number in a merry mood : " My dear Sir, give yourself no trouble in the composition of the paper you
present to us ; for, indeed, it is casting pearls before
swine." '

We shall have to consider when we come to the
last years of Boswell's life the various reasons for his
failure at the Bar.   But one reason may be mentioned
here because it is so essential a part of his character
that we should do wrong not to have it in mind as we
go over the spectacle of his whole life.   Boswell, it
must be remembered, was called to the Scotch Bar ;
but the society of the Scotch, and particularly of the
Scotch lawyers, was never congenial to him.   As early
as March 1767 he writes to Temple : ' It must be con-
fessed that our Court of Session is not so favourable
to eloquence as the English Courts.'   By 1775 he
was apparently quite tired of his work ; ' On my
arrival here [Edinburgh] I had the pleasure to find
my wife and two little daughters as well as I could
wish ; but indeed, my worthy priest, it required some

philosophy to bear the change from England to Scotland. The unpleasing tone, the rude familiarity, the barren conversation of those whom I found here, in comparison with what I had left, really hurt my feelings.'

It is probable that Boswell's opinions about the Scotch lawyers were not entirely concealed from them. And they knew, no doubt, that he had friends among the Edinburgh players, and may have resented the fact. ' The Scottish Themis,' says Scott, speaking of his own early experience, ' is peculiarly jealous of any flirtation with the Muses on the part of those who have ranged themselves under her banners.' We may suppose that Boswell's flirtations, with the Muses at all events, injured his position in legal circles.

The General Assembly [Boswell continues] is sitting, and I practise at its Bar. There is *de facto* something low and coarse in such employment, though on paper it is a Court of *Supreme Judicature*; but guineas must be had. . . . To speak well, when I despise both the cause and the judges, is difficult; but I believe I shall do wonderfully. I look forward with aversion to the little, dull, labours of the Court of Session.

Boswell himself was quite unlike most Scotchmen, and he relates in the ' Life ' the remarks upon this subject made by Johnson at various times :

Johnson : ' I never say, I do not value Boswell more for being born to an estate, because I do not care.' *Boswell* : ' Nor for being a Scotchman.' *Johnson* :

' Nay, Sir, I do value you more for being a Scotchman. You are a Scotchman without the faults of a Scotch- man. You would not have been so valuable as you are, had you not been a Scotchman.' And again, when talking of the Scotch nation, *Johnson* : ' *You* are an exception, though. Come, gentlemen, let us candidly admit that there is one Scotchman who is cheerful.' *Beauclerk* : ' But he is a very unnatural Scotchman.'

Professor Raleigh has emphasised this point in his delightful manner :

If I had to find a paradox in Boswell, I should find it in this, that he was a Scot. His character was destitute of all the vices, and all the virtues, which are popularly, and in the main rightly, attributed to the Scottish people. The young Scot is commonly shy, reserved, and self-conscious ; independent in temper, sensible to affront, slow to make friends, and wary in society. Boswell was the opposite of all these things. He made himself at home in all societies, and charmed others into a like ease and confidence. Under the spell of his effervescent good-humour the melancholy Highlanders were willing to tell stories of the supernatural. ' Mr Boswell's frankness and gayety,' says Johnson, ' made everybody communicative.'

And Boswell himself took no trouble to conceal, but rather published this truth. He saw very clearly certain qualities in the Scotch character which he disliked.

It must be remembered, however, that Boswell professed to be in one sense, perhaps the only right sense, patriotic. He may have hated the Scotch, but he loved Scotland and loved in particular the home of his ancestors. If he preferred to live in England, it was a preference only for the society he found there. During those memorable months when the great Doctor made his tour in Scotland, Boswell had a real anxiety that Johnson should get rid of his prejudices and appreciate the country. He takes the trouble to defend at length Johnson's ' Journey to the Western Islands ' from the anger of Scotchmen, but he does so by asserting that Johnson saw both the good and the bad.

' And let me add [he says in an extravagant vein] ' that, citizen of the world as I hold myself to be, I have that just sense of the merit of an ancient nation, which has been ever renowned for its valour, which in former times maintained its independence against a powerful neighbour, and in modern times has been equally distinguished for its ingenuity and industry in civilised life, that I should have felt a genuine in-dignation at any injustice done to it. Johnson treated Scotland no worse than he did even his best friends, whose characters he used to give as they appeared to him, both in light and shade.

However Boswell may have had ' that just sense of the merit of an ancient nation,' it is clear, as we have said, that he disliked very much his legal work in Scot-land. But it must not be thought that he rapidly became grave and soured by constant irritation. That

process was a slow one in his case. His disposition was
too sanguine to feel very much, as a young man, his
disappointments. He did without doubt, as he grew
older, become less frivolous, and more sedate ; with
this we must suppose that his marriage in 1769 was
in some way connected.

.   .   .   .   .

Before we come to discuss the domesticity of
Boswell we must consider for a time those affairs of
the heart in which he had such a plentiful experience.

About these he was as frank as he was about
all the subjects which he discusses in his letters to
Temple. We have detailed accounts (detailed enough,
apparently, to offend, unfortunately for our purpose,
the delicate ear of the first editor of the letters)
which describe in several cases the precise nature of
Boswell's love or passion or whatever be the appropriate expression. These accounts were intentionally
complete. The eye of Boswell is fixed upon the ther-
mometer of his affections to observe and indicate its
rise and fall. Nothing could illustrate the man so well
as the attitude which he here so nakedly revealed,
typical entirely of Boswell because it is so completely
self-centred. He lived for his own pleasure and says
as much : 'That pleasure is not the aim but the end
of our being, seems to be philosophically demonstrable.
Therefore all the labour and all the serious business
of life should first be considered as means to

that end.' [1] In love he was not less governed by this system than he was in every other phase of life.

It was at the early age of eighteen when Boswell was still at the University that the son of Venus came to him upon the first of many visits. The lady, a Miss W——t, is described as a most desirable companion ; and Cupid in one sense was kind to Boswell—for though his hope of an ideal future in the company of the beloved, the heiress to a fortune of thirty thousand pounds, was not destined to be realised, he was able, if the lady were disinclined to adorn his life, to ' bear it *æquo animo*, and retire into the calm regions of philosophy.'

The subject of matrimony seems often to have occupied the thoughts of Boswell. At times the appeal of unmarried life was strong. ' The bachelor has a carelessness of disposition which pleases everybody, and everybody thinks him a sort of common good— a feather which flies about and lights now here, now there.' But the ideal of a winged good which was to float about thus amiably gave way at times to a more sedate view of living. ' If you think of the comforts of a home, where you are a sort of sovereign, the kind endearments of an amiable woman, who has no wish but to make you happy, the amusement of seeing your children grow up from infancy to manhood, and the pleasing pride of being the father of brave and

[1] *London Magazine*, 1, 40.

learned men, all which may be the case—then marriage is truly the condition in which true felicity is to be found.' In the absence, however, of a felicity which could add so much comfort and pleasure and so small a burden of responsibility to his life, Boswell was happy enough, he proceeds to relate, to have a '*dear infidel.*' That there was no infidelity on the part of this 'charmer' Boswell is able to affirm, while he does not deny that she has a husband; but though, as he says, ' imagination represented it just as being fond of a pretty, lively, black little lady,who, to oblige me, stayed in Edinburgh, and I very genteelly paid her expenses,' he was glad no doubt that circumstances permitted him to arrange his pleasures without hypocrisy.

The course of his amour was not destined to run very smoothly. The ardour of Boswell for the deserted or deserting lady was intermittent and expensive; it was difficult to be rid of her because the tendernesses of a farewell upset the unstable balance of Boswell's susceptibility; ' I was sometimes resolved to let her go, and sometimes my heart was like to burst within me. I took her dear hand; her eyes were full of passion, I took her in my arms.' The dramatic moment is too much for the best-laid plans, and Boswell was grateful, as he well might be, to find himself free after two months. ' I am totally emancipated from my charmer, as much as from the gardener's daughter who now puts on my fire and performs menial offices like any other wench.' The affair with the gardener's daughter is unfortunately not related. She is mentioned only this once where Boswell tells us that a year before this date (March 30, 1767), he had been 'so madly in love as to think of marrying her.' Two other ladies are mentioned in the same letter, Miss Bosville and Miss Blair. He thought of the former, who was his cousin, as a convenient match, but the suit does not appear to have been prosecuted with much vigour. She was kept, as it were, in the second line of battle to fill up a gap when an object of devotion was required. There is another name of the same kind, Zelide, a Dutch lady whom he met at Utrecht and who appears upon the scene periodically. Boswell several times threatened to marry her. How many affairs there were of this class it is difficult to estimate. Exact information on the subject would be valuable as enabling us to adjust the proportion of these matters. From isolated remarks referring to women not elsewhere mentioned, such as ' My Italian angel is constant,' we might suppose that Boswell conducted his amours on the magnificent scale of Solomon. But this can hardly have been the case.

Miss Blair was a Scotch heiress whose estate was not far from Auchinleck. Boswell's father was in favour of the match, which would have been in every way desirable, particularly so if it be considered appropriate that the young lady was in love with Boswell. The

initial stages were highly propitious. Miss Blair with
her mother was persuaded, without great difficulties
we may suppose, to stay at Auchinleck, where Boswell
in the ' romantic groves ' of his ancestors ' adored her
like a divinity.' The heir whose ' grand object is the
ancient family of Auchinleck—a venerable and noble
principle ' intends to carry off the ' neighbouring
princess ' by assault rather than siege, and in the
pursuit of romance allows no time for love to languish.
An emissary [1] is despatched, no other than the faithful
Temple, who is at once to blow the trumpet as a herald,
and as a spy to observe the enemy's fortifications.
' Praise me for my good qualities—you know them.'
These are the instructions.   Romance is to be fed by
mystery and the chase encouraged by the elusiveness
of the quarry.   ' But talk also how odd, how incon-
stant, how impetuous, how much accustomed to
women of intrigue.   Ask gravely, Pray don't you
imagine there is something of madness in that family ? '
A tinge of insanity may be a pleasing dash of colour
in the hero ; or the suggestion may draw the attention
of the fair one to extravagances which are to be noted
as the fantasies of genius.   The ultimate halo, the crown
of glory, is reserved for the explorer of distant lands
and the friend of men distinguished in a continent.

[1] Temple, it appears, was promised payment for his services :
' You shall have consultation guineas, as an ambassador has his
appointments.'   This seems to imply more than the mere travelling
expenses which Dr. Rogers suggests as an explanation.

' Talk of my various travels, German princes—Voltaire
and Rousseau.'   The effect upon the audience of this
elaborate comedy is to be duly registered in order that
the manager may arrange the sequence appropriately
and the principal actor appear in splendour at the
dramatic moment. ' Observe her well. See how
amiable ! Judge if she would be happy with your
friend.   Think of me as the great man at Adamtown—
quite classical too ; study the mother. Remember
well what passes. . . .   Consider what a romantic
expedition you are on ; take notes.'   By the final
injunction, the biographer's own peculiar weapon is
to be directed at the prize and the lady captured by
a sheet of memoranda.

    An accident, however, occurs and trivial circum-
stance is swollen to importance by the fever of im-
patience.   The fervour of a suitor's letter demands
immediate reply ; but the letter remains for some days
in the post.   Letter follows letter, and the perturbation
increases when jealousy summons the image of a
yellow nabob.   The actor doubts if he has chosen the
proper *rôle*, and fears the effect of his ' Spanish stateli-
ness.'   But the ardent lover is able to exclaim, ' I
am entertained with this dilemma like another chapter
in my adventures,' and consolation comes in a letter
from the Signora ' written with all the warmth of
Italian affection.'   Finally the matter is explained and
there is the pleasure of restoring harmony.   Lucky

that these matters run never smoothly, for there will be further opportunity of experiencing the tortured joy of a quarrel and the supreme delight of recon- ciliation. An uninteresting interval is amused by a renewal of intimacy with the ' dear infidel ' before another coolness is arranged. The self-possession of the lady now provokes ' a strange sultanish letter, very cold and very formal,' and after an absence of three weeks the suitor pays an eminently agreeable visit to the prospective bride, though still apparently in a rather sultanish mood : ' I am dressed in green and gold. I have my chaise in which I sit alone with Mr. Gray, and Thomas rides by me in a claret-coloured suit with a silver-laced hat.' The final joy was however withheld. ' The princess and I have not yet made up our quarrel, she talks lightly of it.' The adorer is prepared conditionally to soar to the last heights of adoration. ' If she feels as I wish her to do, I shall adore her while my blood is warm ' : but the philosopher is determined to escape the inconvenience of a wounded heart : ' I shall just bring myself, I hope, to a good, easy tranquillity.' The ' princess ' by this time has ceased to be a dupe ; she may have seen that the courtship was arranged to give the colouring of romance to conventional matrimony, and alter the pompous comedy of surrender to a serious farce for one party and for the other probably to a serious tragedy. Her manner in any case became more reserved : ' She

refused sending me a lock . . . and she says very
cool things upon that head.' The burning lover
begins to congratulate himself upon escape from so
unsatisfying a mate, and the beautiful princess is
discovered to be a jilt. ' Wish me joy, my good
friend, of having discovered the snake before it was
too late. . . . After this I shall be upon my guard
against ever indulging the least fondness for a Scot
lass ; I am a soul of a more Southern frame. I may
perhaps be fortunate enough to find an Englishwoman
who will be sensible of my merits and will study to
please my singular humour.' Zelide and Miss Bosville
are mentioned in the same letter, the former to illustrate the truth that ' an old flame is easily rekindled '
and the latter as a possibility to be kept in mind.

But a volatility amazing even in Boswell produces
on the following day a letter which is full of the charms
of Miss Blair. The more violent the quarrel the more
pleasing the peace-making. A meeting is arranged at
Edinburgh ; a declaration is made and the now enthusiastic suitor reports, ' I ventured to seize her hand.
She is really the finest woman I ever saw.' The
' princess ' however is still reserved, and determined
efforts have to be made at the theatre.

Next evening I was at the play with them ; it
was ' Othello.' I sat close behind the princess, and
at the most affecting scenes I pressed my hand upon her
waist ; she was in tears and rather leaned to me. The

jealous Moor described my very soul. I often spake to
her of the torment she saw before her.

But even after this touching scene there is cause for
disquiet. ' Still,' he says, ' I thought her distant, and
still I felt uneasy.'

The encouragement however was sufficient to give
confidence to the attack, and there follows a *tête-à-tête*
in which ' pleasure from the intimacy of often squeezing
and kissing her fine hand, while she looked at me with
those beautiful black eyes,' was somewhat darkened by
a disconcerting surprise. ' I then asked her to tell
me if she had any particular liking for me. What
think you, Temple, was her answer ? " No ; I really
have no particular liking for you ; I like many people
as well as you—I like Jeany Maxwell better than you." '
Consolation must now be sought where love is denied.
Boswell : ' If you should happen to love another,
will you tell me immediately and help me to make
myself easy ? ' *Princess* : ' Yes, I will.' But the lady's
sympathy shows a want of imagination which is
highly unsatisfying. *Boswell* : ' I must, if possible, endeavour to forget you. What would you have me do ? '
Princess : ' I really don't know what you should do.'

It would appear that honour had no escape from
such a defeat but in renewing the encounter. The
history of the last period of this wooing, of the nadir
of the wooer's fortunes and his cheerfulness in spite
of repulses, is told to Temple six weeks later. A new

rival appears upon the scene, and there is rumour of an engagement. The rejected suitor writes to ascertain the truth of this alarming story. But his appeal is neglected. Dignity now demands that disappointment shall be concealed, and an alliance is formed with the presumably successful rival, Sir Alexander Gilmour. ' I endeavoured to laugh off my passion, and I got Sir Alexander Gilmour to frank a letter to her, which I wrote in a pleasant strain, and amused myself with the whim.' The lady now appears in London and at the same moment the Nabob. He too is to be an ally, and a final scene is arranged. ' We gave our words as men of honour that we would be honest to each other so that neither should suffer needlessly ; and to satisfy ourselves of our real situation, we gave our words of honour that we should both ask her this morning, and I should go first.' The result can hardly have been doubtful. Boswell tells his adorable princess, ' I have great animal spirits, and bear it wonderfully well,' and proceeds to write ' A Crambo Song on Losing my Mistress.'

> Although I be an honest laird,
>   In person rather strong and brawny,
> For me the heiress never cared,
>   For she would have the knight, Sir Sawney.
>
> And when, with ardent vows, I swore,
>   Loud as Sir Jonathan Trelawney,
> The heiress showed me to the door,
>   And said, she 'd have the knight, Sir Sawney.

H

> She told me with a scornful look,
>   I was as ugly as a tawney;
> For she a better fish could hook,
>   The rich and gallant knight, Sir Sawney.

We might suppose that Boswell in spite of his cheer-fulness would have been at heart rather dejected by these events ; but he writes to Temple, ' My mind is now twice as enlarged as it has been for some months. You cannot say how fine a woman I may marry ; perhaps a Howard or some other of the noblest in the kingdom.'

The realities were hardly so elevated as these dreams, for in the following spring (1768), it is Zelide again, and not she alone. ' Zelide may have had her faults but is she always to have them ? May not time have altered her for the better as it has altered me ? But you will tell me that I am not so greatly altered, as I have still many unruly passions. To confess to you at once Temple, I have, since my last coming to town been as wild as ever.' But flowers were to be fresh at last in the month of August. ' I am exceedingly lucky in having escaped the insensible Miss Bosville and the furious Zelide, for I have now seen the finest creature that ever was formed, *la belle Irlandaise*. Figure to yourself, Temple, a young lady just sixteen, formed like a Grecian nymph, with the sweetest countenance full of sensibility . . .' Everything was favourable. ' Here every flower is united.' The diplomat who

had been fatigued before by the restraint of a wise
cautiousness is resolved that this time there shall
be no reserve. ' Ah, my friend, I am now as I ought
to be ; no reserved prudent conduct as with Miss
Bosville. No ! all youthful, warm, natural, in short,
all genuine love.' And the ardent hunter seems to
have been more successful than the wily angler. ' I
repeated my fervent passion to her again and again ;
she was pleased and I could swear that her little heart
beat. I carved the first letter of her name on a tree ; I
cut off a lock of her hair, *male pertinax*. She promised
not to forget me, nor to marry a lord before March.'
Moreover, the unspoilt joy of advance without contest
was more pleasant than the doubts and hopes of expectation, while a puritanical idealism and the solemnity
of an oath were a welcome change for less spiritual
delights.

This is the most agreeable passion I ever felt ;
sixteen, innocence, and gaiety make me quite a
Sicilian swain. Before I left London I made a vow in
St. Paul's Church that I would not allow myself in
licentious connections of any kind for six months, I
am hitherto firm to my vow, and already feel myself
a superior being . . . in short, Maria has me without
any rival ; I do hope the period of my perfect felicity,
as far as this state can afford, is now in view.

Whether this ' perfect felicity ' was attained and
how long it lasted we do not know. Maria no doubt
had her day like the others ; the sequel to the vow in

St. Paul's we may conjecture. Boswell, if his name
endured for no other talents, would remain with us for
ever as an incomparable genius for reviving affection.
In December we learn : ' Miss Blair is Miss Blair still,'
—still a fit subject for this curious pastime. ' I was
two or three times at Adamtown, and, upon my word,
the old flame was kindled.' Miss Blair apparently
had been piqued because her suitor had made such a
joke of his love for the heiress in every company.
' Temple, to a man again in love, this was engaging.
I walked whole hours with the princess ; I kneeled ;
I became truly amorous.' These brief sentences
adequately describe the last recorded love-scene. If
Boswell corresponded with Temple between December
1768 and May 1770 the letters have been lost ; and so
the outrageous story ends abruptly—and it is fortunate
perhaps for the readers of this book, for it is a story so
fascinating and so absurd and so richly human that no
part of it can be omitted.

Boswell in fact was destined to be married to his
cousin, Miss Montgomerie. The Montgomeries were
an aristocratic family related to Lord Eglinton, and
Boswell was proud of the connection: he speaks in a published pamphlet of ' having the honour and happiness
to be married to his Lordship's relation, a true Mont-
gomerie.' We know very little about Mrs. Boswell.
Johnson's curt judgment in a letter to Mrs. Thrale is
probably right in placing her with the great bulk of

mediocre humanity : 'Mrs. B—— has the mien and manners of a gentlewoman ; and such a person and mind as would not be in any place either admired or contemned. She is in a proper degree inferior to her husband : she cannot rival him, nor can he ever be ashamed of her.' But if undistinguished, as in Johnson's view a good wife should be, the lady had some excellent qualities ; and Johnson himself would have been the first to praise them. If he urged Boswell on more than one occasion to be considerate of his home, it was because he knew that the home was both pleasant and valuable to his friend : ' I need not tell you what regard you owe to Mrs. Boswell's entreaties ; or how much you ought to study the happiness of her who studies yours with so much diligence, and of whose kindness you enjoy such good effects.' Boswell, too, loudly sings the praise of his wife : ' I am fully sensible,' he writes to Temple, ' of my happiness in being married to so excellent a woman, so sensible a mistress of a family, so agreeable a companion, so affectionate and peculiarly proper helpmate for me.' After her death he writes : ' I had no occasion almost to think concerning my family, and every particular was thought of by her better than I could ' ; and he refers to her in the ' Life of Johnson ' as ' my very valuable wife, and the very affectionate mother of my children, who, if they inherit her good qualities, will have no reason to complain of their lot.'

That Mrs. Boswell had in abundance the matronly
virtues is sufficiently clear. She had besides considerable intellectual gifts. Boswell calls her, ' A lady of
admirable good sense and quickness of understanding ' ;
he kept a common-place book, ' Uxoriana,' to preserve
her witty sayings, and after her death regretted her
' admirable conversation.' From her own expressed
opinion of her husband's friendship with Dr. Johnson
we are obliged to think well of her intelligence : it
was a female opinion, as Boswell remarks, with something of resentment for the intrusion of this uncomfortable guest : ' His irregular hours and uncouth
habits, such as turning the candles with their heads
downwards, when they did not burn bright enough,
and letting the wax drop upon the carpet, could not
but be disagreeable to a lady.' And no doubt she
failed to appreciate the devotion of Boswell to this
ungainly and unpleasing animal. But her observation,
in the manner of the times, is admirably pointed :
' I have seen many a bear led by a man, but I never
before saw a man led by a bear.'

The marriage took place in the autumn of 1769 ;
Boswell was then twenty-nine years of age. The
situation is summed up in his own remarks in the
London Magazine for April 1781 :

After having for many years cherished a system
of marrying for money, I at last totally departed from

it, and married for love.   But the truth was that
I had not been careful enough to weed my mind ; for
while I cultivated the plant of interest, love all the
time grew up along with it and fairly got the better.
Naturally somewhat singular, independent of any
additions which affectation and vanity may perhaps
have made, I resolved to have a more pleasing species
of marriage than common, and bargained with my bride
that I should not be bound to live with her longer than
I really inclined ; and that whenever I tired of her
domestic society, I should be at liberty to give it up.

That Boswell was always fond of his wife is clear
enough. ' Eleven years have elapsed and I have
never yet wanted to take advantage of my stipulated
privilege.'   He never speaks of her without affection,
and was deeply distressed by her death in 1789.   But
for how long he continued to love her fervently it is
difficult to tell ; not, one would suppose, for a great
length of time, or he could hardly have written in the
London Magazine : ' Whatever respect I may have
for the institution of marriage, and however much
I am convinced that it upon the whole produces
rational happiness, I cannot but be of the opinion that
the passion of love has been improperly feigned as
continuing long after the conjugal knot has been tied.'
Nor, if Boswell had continued to love his wife passion-
ately, would he have found it disagreeable to return
to Edinburgh, after visits to London.

But Boswell no doubt wanted to be a faithful

husband : ' I can unite little fondnesses with perfect conjugal love.' [1]   His idea of fidelity would seem to involve no kind of restriction upon his natural inclinations except in so far as that he should appear to be a good husband in the eyes of the world and particularly of his wife.   However sensible this view may have been, it was not such as commonly finds favour among the female sex.   But he was undoubtedly in his own view a faithful husband and he had really at heart the welfare of his wife.   ' Upon the whole I do believe,' he says, ' I make her very happy.' [2]

[1] *Letters to Temple*, p. 159.   [2] *Ib.* p. 137.

CHAPTER IV

A BIOGRAPHY of Boswell, though it might profess to be complete, could say little about his domestic life. If he has told us very little about it, there is, however, no reason that we should seek to know more. It was a very essential part of Boswell that he should have a wife and family : a wife, because she adds a certain flavour of respectability and is a definite asset to the social position of a man, still more perhaps because she increases responsibility and so intensifies the sensation of importance ; a family, because to the man of estate there must be born an heir. But the mere fact of his being married was, in a sense, of far less consequence to him than to most men.

There were two aspects of his life which were dissociated in a peculiar degree from each other—the life in Scotland, where he laboured at the Law and was eventually to be Laird of Auchinleck, and where his home was the basis of operations ; and the life in London, which he visited as often as he was able, to live the gay life he loved, and to talk to his literary friends, especially to Dr. Johnson. The pleasure

he had in the society of his English friends was far
more to him than another man's recreation or hobby.
It occupied more time, and it was time spent away
from his domestic circle and, for the most part, away
from his work. He is never tired of telling of his
love of London.

I had long complained to him [Johnson] that I
felt myself discontented in Scotland, as too narrow a
sphere, and that I wished to make my chief residence
in London, the great scene of ambition, instruction,
amusement : a scene which was to me, comparatively
speaking, a heaven upon earth ! *Johnson* : ' Why, Sir,
I never knew anyone who had such a gust for London
as you have.'

It must be our business then to follow for a little
the life of Boswell among his London friends, to see
the relations in which he stood to them and the progress of his intimacy with Dr. Johnson.

In the ' Life ' there are recorded the consecutive
visits of Boswell to England with relation always to
Dr. Johnson in particular, but referring also to other
celebrities whom he met, and to his own pleasures and
amusements. The group of men who were in the first
place the friends and admirers of Dr. Johnson, and
with whom Boswell naturally associated so far as he
was able, were for the most part distinguished men in
the best literary society, and members of that club
which was started by Johnson and Reynolds in 1762
or 1763.   Burke, Beauclerk, Langton, Goldsmith,

Hawkins, were original members ; Garrick was elected in 1773, as was Boswell himself. Malone, whose wise help was invaluable to Boswell in preparing for the press his *magnum opus*, and who was its first editor, became a member later.

The pleasure which it gave Boswell to belong to this club of distinguished men is revealed in his own account of his election. ' The gentlemen went away to their club, and I was left at Beauclerk's till the fate of my election should be announced to me. I sat in a state of anxiety which even the charming conversation of Lady Di Beauclerk could not entirely dissipate. In a short time I received the agreeable intelligence that I was chosen. I hastened to the place of meeting, and was introduced to such a society as can seldom be found.'

From a conversation reported in the ' Tour to the Hebrides ' it would appear that Boswell was not elected without some difficulty. ' He [Johnson] told me, " Sir, you got into our club by doing what a man can do." '

(Boswell's note on this is : ' This I find is considered as obscure. I suppose Dr. Johnson meant that I assiduously and earnestly recommended myself to some of the members, as in a canvass for an election into Parliament.')

' Several of the members wished to keep you out. Burke told me he doubted if you were fit for it . . .' Boswell : ' They were afraid of you, Sir, as it was you who proposed me.' *Johnson* : ' Sir, they knew that if they refused you, they 'd probably have never got in another. I 'd have kept them all out.'

Boswell, of course, did not get on equally well with all of Johnson's friends. Goldsmith especially he seems to have disliked, and at a later date Mrs. Thrale, Miss Burney and Baretti ; we may suppose that the feeling was mutual, especially after the appearance of the ' Life of Johnson,' in which Boswell made little attempt to conceal his feelings. With Hawkins, who was chosen to write the official biography of Johnson, he was eventually to quarrel. But he had strong supporters in the club. ' Now you are in,' Johnson told him, ' none of them are sorry. Burke says you have so much good humour naturally, it is scarce a virtue.' Beauclerk too appreciated him. ' Beauclerk was very earnest for you.' His greatest friend of this *coterie* besides Dr. Johnson was Sir Joshua Reynolds. Sir Joshua seems always to have understood and insisted upon the value of Boswell. He was prepared to take up the cudgels. ' He thaws reserve wherever he comes and sets the ball of conversation rolling.' [1] The club, whatever else it might think about Boswell, was obliged to admit that he was excellent company.

There were some, no doubt, who had a high opinion of Boswell's abilities ; it was admitted by everyone

[1] *Life of Reynolds*, ii, p. 12.

that he had written a good book, and not all, like Gray and Walpole, [1] can have thought that he wrote it by chance. And Boswell too, if not a good literary critic, was interested in books and able to talk about them. The opinions to which he gave expression in the ' Life of Johnson ' about various books which came under discussion are often more appreciative and better supported by reason than the dicta of Johnson, and he sometimes shows considerable sagacity. His views about Johnson's own books, and especially his criticism of Johnson's style and the high estimate he formed of the ' Lives of the Poets,' are excellent.

But it was far more for his social than for his literary qualities that Boswell was valued. In the circle of Johnson's admirers he was in a sense the most important figure ; he had a greater admiration than any other and was rewarded by Johnson with a greater degree of affection. He came to understand Johnson. Hannah More relates that she was on one occasion made umpire in a trial of skill between Garrick and Boswell, which could most nearly imitate Dr. Johnson's manner.[2] ' I remember I gave it for Boswell in familiar conversation, and for Garrick in reciting poetry.' To have beaten Garrick was a great performance and shows how Boswell must have studied Johnson. He was, as it were, his chief exploiter. It was he above

[1] *Letters of Horace Walpole*, v, p. 85.
[2] *Memoirs of Hannah More*, i, p. 213.

all the rest who could make Johnson talk.[1] He knew
what would provoke a discussion, and was so reckless
of appearing foolish that he would introduce any
subject. He made opportunities for Johnson to exhibit his powers. The description of how he arranged
the meeting with Wilkes, though more famous almost
than any other passage of the ' Life,' is too important
as illustrating the whole attitude of Boswell to be
omitted here. It is not inappropriate to say that the
very name of Wilkes was to Johnson like a red rag to a
bull. He hated what he considered to be a pretentious
notoriety, and what he no doubt talked about as ' this
cant of liberty ' was the signal for an outburst of
violence in his best manner. Boswell conceived the
idea of bringing these two together, and probably
hoped to witness an incomparable contest. But how
was this to be done ?   ' I was persuaded that if I had
come upon him with a direct proposal, " Sir, will you
dine in company with Jack Wilkes ? " he would have
flown into a passion and would probably have answered,
" Dine with Jack Wilkes, Sir ! I 'd as soon dine with
Jack Ketch." '   But it was easy to see the weak point
in the Doctor's armour. ' Notwithstanding the high
veneration which I entertained for Dr. Johnson, I
was sensible that he was a little actuated sometimes by
contradiction, and by means of that I hoped I should

[1] The evidence for what is stated in this sentence and the next
is discussed later under Boswell's biographical qualities.

gain my point.' Boswell, who knows exactly what will provoke his friend, has thought out beforehand precisely what he shall say, and opens with a proposal which Johnson is sure to accept. ' Mr. Dilly, Sir, sends me his respectful compliments, and would be happy if you would do him the honour to dine with him on Wednesday next along with me, as I must soon go to Scotland.' *Johnson* : ' Sir, I am obliged to Mr. Dilly. I will wait upon him.' The dictator is in a gracious mood, and the moment favourable to excite a rebuke in defence of that formal courtesy which he loved to practise. ' Provided, Sir, I suppose,' adds Boswell, ' that the company which he is to have is agreeable to you.' The apparent artlessness of the remark in the true Boswellian fashion, with the exaggerated respect that so often irritated Johnson, took effect at once. *Johnson* : ' What do you mean, Sir ? What do you take me for ? Do you think I am so ignorant of the world as to imagine that I am to prescribe to a gentleman what company he is to have at his table ? ' An excuse must now be made which is certain to meet with sledge-hammer reasoning or piercing sarcasm, and it will then be safe to lead up to the disagreeable intelligence. ' I beg your pardon, Sir, for wishing to prevent you from meeting people whom you might not like. Perhaps he may have some of what he calls his patriotic friends with him.' *Johnson* : ' Well, Sir, what then ? What care *I* for his *patriotic friends*? Poh!' *Boswell* : 'I should not be surprised to find Jack Wilkes there.' The possibility may have been disconcerting, but retreat was now out of the question. *Johnson* : ' And if Jack Wilkes should be there, what is that to me, Sir? My deaɪ friend, let me have no more of this. I am sorry to be angry with you, but really it is treating me strangely to talk to me as if I could not meet any company whatever, occasionally.' So the matter was settled. Boswell asks forgiveness and clinches the matter : ' Pray forgive me, Sir ; I meant well. But you shall meet whoever comes.' 'Thus,' he tells the reader, with evident satisfaction, ' I secured him.'

The man who could do this was clearly of importance to those who were interested, even though in a less degree than himself, in Dr. Johnson. We may suppose that the circle of Johnson's literary friends welcomed Boswell as much for his peculiar homage to the Doctor as for his own social talents.

.   .   .   .   .

We must now more nearly examine that friendship, which is as much the concern of our own age as it was of Boswell's. We have considered already what it was that caused these two men to be friends ; but the meanest picture of Boswell must include some account of his behaviour towards Johnson ; we must review the progress of their friendship and remark the more characteristic attitudes of the biographer.

In the pages of the ' Life of Johnson ' is recorded in detail, and almost without reserve, the story of the relations between these two friends.   It is a story full of humour, telling of all the little peculiarities of a great man, of all the whims and foibles which we are accustomed to observe in old age and which we both like and laugh at ; but it is the story also of a deep and anxious affection.

If the course of friendship ran smoothly on the whole for Johnson and Boswell, as might be expected when one of the two was so well balanced and so practically wise as the older man, yet, as must always be the case with people who are not either quite perfect or quite colourless, there were rough places here and there ; and these, if responsible for no great misery, were, however, the cause of some unhappiness to both.   Boswell, at all events, realised very keenly the great gulf between them ; between his own sensitive, uncertain nature and Johnson's rude strength.   He, probably more than most men, wanted sympathy, wanted to be understood. With what relief he speaks from his heart to Temple : ' I have not had such a relief as this for I don't know how long. I have broke the trammels of business, and am roving unconfined with my Temple.' It is unfortunate for Boswell that he expressed himself so extravagantly. We sympathise with those who are self-contained about sentiment and particularly about their own sorrows, but we have few kind feelings for

I

those who exaggerate. And Boswell, because he was difficult to understand, was more than usually isolated : to Johnson, at all events, there must have been many matters about which he could not talk, and he was nettled sometimes by the other's blunt advice. It was unpleasant to be told by one whom he so much respected, at the moment of his first serious publication, 'The Corsican Journal,' to 'empty his head of Corsica which had filled it too long.' It must have been more than annoying when he had written to Johnson in a despondent mood (there is no reason to doubt that he was genuine in despondency) to receive his answer : 'I had hoped you had got rid of all this hypocrisy of misery. What have you to do with Liberty and Necessity? Or what more than to hold your tongue about it? Do not doubt that I shall be most heartily glad to see you here again, for I love every part about you but your affectation of distress.'

Much as we must admire the honest wrath of Johnson, and the desire which he had to cure the affectation of Boswell, we cannot but regret sometimes that he was not more discriminating. It was much, no doubt, to be assured of affection, but affection alone could not take the place of an understanding sympathy; and if this had come from one whom he so much respected, it would have been invaluable to Boswell. As it was, he realised that Johnson must partially disapprove of him, and it was because he knew, and felt this disapproval, as much as from any inherent quality of his temperament, that he so often wanted a proof of affection.

Whatever may have been their cause—it may have been no more than the mere need for friendship coupled with the peculiar unreserve of Boswell's character— the result of these demands was sometimes to irritate Johnson.

I said to him : ' My dear Sir, we must meet every year, if you don't quarrel with me.' *Johnson* : ' Nay, Sir, you are more likely to quarrel with me than I with you. My regard for you is greater almost than I have words to express ; but I do not choose to be always repeating it ; write it down in the first leaf of your pocket-book, and never doubt of it again.'

On one occasion Johnson was really angry. Boswell conceived the idea of making an experiment to test his affection. It was apparently his custom to write to Johnson upon his return to his family. He wanted to see what the Doctor would do if he neglected the usual civility. Johnson, of course, was eventually the first to write ; and Boswell, thus gratified, answered him by a letter which frankly explained his motives :

I was willing . . . to try whether your affection for me would, after an unusual silence on my part, make you write first. This afternoon I have had very high satisfaction by receiving your kind letter of inquiry, for which I most gratefully thank you. I am doubtful if it was right to make the experiment, though I have gained by it.

We may forgive Johnson for being annoyed by this letter.

Those who make very large demands upon their friends for a display of affection are, as a rule, rather tiresome companions; it may possibly be good to be sensitive, but it is bad to be easily offended, which is often the case with such people. But if Boswell, like many who take a decided lead in friendship, required many proofs to make him believe that it was more than a one-sided affair, he of all men was the most difficult to offend. We cannot do better than read his own accounts of his quarrels with Johnson. There is that famous one, in the first place, of the dinner at Sir Joshua's.

On Saturday, May 2, I dined with him at Sir Joshua Reynolds', where there was a very large company, and a great deal of conversation; but owing to some circumstance which I cannot now recollect, I have no record of any part of it, except that there were several people there by no means of the Johnsonian school; so that less attention was paid to him than usual, which put him out of humour; and upon some imaginary offence from me he attacked me with such rudeness, that I was vexed and angry, because it gave those persons an opportunity of enlarging upon his supposed ferocity and ill-treatment of his friends.

We may doubt whether Boswell gives the true reason

for his vexation. He was able to stand a great deal of 'buffeting' at Dr. Johnson's hands; but it was probably necessary for him to feel that the company were good-natured in their merriment. We do not resent that men should laugh *at* us if they laugh *with* us at the same time. It was no doubt the contemptuous and half-concealed mirth of strangers which Boswell felt to be unbearable. And if he felt like this we may sympathise with a short period of sulking. ' I was so much hurt, and had my pride so much roused, that I kept away from him for a week; and, perhaps, might have kept away much longer, nay, gone to Scotland without seeing him again, had not we fortunately met and been reconciled. To such unhappy chances are human friendships liable.'

The oddest thing of all about Boswell, when we reflect upon the scenes of his humiliation, is his pride. It is not the least unlikely that, as he suggests, if circumstances had not ordained otherwise he would have waited, and waited for a long time, for Johnson to make advances. It was not merely the pride of the worm in the proverb which may be roused at the last. The worm would not consciously go out of his way to incur insulting anger as Boswell did when he arranged the dinner with Wilkes and on many other occasions. Boswell's was a pride which was constantly giving him pain and was capable, when goaded to obstinacy, of going to considerable lengths.

At Sir Joshua Reynolds' dinner he must have suffered acutely. Croker tells the story of Boswell's discomfiture as it was told to him at fourth-hand by the Marquess of Wellesley. ' The wits of Queen Anne's reign were talked of, when Boswell exclaimed, " How delightful it must have been to have lived in the society of Pope, Swift, Arbuthnot, Gay, and Bolingbroke! We have no such society in our days." Sir Joshua answered, " I think, Mr. Boswell, you might be satisfied with your great friend's conversation." " Nay, Sir, Mr. Boswell is right," said Johnson, " every man wishes for preferment, and if Boswell had lived in those days, he would have obtained promotion." " How so, Sir ?" asked Sir Joshua. " Why, Sir," said Johnson, " he would have had a high place in the Dunciad." ' It was a hard blow. How deep was the wound we cannot tell, because we do not know how it was said or how received. It is curious at first sight that Boswell should have been more sulky about this than about many a rough retort recorded in the ' Life.' It is even more remarkable that he should have concealed this story of his humilia- tion while he told others with perfect frankness. To do so was entirely contrary to his principle and practice. The idea that ' the several people there by no means of the Johnsonian school ' should read the story, recall the circumstances and laugh, not good-naturedly but with contempt and malice, must have overcome for once the biographer's ' sacred love of truth.' From these facts, in any case, we may fairly argue that Boswell suffered from his pride as a proud man must have suffered from the Doctor's rude snubs. It is to Boswell's credit that he was willing to run the gauntlet and even to bare his breast for the wound, not only because if he was to have the honour he must endure the pain, but at least as much because he knew that it was his vocation to goad the giant into action, to strike and fan the spark that would ignite the powder. It is to Boswell's credit that he had a part in the fray : he bled from honourable wounds. But since men had been so ill-natured as to despise them it was difficult to display the gashes and the scars ; and because from a noble motive he did what was most difficult and most valuable we must praise Boswell exceedingly.

It is further to Boswell's credit that, if he winced for a moment under the sledge-hammer and pouted at the executioner, his natural good-humour and generosity made reconciliation easy.

On Friday, May 8, I dined with him at Mr. Langton's. I was reserved and silent, which I suppose he perceived and might recollect the cause. After dinner, while Mr. Langton was called out of the room, and we were by ourselves, he drew his chair near to mine, and said, in a tone of conciliating courtesy, ' Well, how have you done ? ' *Boswell* : ' Sir, you have made me very uneasy by your behaviour to me when we were last at Sir Joshua Reynolds'. You know, my dear Sir, no man has a greater respect and affection for you, or would sooner go to the end of the world to serve you. Now to treat me so——.' He insisted that I had interrupted him, which I assured him was not the case and proceeded—' But why treat me so before people who neither love you nor me ? ' *Johnson* : ' Well, I am sorry for it. I 'll make it up to you i' twenty different ways as you please.'

Johnson certainly seems to have made himself most agreeable on this occasion, and it would have been churlish of Boswell to have resisted these advances; but nothing could be more truly generous than the way in which he reminded Johnson of his affection and respect. Boswell now proceeds to appease his pride by using the occasion to make a *bon mot*. ' I said to-day to Sir Joshua, when he observed that you *tossed* me sometimes—" I don't care how often or how high he tosses me, when only friends are present, for then I fall upon soft ground : but I do not like falling on stones, which is the case when enemies are present." I think this is a pretty good image, Sir.' Johnson assents, with unusual courtesy, ' Sir it is one of the happiest I have ever heard.' And Boswell is now completely satisfied. The account proceeds by giving Johnson a testimonial for good-nature and assuring its readers that the best of relations were at once re-established. ' The truth is, there was no venom in the wounds he inflicted at any time, unless they were irritated by some malignant infusion from other hands. We were instantly as cordial again as ever, and joined in hearty laugh at some ludicrous but innocent peculiarities of one of our friends.'

The story of this quarrel, if there were no other evidence, would show that Boswell endured not a few rebuffs.   The fact indeed has never been challenged. Johnson's method of talking for victory often took the form of mere rudeness, and Boswell was frequently the subject of his rough wit.   For Boswell it was a question whether the fun and the interest of making Johnson angry were worth the sacrifice of dignity involved. In retrospect it always was so, and, at the moment too, very often.   He tells us how, on one occasion, he had quoted Shakespeare in the course of discussion, and Johnson, who was angry, had made the characteristic reply, ' Nay, if you are to bring in gabble I 'll talk no more ' ; it is evident that this was regarded by him as a successful issue to the argument.   Johnson had become angrier and angrier, and Boswell, far from trying to appease him, was glad to bring him to a state of entire unreasonableness. He was conscious of this when he commented with evident pleasure, ' My readers will decide upon this dispute.'

There is something of the same spirit in the tale which Boswell tells of the quarrel on the moor during the Tour in the Hebrides. Boswell towards the end of a day had the not unnatural intention of going on ahead to make preparations at the inn.

It grew dusky ; and we had a very tedious ride for what was called five miles ; but I am sure would measure ten. We had no conversation. I was riding forward to the inn at Glenelg, on the opposite shore to Skye, that I might take proper measures, before Dr. Johnson, who was now advancing in dreary silence, Hay leading his horse, should arrive. Vass also walked by the side of his horse, and Joseph followed behind : as therefore he was thus attended, and seemed to be in deep meditation, I thought there could be no harm in leaving him for a little while.

Boswell indeed seems to have been particularly thought-ful and even shows some delicacy in not interrupting Johnson's meditations to tell him his plan. The sequel must have surprised him very much. ' He called me back with a tremendous shout, and was really in a passion with me for leaving him. I told him my intentions, but he was not satisfied, and said, " Do you know I should as soon have thought of picking a pocket as doing so ? " ' This did not annoy Boswell in the least, though it took place in the presence of their servants ; he was accustomed by this time to the Doctor's moods, and could only be amused. He replied with a composure which he must have known would irritate Johnson exceedingly ; ' I am diverted with you, Sir.' The force of the desired explosion may have been underestimated. ' *Johnson*: " Sir, I could never be diverted with incivility . . ." His extraordinary warmth confounded me so much, that I justified myself but lamely to him. Matters in fact were rather more serious than Boswell had supposed, and he must now make an effort to pacify his companion— but without effect. ' I resumed the subject of my leaving him on the road, and endeavoured to defend it better. He still was violent on that head, and said, " Sir, had you gone on, I was thinking that I should have returned with you to Edinburgh, and then have parted from you, and never spoken to you more." ' The storm was indeed a bad one that did not clear up entirely by bedtime. Boswell felt distinctly uneasy in the volcanic atmosphere ; but he easily effected a complete reconciliation.

Thursday, September 2. I had slept ill. Dr. Johnson's anger had affected me much. I considered that, without any bad intention, I might suddenly forfeit his friendship ; and was impatient to see him this morning. I told him how uneasy he had made me by what he had said, and reminded him of his own remark at Aberdeen upon old friendships being hastily broken off. He owned he had spoken in a passion . . .; and he added, ' Let 's think no more on 't.' *Boswell*: ' Well then, Sir, I shall be easy. Remember I am to have fair warning in case of any quarrel. You are never to spring a mine upon me. It was absurd in me to believe you.' *Johnson*: ' You deserved about as much as to believe me from night to morning.'

The mixture of amusement and anxiety in Boswell's conduct and the affectionate and good-humoured reconciliation are all extremely typical of the relations between these two friends. Johnson indeed had far

too much sense of Boswell's good qualities and value
ever to fall out with him seriously, and it would have
been hard to do so.   There was never one real mis-
understanding between them up to the end.   Their
intercourse, consisting of the visits of Boswell to
London and a number of letters on both sides, had but
one break, from November 1769 to April 1771.   Boswell
had just been married, and omitted in 1770 to pay his
usual visit to London ; he tells us that there was no
coldness on either side, no reason for not writing
beyond the common one of procrastination.

The correspondence of Boswell and Johnson is on
the whole of an irregular nature ; there is more than
one interval, longer than we might expect, between
two men who were such active friends as they, in
an age when letter-writing was cultivated for its own
sake.   Arguing from this fact and considering that
he was not present at Johnson's death-bed, Boswell
has been accused of neglecting his friend at the end
of his life.   But from the state of mind which he
described much earlier in the *London Magazine*, we
can otherwise account for these lapses :

To pay a visit or write a letter to a friend does not
surely require much activity. Yet such small exertions
have appeared so laborious to a Hypochondriack, that
he has delayed from hour to hour, so that friendship
has grown cold for want of having its heat continued,
for which repeated renewals, however slight, are
necessary ; or, perhaps, till death has carried his friend

beyond the reach of any token of his kindness, and the regrets which pained him in the course of his neglect are accumulated and press upon his mind with a weight of sorrow.[1]

We may suppose that whenever Boswell for a short time failed in his careful attention it was through no lack of affection, but rather through a kind of indolence and want of purpose in the manner of it, which is far from being uncommon.

The greatest event in this long friendship, and the time which has left us the fullest record, is the 'Tour to the Hebrides,' in 1773. In Boswell's journal we see more nearly than elsewhere the relations between the two friends and the nature of their companionship. In the foreground is the extreme amiability of Boswell— it was by this that he was fitted to perform that most difficult office of friendship, to travel with Dr. Johnson. We may read his own account of himself at this time :

Think then, of a gentleman of ancient blood, the pride of which was his predominant passion. He was then in his thirty-third year, and had been about four years happily married. His inclination was to be a soldier ; but his father, a respectable judge, had pressed him into the profession of the law. He had travelled a good deal, and seen many varieties of human life. He had thought more than anybody supposed, and had a pretty good stock of general learning and knowledge. He had all Dr. Johnson's

[1] *London Magazine*, xlvii, 106.

principles, with some degree of relaxation. He had rather too little, than too much prudence ; and, his imagination being lively, he often said things of which the effect was very different from the intention. He resembled sometimes.

'The best good man, with the worst natur'd muse.'

He cannot deny himself the vanity of finishing with the encomium of Dr. Johnson, whose friendly partiality to the companion of his ' Tour ' represents him as one 'whose acuteness would help my enquiry, and whose gaiety of conversation, and civility of manners, are sufficient to counteract the inconveniences of travel, in countries less hospitable than we have passed.' Dr. Johnson in a letter to Mrs. Thrale wrote of him in terms of the highest esteem : ' Boswell will praise my resolution and perseverance, and I shall in return celebrate his good humour and perpetual cheerfulness . . . It is very convenient to travel with him, for there is no house where he is not received with kindness and respect.' [1]

No one certainly could have been more attentive than Boswell was : he had a sense of responsibility in being in charge of the great writer, which made him anxious not only that Johnson should be welcomed in a fitting manner, but that he himself should appear as a worthy companion. His deep sense of respect, his desire for approval and dread of reproof are constantly

[1] *Piozzi Letters*, i, 198.

obvious. This attitude is well illustrated by the account of his carouse in Corrichatachin :

We were cordial and merry to a high degree, but of what passed I have no recollection, with any accuracy. . . .

Sunday, September 26. I awaked at noon with a severe headache. I was much vexed that I should have been guilty of such a riot, and afraid of a reproof from Dr. Johnson. I thought it very inconsistent with that conduct which I ought to maintain as the companion of the Rambler.

The interview, however, was a very pleasant one. Boswell found ' the Rambler ' in his most agreeable mood and was glad to escape the reproof he had anticipated. ' About one he came into my room and accosted me, " What, drunk yet ? " ' His tone of voice was not that of severe upbraiding ; so I was relieved a little. ' Sir,' said I, ' they kept me up.' He answered, ' No, you kept them up, you drunken dog : ' This he said with a good-humoured *English* pleasantry.

Boswell, it need hardly be said, was very proud of introducing Johnson to the men of Scotland : it raised him, as he no doubt understood, in their esteem, and he took trouble that Johnson should appear to them in the most favourable light. He had also a further gratification. He was more than a mere showman. He came to have proprietary rights in Dr. Johnson. Boswell's joy was the joy of possession :

and he even became jealous. There is a story told
by Miss Burney, of a later date, when Boswell, it
must be admitted, behaved rather badly. A party
gathered at Streatham where Johnson was staying.
Boswell arrived to spend the morning. The Doctor's
intimacy with Miss Burney was new to Boswell and
the latter now found that his rights were being
infringed. ' A collation was ordered.'

Mr. Boswell [it is related] was preparing to take a
seat that he seemed, by prescription, to consider as
his own, next to Dr. Johnson ; but Mr. Seward, who
was present, waved his hand for Mr. Boswell to move
farther on, saying, with a smile, ' Mr. Boswell, that
seat is Miss Burney's.'

He stared, amazed : the asserted claimant was
new and unknown to him, and he appeared by no means
pleased to resign his prior rights. But, after looking
round for a minute or two with an important air of
demanding the meaning of this innovation, and receiving no satisfaction, he reluctantly, also resentfully,
got another chair, and placed it at the back of the
shoulder of Dr. Johnson, while this new and unheard-
of rival quietly seated herself as if not hearing what
was passing, for she shrunk from the explanation that
she feared might ensue, as she saw a smile stealing
over every countenance, that of Dr. Johnson himself
not excepted, at the discomfiture and surprise of Mr.
Boswell.

We must not forget that Boswell, before everything
else, was the biographer, looking ever with inquisitive
eye upon the great man's movements, marking with

zealous care any detail that might be significant, and appreciating very keenly the humour of every scene. The furthest point one may suppose that his curiosity reached, or indeed was able to reach, is recorded in an account of breakfast at Lochbuy. The comedy arose from an unusual proposal on the part of Lady Lochbuy as to the provision to be made for Johnson's entertainment; Boswell encouraged it to see what the Doctor would do, deriving at the same time much pleasure from the dispute between the lady and her brother.

She proposed that he should have some cold sheep's head for breakfast. Sir Allan seemed displeased at his sister's vulgarity, and wondered how such a thought should come into her head. From a mischievous love of sport, I took the lady's part; and very gravely said, ' I think it is but fair to give him an offer of it. If he does not choose it, he may let it alone.' ' I think so,' said the lady, looking at her brother with an air of victory. Sir Allan, finding the matter desperate, strutted about the room and took snuff. When Dr. Johnson came in she called to him, ' Do you choose any cold sheep's head, Sir ? ' ' No, Madam,' said he, with a tone of surprise and anger. ' It is here, Sir,' said she, supposing he had refused it to save the trouble of bringing it in. They thus went on at cross purposes till he confirmed his refusal in a manner not to be misunderstood.

The malicious experiment of Boswell had the desired conclusion. ' I,' he says, ' sat quietly by, and enjoyed my success.'

K

Dr. Johnson was irritated sometimes by Boswell's curiosity.   Dr. Campbell even records that Johnson on one occasion was driven away by Boswell's continual questions.[1]   But it would seem that far more often Johnson found means of protecting himself.   Miss Burney gives an enlightening summary of the prospect in case Johnson should notice Boswell imitating him.

Dr. Burney thought that Dr. Johnson, who generally treated Mr. Boswell like a schoolboy, whom, without the smallest ceremony, he pardoned or rebuked alternately, would so indignantly have been provoked as to have instantaneously inflicted upon him some mark of his displeasure.   And equally he was persuaded that Mr. Boswell, however shocked and even inflamed in receiving it, would soon, from his deep veneration, have thought it justly incurred, and after a day or two of pouting and sullenness would have compromised the matter by one of his customary simple apologies of ' Pray, Sir, forgive me.'   Dr. Johnson though often irritated by the officious importunity of Mr. Boswell, was really touched by his attachment.

It was presumably in some degree because he realised that Johnson was fond of him that Boswell was able to endure his rudeness.   It must be remembered, however, that it was deliberately in most cases brought upon himself, and there was then no real cause to take offence.   You cannot complain if

---

[1] *Campbell's Diary*, p. 70.

by your own fault you have made a man angry, whatever he may say—especially if he is thirty years older than yourself. It is one of Boswell's chief merits that he was able to see this. He may have been often annoyed, but he came afterwards to see that it was but the natural result of his method of treating Johnson—the method which enabled him to write in the end the immortal ' Life.'

Boswell in the *rôle* of biographer will claim a more detailed attention later in this book. It will suffice to say here that the attitude which he presented in the scene at Lochbuy, and on all those occasions when he led Johnson to talk or arranged some situation for the sake of observing his behaviour, is that which is most typical of Boswell, that by which he was famous, or, as some might have said, notorious among his contemporaries.

The relations between these two friends which we see so pleasantly revealed in Boswell's journal of the ' Tour to the Hebrides,' in 1773, containing as they did all that is best between the old and the young, re-mained unimpaired to the death of Johnson in 1784 : Boswell never neglected to pay at least one visit in the year to England, and preserved to the end his affection, his careful and kind attention, his pride and respect, and above all his humour and curiosity. It would be idle to suggest, though it may be difficult to understand or explain the fact, that his absence from Johnson's death-bed is significant in any way of a declining interest and affection.

Boswell himself was feeling ill and melancholy during a considerable part of the year, and was much upset by Johnson's charges of affectation : it is easily conceivable that he shrank from the pain of being present at the death-bed of his friend, and believed too that his own distress could only irritate the other.[1] But, whatever may have been the cause of his absence, it is impossible, if we consider his own words about the final parting, to doubt the sincerity of his affection.[2]

He asked me whether I would not go with him to his house ; I declined it, from an apprehension that my spirits would sink. We bade adieu to each other affectionately in the carriage. When he had got down upon the foot-pavement, he called out, ' Fare you well,' and without looking back, sprung away with a kind of pathetic briskness, if I may use the expression, which seemed to indicate a struggle to conceal uneasiness, and impressed me with a foreboding of our long, long separation.[3]

Johnson in one of his last letters said : ' I consider your fidelity and tenderness as a great part of the comforts which are yet left me ' ; and Boswell,

[1] *Life of Johnson*, iv, pp. 378–80.
[2] It must be remembered that Boswell spent nearly two months with Johnson in this last year. In March he wrote to Dr. Percy about going to London, ' chiefly to attend upon Dr. Johnson with respectful attention.' (Nichols, *Literary History*, vii, p. 302.)
[3] *Life of Johnson*, iv, p. 339.

speaking of his death, says enough when he says no more than this : ' I trust I shall not be accused of affectation when I declare that I find myself unable to express all that I felt upon the loss of such a Guide, Philosopher, and Friend.'

The loss was indeed a severe one for Boswell. He made a friend of Johnson at the age of twenty-two and was forty-four at the date of Johnson's death. For more than twenty years he had been accustomed implicitly to trust the judgment of the older man.

Its mere duration in time is some testimony to the value of the friendship, the more so when we remember that Boswell when he died himself was but fifty-five years old. The friend who was the hero of Boswell's youth, and his constant adviser, saw within the space of a few years the beginning of his professional life at the Scotch Bar, the publication of his first serious book, his marriage to an admirable lady, and his election to the Literary Club ; he died but two years after Boswell had become the Laird of Auchinleck, at a time when he was showing an increased activity, and before the political and legal hopes that he indulged had brought about by their failure the disappointment of his later life.

From the few facts which have been related here something may be gleaned, if not a complete conception of the part which Johnson played in Boswell's life. Boswell has revealed himself as a friend and in particular as the friend of Johnson. So great a devotion is a real asset in life. Whatever its definite value may be as regards events, and it is often small, it serves to fix more clearly and fuse together the intricate moving forms of a land of dreams into a simple mundane shape. It may be an end in itself. And devotion in Boswell's case belonged to the essence of his genius. It was an important part of that abnormal ingredient in him which was to blaze forth in an imperishable flame.

What Johnson accomplished for Boswell was primarily in the realm of ideals. The aspirations of Boswell were concentrated by his admiration. But what was the final result ? When Johnson died, the ship that carried that heavy load of Boswell's hopes was sailing steadily towards a definite harbour, though not the harbour he intended to reach : what had Johnson to do with this ? Was his the hand at the helm ?—the breath in the sails ?

CHAPTER V

BIOGRAPHY is by its nature historical and suited to an historical method. The history of an institution is written in respect of its functions. The Christian Church, for instance, played a certain part in the life of society at the end of the fourth century, and another part when Clement proclaimed a Crusade to all Western Europe. The historian of the Church may well be expected to hold in view the later development during the whole course of his inquiry before that climax ; he must analyse the primitive organism, having regard to its future growth, and explain how it was that those organs grew. The biographer has similar duties. We commonly consider the lives of men with reference to a few conspicuous events or remarkable achievements ; and we want to know what were the essential qualities of the man and how they grew to those results. In Boswell's case the central theme is single, for he accomplished one thing of overwhelmingly greater importance than anything else in his life. But the growth which came to this glorious end was by no means a simple and serene development.

It is concerned with an amazing war between the conventional and the real, the false and the true. We have now to investigate more closely the details of that struggle, and incidentally the effect on Johnson.

Boswell, in the first place, had a number of what may be called conventional prejudices ; he had the common prejudices of the landed gentleman in the eighteenth century. He was brought up to believe that he would one day become the Laird of Auchinleck. He was proud of his family name and ancient lineage ; he believed altogether the conventional idea, that a man was not only in a higher position and a greater person, but, in some indefinable way, better from the possession of land. Soil and mansion were not merely the insignia of the governing class or the boast of blood, but, further, the supreme expression of an ideal— the commonest practical ideal of the British people, ' to be as our fathers.' ' Holding an estate,' says Boswell, in the first of the political letters which he addressed to his compatriots,[1] ' transmitted to me through my ancestors, by charters from a series of kings, the importance of a charter, the prerogative of a king, impresses my mind with seriousness and duty ; and while animated, I hope, as much as any man, with genuine feelings of liberty, I shall ever adhere to our excellent Monarchy, that venerable institution under

[1] For Boswell's political career see pp. 174–182. He published this letter in 1783, and a second two years later.

which liberty is best enjoyed.' The truth expressed by these extravagant words is that Boswell accepted, as a consequence of having inherited an estate, a certain outfit of principles and practical objects which was to be worn in the same way that a parson wears a black coat or a coachman a livery. In politics, therefore, he was a Monarchist and Tory. Property and the Constitution, these were his interests.

In the second political letter he shows that he strongly disapproved of innovation and of change in general ; disapproved because he disliked and mistrusted them as by convention a man of property ought to do. Reform, however necessary, is never respectable. Boswell liked an order and formality which should go on for ever exactly as he knew it. It was for this reason and not from any æsthetic pleasure that he delighted in the ceremonial of the dinners in the Inner Temple and in the services which he was wont to attend in St. Paul's Cathedral each year, if he were able, upon Easter Day.

The same views found expression in a series of essays which Boswell wrote for the *London Magazine*. It is in fact in these essays rather than in his biographical writings that we should look for Boswell's opinions on general subjects. Comprehensive though the ' Life of Johnson ' is, it necessarily refrains from giving the author's view on many occasions, and when Boswell speaks for himself he does so incidentally, and not directly.   In the *London Magazine* he is free, and consequently the range is wider and the matter more diffuse.

'The Hypochondriack '—for such is the title under which Boswell wrote — appeared in twenty-seven numbers of the *London Magazine* from October, 1777, to December, 1779.   The articles are not very long—three pages of close double-columns is the average length ; but altogether they must contain enough printed matter to fill one volume of a moderate size in our day.   The title explains the attitude of the writer in the whole series ; Boswell wrote as a hypochondriac to others who suffered as he did from periodical depression, to divert them, as he said, by good-humour.   'I may, without ever offending them by excess of gaiety, insensibly communicate to them that good-humour which, if it does not make life rise to felicity, at least preserves it from wretchedness.'

It is remarkable that Boswell formed the plan of writing these papers at an earlier stage of his existence, during the years which he spent abroad from 1763–5. The tenth of the series was actually written then and was intended, so he tells us, to be published, in the *London Magazine* as Number X of 'The Hypochondriack.'   The fact that it fulfilled its destiny, and that, though written in a rather more frivolous style, it is in no way out of place, is a testimony, if any further were needed besides the *magnum opus*, to the capacity that Boswell had for carrying a literary project to its due accomplishment.

The qualities required of a biographer, which Boswell had in so supreme a measure, are not those which necessarily make a good essayist. But Boswell was by no means contemptible as a writer of essays. A great thinker he never professed to be, and never could have become ; he had, however, what for his purpose was even more valuable than profound thought or comprehensive originality—the art of self-expression. We are obliged to read anything that Boswell wrote because, by some enchanter's magic, he is there talking to us. This is not the place to probe the mystery of Orpheus with his lute ; perhaps, in any case, it is better that the mystery should remain for ever dark ; for the charm of Orpheus might be perceptibly less if we knew its mechanism. And it may be no more than an accomplishment which, when exercised with par-ticular grace, gives, in the common way, the capricious illusion of facility. Whatever it be in the art of letters, Boswell had it. He inevitably produced his effect ; and it is himself. We are made to feel good-humoured and agreeable ; and we wish to leave it at that and trouble our heads no further. A less easy style will draw our attention to the technique of words. With Boswell, it is clear midday on the dial, and we have no desire to bother with the wheels inside.

' The Hypochondriack,' however, is scarcely so gay

as one might expect. Truly this is not the serious business of life ; he is out for a spree. 'The pleasure of writing a short essay,' says the lively physician of melancholy, 'is like taking a pleasant airing that enlivens and invigorates by the exercise which it yields, while the design is gratified in its completion.' Boswell the essayist has not the solemn responsibility of showing a great example to the world ; and he has no need to be the grave judge. Yet there is a very serious background to the thoughts of this jolly author. When he chooses a theme he searches in the depths. Religion, Death and Conscience, Fear, Truth, Pleasure and Pride, Matrimony and Offspring, Youth and Age, Pity and Prudence, Excess, Drinking, Flattery, and Hypochondria itself—such are the subjects with which he sets forth to divert his fellow-sufferers. And having chosen thus, Boswell naturally, on many occasions, says earnestly what he sincerely thinks. He faithfully describes in one place the discomfort of his own depression :

To be overpowered with languor must make a man very unhappy. He is tantalized with a thousand ineffectual wishes which he cannot realise. For as Tantalus is fabled to have been tormented by the objects of his desire being ever in his near view, yet ever receding from his touch as he endeavoured to approach them, the languid Hypochondriack has the sad mystification of being disappointed of realising every wish, by the wretched defect of his own activity. While in that situation time passes over him only to be loaded with regrets. The important duties of life, the benevolent offices of friendship are neglected, though he is sensible that he shall upbraid himself for that neglect till he is glad to take shelter under cover of disease.

In this account there is no ill-placed levity and no extravagance such as we might fear to find. It is a simple and effective account of an unpleasant experience. The advice which he gives to hypochondriacs from time to time is similarly grave and sympathetic, and concerned with defeating the dangers of their state of mind ; his view is that the disease is nearly always curable ; he unwillingly admits that there are cases beyond hope, and condemns pessimistic fatalism :

We should guard against imagining that there is a volcano within us, a melancholy so dreadful that we can do nothing in opposition to it.

It would be a mistake to suppose when we read such grave advice that Boswell had a serious view of himself as the spiritual adviser of hypochondriacs. His object, as he tells us, was to divert them ; and in that frame of mind no doubt he began to write. He became grave and even earnest because he had a very strong vein of seriousness. In the ordinary way of life he was light-hearted enough, and easily dispensed with his thoughts when they began to be uncomfortable : but when he had set himself to write from a text he persevered with his serious reflections and they found expression. He was able to reach considerable heights ; a famous epitaph, when he is writing upon a motto from Cicero about the duties of Conscience, stirs him to a noble feeling :

The epitaph upon Sir Christopher Wren in St. Paul's Church, of which he was the architect, has been justly admired as sublime : ' Lector, si monumentum requiris, circumspice ' ; ' Reader, if you would see his monument, cast your eyes around you,' so that the whole Church is made his Mausoleum. In my opinion there is a similar sublimity about this sentiment, by which a man, upon the ancient principle of τίμα σεαυτὸν, ' reverence thyself,' is taught to expand his mind into a grand theatre of self-observation.

Occasionally Boswell, on account of this same seriousness, has an outburst of Johnsonian anger. He tells of a French writer that he published a book, ' Réflexions sur ceux qui sont morts en plaisantant,' that he succeeded in collecting a good number of instances both ancient and modern : ' But I,' says Boswell ' hold all such extraordinary appearances to be unnatural, affected, and thoughtless.'

However, when all is said about the gravity of the Hypochondriack, he is essentially the easy, good-humoured companion he set out to be. He is often dignified, never indecorous ; rarely is he even light-hearted, for while he supports the cares of this world with smiling equanimity he leaves the impression that they matter ; still more rarely is he flippant. The effect is never depressing. He is for the most part a soothing optimist ; and if that seem scant praise, be it remembered that one may resist the optimist's persuasion and yet fall a victim to the cheerful manners that accompany it. Such is the attitude of Boswell as an essayist ; and, when we consider what he chose to write about, it is a remarkable performance.

The lightness of touch which was necessary for Boswell's purpose was obtained partly by anecdote and image. A wide acquaintance with books evidently supplied Boswell with a store of anecdotes ; and he both selected them well and used them relevantly. One instance, where Boswell, in an essay about Excess, is speaking of the dangers of wealth, will suffice to illustrate his method :

The Dutch, who have much sagacity of contrivance in many respects, have in what they call a ' verbeetering huys ' (that is to say, a correcting and amending house, a house for making people better) an admirable method of curing laziness. A fellow who will not work is put into a large reservoir, which takes him up to the chin ; a cock is then turned so as to let more water run in upon him, and he is then shown a pump. If he exerts himself with active force he prevents the water from rising, and breathes freely ; but if he does not ply the pump, the water soon gets up upon him and he is suffocated. An inundation of wealth will be equally fatal to a man's happiness, if he does not throw it off by vigorous exertion. *Aurum potabile* will

choak him ; and, when drowning in Pactolus's streams,
it will be no consolation to him to know that they
have golden sands.

Boswell's images, sometimes employed in imitation
of Dr. Johnson's manner, if they are apt to be slightly
extravagant, are generally pointed and help the sense.
' A Dogmatist,' he says, ' is a man that has got a pair
of shoes that fit him exactly well, and therefore he
thinks them so very good that he flies in a passion
against those who cannot wear them.'   An image is
often used far more gracefully to bring the argument
to a head as in the following admirable passage :

But old men forget in a wonderful degree their
own feelings in the early part of life, are angry because
the young are not as sedate in the season of effervescence
as they are, would have the fruit where in the course
of nature there should be only the blossom, and complain because another generation has not been able
to ascend the steep of prudence in a fourth part of the
time which they themselves have taken.

These few quotations may suffice to show that
Boswell's essays are worthy of some attention.   They
can be read with pleasure because Boswell was both a
capable writer and an agreeable man.   And, moreover,
Boswell was a good man.   It is a somewhat ridiculous
exclamation, because the fact is so striking and so in-
disputable.   One might dispute the proposition that
to write an unrivalled biography a man must be good :

it would probably be a foolish discussion, for the common sense of mortals refuses to believe that one who has done a supremely good thing is not himself essentially good. But to dispute it in the case of Boswell—when we consider how many hearts he has won, and with how excellent a wooing, surely that would be preposterous ! He was not wholly good more than other men, nor less than the majority ; but he possessed a quantity of good that might be envied of the best. And this is true, not of the man only, but of the writer. The test is a very simple one : the plain fact is that it is impossible to read Boswell without feeling better. Boswell does not edify in the spiritual fashion of Michael Angelo or Milton ; but he edifies just as truly. With Boswell we never want to leave the world for something better, but we want to live in it and enjoy life to the full ; and we want especially to love other men. It is not a small matter that we should feel this : and as we may feel it in the ' Life of Johnson,' we may feel it also, though in a less degree, in the essays.

But ' The Hypochondriack ' is not to be read for the sake of the author's opinions, nor even for the arguments by which he supports them. For Boswell writes from a conventional point of view. His conclusions are not his very own. He has never been tossed in the great void and fought long doubtful battles for a sure place to stand on. His children

L

have not been begotten with pangs, but adopted for pleasure.

And here we return to the main battle. Boswell was conventional. But this is by no means a sufficient explanation. Clearly, in some respects, it is not even true. What then is the range of Boswell's conventionality and what are its limits ?

Beliefs are the result, as a rule, either of tradition, or of emotional experience, or of mere desire. In a few rare spirits they may be determined in more intellectual fashion ; but Reason is seldom mistress, and very often she is servant and nurse. By reason, we seek to justify our prejudices and convictions. With varying degrees of intellectual dishonesty we make use of reason to reject what we dislike and nourish what we prefer.

Boswell's case was somewhat uncommon. He was clearly not very critical. Having once adopted an attitude he marched through life without looking back. We have seen something of the outlook he adopted conventionally. He deceived himself, however, far less than most men of those opinions. And in the effort to believe what he wished to believe, Boswell used reason in a curiously deliberate fashion. He accepted the conventional beliefs and standards in an unconventional manner—not chaotically and aimlessly, but perceiving what the conventional aim essentially was, and approving it as a mode of living.

Boswell's philosophy of life, as far as he had a

philosophy, was to have in all (including, that is, the future life of happiness which he flattered himself that he would be able to enjoy) the maximum amount of pleasure. Pleasure and happiness, these are ends in themselves ; and except in so far as pleasure must be restrained for the sake of happiness either in this state of being or in another—and Boswell can hardly be said to have practised restraint in any remarkable degree—they are not distinguished. Pleasure he speaks of as 'not only the aim but the end of our being.' 'To be happy,' he says, ' as far as mortality and human imperfection allow, is the wisest study of men.'

In the 'Hypochondriack' essays we see how entirely Boswell's philosophy of life is a philosophy of comfort. With regard, for instance, to Love—a subject which, since three papers of 'The Hypochondriack' are devoted to it, must have been considered important— though too logical to be entirely conventional, his doctrine is frankly based upon his view of happiness :

As no disorder of the imagination has produced more evils than the passion of love, it behoves us to guard ourselves with caution against its first appearance.

However coldness or indifference is unpleasant, yet excess of love or fondness is bad, not only as it is not lasting, but also because it is disagreeable at the time.

It is in his religious views that we see best this

attitude of Boswell. While his opinions were on the one hand completely conventional, they yet depended quite consciously upon this doctrine of happiness.

The religious fear which I mean to inculcate, is that reverential awe for the Most High Ruler of the Universe, mixed with affectionate gratitude and hope, by which our minds are kept steady, calm, and placid, at once exalted by the contemplation of greatness, and warmed by the contemplation of goodness, while both are contemplated with a reference to ourselves.[1]

However ' romantic ' Boswell may have been in other matters, there is no shadow of romance in his conception of a Deity. His admiration for what seems to be merely a superior human being admitted of no spiritual disquiet. Rather the ' steady, calm, and placid ' temper so produced was to serve as an antidote to hypochondria.

In order to have these comforts which not only relieve but ' delight the soul,' the Hypochondriack must take care to have the principles of our holy religion firmly established in his mind, when it is sound and clear, and by the habit and exercise of piety to strengthen it, so that the flame may live even in the damp and foul vapour of melancholy.[2]

Further instructions as to how these comforts are to be enjoyed are given in the ' Life ' where his final view is expressed :

[1] *London Magazine*, vol. xlvi, pp. 492–3.
[2] *Ibid.*, vol. xlix, p. 542.

This I have learned from a pretty hard course of experience, and would, from sincere benevolence, impress upon all who honour this book with a perusal, that until a steady conviction is obtained that the present life is an imperfect state, and only a passage to a better, if we comply with the divine scheme of progressive improvement ; and also that it is part of the mysterious plan of Providence that intellectual beings must be ' made perfect through suffering ' ; there will be a continual recurrence of disappointment and uneasiness. But if we walk with hope in ' the mid-day sun of revelation ' our temper and disposition will be such that the comforts and enjoyments in our way will be relished, while we patiently support the inconveniences and pains.

The argument is clear : we must choose the path where ' uneasiness ' is avoided and ' comforts and enjoyments ' are in store for us. The part to be played by the intellect is not doubtful. The power of reasoning may be valuable up to a certain point ; beyond that point it is unsafe for it to pass :

After much speculation and various reasonings, I acknowledge myself convinced of the truth of Voltaire's conclusion, ' *Après tout, c'est un monde passable.*' But we must not think too deeply ;

Where ignorance is bliss, 'tis folly to be wise

is, in many respects, more than poetically just. Let us cultivate, under the command of good principles, ' *la théorie des sensations agréables* ' ; and, as Mr. Burke once counselled a grave and anxious gentleman, ' live pleasant.'

' We must not think too deeply '—because it is not pleasant. ' I most willingly admit,' he says elsewhere, ' that of all kinds of misery, the misery of thought is the severest.' He wished to escape from thought, and found his religion a very pleasant substitute. It enabled him to believe all that he found most pleasant in beliefs, and to reject what he found disquieting. The fear of death, he discovered, could best be alleviated by believing in the divine revelation ; accordingly he proceeded to adopt this belief.

But the pleasure which Boswell obtained in this way was not merely the pleasure of a mind lulled to tranquillity, it was the pleasure also of possessing a point of view. He wanted to be entirely respectable. And respectability was to be achieved by adopting wholesale the respectable beliefs. Boswell perhaps could never have been otherwise than conventional in his ethical and religious thought ; but he did at one time think, and he deliberately ceased to think ; with the consequence that all those views which he might or might not have arrived at by thought and experience, instead of being deeply founded within him, were only an ill-balanced superstructure.

·   ·   ·   ·   ·

The effect of Johnson upon this development was a very remarkable one. Johnson himself was pre-eminently a conformist, and it was partly, no doubt, from his example that Boswell derived his desire to be respectable—to be, as he expressed it, ' an uniform pretty man.'

Boswell's own words show us that he was influenced in this way. A meeting had been arranged between Johnson and one of Boswell's friends, George Dempster, who held the sceptical views of Hume and Rousseau ; a discussion took place in which Johnson, whether by force of argument or power of lungs, was victorious. ' I had infinite satisfaction,' says Boswell, ' in hearing solid truth confuting vain subtilty. I thank God that I have got acquainted with Mr. Johnson. He has done me infinite service. He has assisted me to obtain peace of mind, he has assisted me to become a rational Christian.'

How much are we to assume from this ? How much of Boswell's respectability came directly from Johnson ?

There could be nothing more unreasonable than to dogmatise about the extent of a personal influence. How subtle and intricate it is in the thousand chances of a mind's development, of acquiescence and rebellion, of mere time and place ! how difficult to see the beginning and the end, to know even approximately the value of any one force in a number of causes ! The distinction alone between a conscious or unconscious acceptance, what a difference it makes !

That which determines individuality in men more than any other factor is the freedom of choice. But there is more than one way of choosing. There are some who choose to march upon the high road where tall fences on either side prevent the possibility of wandering astray ; and there are others who select the by-paths deliberately. All who choose are in search of treasure. Those who have rejected the high roads hardly know what they so urgently desire ; but when they come upon a rare flower in the wilderness which pleases them particularly they cull it ; they are then refreshed and go forward with more certain step, and there hangs about them something of the fragrance they inhaled, so that other men when they meet them are reminded of that flower which they too have seen and smelt.   The rest press forward more directly ; when they have chosen the way there is no deviation ; they will pause for nothing unless it be of precious metal. And when their quest is rewarded they surround themselves with a cloud of gold-dust, as it seems to them, and cannot be seen except through this strange mist.

Boswell, it would seem, was among these last. He chose freely, but did not wander far afield. He was one of those in pursuit of ideal treasure ; and when he found in Dr. Johnson all that he desired, and the ideal was satisfied, he impregnated himself with the priceless essence. But, inasmuch as it was the essence he had chosen to seek, even this exterior atmosphere was entirely of himself.

We expect, indeed, to see in Boswell beyond his own real nature the marks of a stronger personality. But we may admit the Johnsonian flavour without impugning the originality of Boswell or degrading him to the level of a mere imitator. All the conventional prejudices, the strong conformity which was so pronounced in Johnson, existed in Boswell independently. The ' old Tory sentiments ' inasmuch as they exceeded the sentiments of Johnson (which they occasionally did, *e.g.* on the subject of slavery), were definitely a part of the true Boswell. It is remarkable that in the ' Letters to Temple ' the opinions of Johnson are very rarely mentioned ; Boswell on one occasion was ' confirmed in his Toryism ' ; and Johnson is quoted two or three times : but his name appears far less often than we should expect. It is clear, indeed, when we read the ' Life of Johnson,' that Boswell, however he might be a worshipper, was far from being a slave : his passion for truth would not allow him to pass lightly by an opinion he disapproved, and his conviction that Johnson was wrong, or at least that his own opinions remained unaltered, is frankly if respectfully stated more than once.

He knew that Johnson's opinions might be formed

only to refute an adversary : 'But it is not improbable that if one had taken the other side he might have reasoned differently.' Not infrequently Boswell ventures to criticise his philosopher's argument. On one occasion, when predestination had been discussed, he even goes so far as to excuse Johnson's prejudices :

He avoided the question which has excruciated philosophers and divines beyond any other. I did not press it further, when I perceived that he was displeased, and shrunk from any abridgment of an attribute usually ascribed to the divinity, however irreconcilable in its full extent with the grand system of moral government. His supposed orthodoxy here cramped the vigorous powers of his understanding. He was confined by a chain, which early imagination and long habit made him think massy and strong, but which, had he ventured to try, he could at once have snapped asunder.

Boswell's attitude in this passage is very far from being intellectually dependent on Johnson or on anyone else. And it is not an unusual attitude. We sometimes see another side—Boswell, apparently in fetters, a prisoner in the citadel of respectability. But it cannot be asserted too often that Boswell was essentially an independent individual, one who was capable of pursuing his own true vision, inflexible and careless of the consequences.

There is no need to infer from this that the influence of Johnson was negligible, or even small. We cannot suppose that the guide, philosopher and friend of Boswell, for whom he had a 'mysterious veneration,' whose ' just frown ' he so greatly dreaded, whom upon so many occasions he eagerly consulted, can have been of small account. Boswell himself was far from thinking so ; he knew the value of Johnson to him when, reflecting that death must soon rob him of his friend, he wrote to Temple, in Johnsonian words : ' it will be like a limb amputated.'

If influence is to be defined it may be said perhaps that it is a quality which makes us see what we should not have seen without it. We cannot doubt that Boswell learnt many things by his intercourse with Dr. Johnson. The influence of Johnson was in the first place, as we remarked above, an influence for truth, for honesty. It helped Boswell in his early life to see the self which he came in the end to understand so well. He must long have remembered the letter which he received from Johnson at Utrecht.

Boswell, in his desire to make an impression as the young genius, then regarded himself as a peculiar mortal who had no need to regulate his conduct by the ordinary standards. Johnson begins by describing this state of mind :

There lurks, perhaps, in every human heart a desire of distinction, which inclines every man first to hope, and then to believe, that Nature has given him something peculiar to himself. . . . You know a gentleman who, when first he set his foot in the gay world, as he prepared himself to whirl in the vortex of pleasure, imagined a total indifference and universal negligence to be the most agreeable concomitants of youth, and the strongest indication of an airy temper and a quick apprehension.

The result which he particularly deplored was Boswell's idleness :

Vacant to every object, and sensible of every impulse, he thought that all appearance of diligence would deduct something from the reputation of genius ; and hoped that he should appear to attain, amidst all the ease of carelessness, and all the tumults of diversion, that knowledge and those accomplishments which mortals of the common fabrick obtain only by mute abstraction and solitary drudgery.

He then alludes to the wrong conclusions which might be drawn by one in Boswell's mental condition from the difficulties which attend a return to a normal course of life :

He tried this scheme of life awhile ; was made weary of it by his sense and his virtue ; he then wished to return to his studies ; and finding long habits of idleness and pleasure harder to be cured than he expected, still willing to retain his claim to some extraordinary prerogatives, resolved the common consequences of irregularity into an unalterable decree of destiny, and concluded that Nature had originally formed him incapable of rational employment.

And finally he gives some very solemn advice :

Let all such fancies, illusive and destructive, be banished henceforward from your thoughts for ever.

Resolution will sometimes relax, and diligence will sometimes be interrupted ; but let no accidental surprise or deviation, whether short or long, dispose you to despondency. Consider these failings as incident to all mankind.

Boswell was too honest not to realise the truth of what Johnson said, and we cannot but think of this letter when we read a number of years later, in the *London Magazine* of 1778, an attack written by Boswell upon the association by Aristotle of melancholy with genius ; for this essay seems to aim at undermining the same kind of affectation as that which Johnson had seen in him.

Similarly the effect of Johnson in making Boswell more respectable was produced less by example than by dislike of affectation. Johnson was pre-eminently a conformist ; and Boswell desired the same happy state for himself. But Johnson was honest in his conformity, and he cared less for the conformity than for the honesty. And so he was able, when he saw Boswell affecting sentiments which he did not wholly feel, to reprove him. It was not that the sentiments in themselves were not good sentiments, for they often were, but that in Boswell they were unreal.

Boswell : ' Perhaps, Sir, I should be the less happy for being in Parliament. I never would sell my vote, and I should be vexed if things went wrong.' *Johnson :* ' That 's cant, Sir. It would not vex you more in the House than in the Gallery : publick affairs vex no man.'

Boswell was probably annoyed at this retort ; it is very annoying to be told the truth about oneself. He now tries to make Johnson admit that he has been vexed himself ' by all the turbulence of this reign.'

Johnson : 'Sir, I have never slept an hour less, nor ate an ounce less meat. I would have knocked the factious dogs on the head, to be sure ; but I was not *vexed.*'

The argument is too strong :

Boswell : ' I declare, Sir, upon my honour, I did imagine I was vexed, and took a pride in it ; but it *was*, perhaps, cant ; for I own I neither ate less, nor slept less.' *Johnson :* ' My dear friend, clear your *mind* of cant. You may *talk* as other people do ; you may say to a man, " Sir, I am your most humble servant." . . . You may *talk* in this manner ; it is a mode of talking in society : but don't *think* foolishly.'

The result of Johnson's honesty acting upon Boswell's conventional affectations was not to make him less but rather more conventional. It gave him a surer foundation. An affectation does not as a rule become less affected but rather the reverse. But Boswell's affectations tended rather to become the substantial and real expression of a mind as he came to understand that they were affectations. He saw that the manners and opinions which he affected because they pleased him had a value in life and a value for him. The lessons which he learnt from Johnson in this way were, for the most part, moral ; they were concerned with the piety and goodness which were so much a part of Johnson himself. Boswell was able to reinforce a set of religious beliefs with a little real piety, and a set of moral axioms with a little real goodness. If it were necessary to point to one definite quality in the Johnsonian atmosphere which we might suppose to be of special value to Boswell, it would be the genuine kind-heartedness and benevolent interest, the ' tenderness ' which we find so carefully recorded in the ' Life.' It was to some purpose that the naturally egotistical Boswell was reminded of a duty towards other men, was told more than once without compromise that he must be kind to his father and kind to his wife.

But it is not so much in any minute particular that Johnson was reflected by his biographer, but rather in a more general way, in a whole attitude towards life, in the one significant fact that Boswell himself as we see him, not only in the biographical writings but in his own letters too, is essentially a moralist. The one difficulty which his conscience found in writing the ' Life ' was that he might, by showing the failings of so great a man, give support to those who were inclined to the same faults so that they should conceive themselves to be justified by that example. And so he points out with zealous care that, where the ' practice ' of Johnson does not agree with his ' principle,' it is not because the principle is not good but that even so great a man was not quite perfect ; *humanum est errare.*

Undoubtedly the influence of Johnson was a moral influence ; this in itself may be considered as one aspect of its complete respectability.   Johnson wanted Boswell to be a sober, honest, contented citizen, a hard-working, successful lawyer, a good son, a good husband, a good friend and a religious man. ' I have always loved and valued you,' he wrote in 1769, ' and shall love you and value you still more, as you become more regular and useful.'   And again, in 1771 :

I never was so much pleased as now with your account of yourself ; and sincerely hope, that between publick business, improving studies, and domestick pleasures, neither melancholy nor caprice will find any place for entrance. Whatever philosophy may determine of material nature, it is certainly true of intellectual nature that it ' abhors a vacuum ' ; our minds cannot be empty ; and evil will break in upon them, if they are not preoccupied by good. My dear Sir, mind your studies, mind your business, make your lady happy, and be a good Christian.

There was no place for any intellectual unquiet—and herein it was essentially respectable — in Johnson's scheme of life as he presented it to others. If a subject were unpleasant to think of, it were better not to heed it. He wished himself to walk through life in a calm, majestic, and dignified way, with firm knowledge of good and a resolute purpose to follow it. He never, if we may judge from Boswell, was in any serious doubt as to the right course, and he seems to have thought the matter as easy for Boswell as it was for him. It is because he himself desired to be like this that Boswell found Johnson such a valuable friend. But it was unfortunate, as it turned out, that he attached so much importance to mere success in the world, in his profession, in politics ; in these, with the encouragement of Johnson, he so completely believed, that when he discovered that he had failed, or had at least fallen far short of his ambitions, he was bitterly disappointed.

M

CHAPTER VI

LORD AUCHINLECK died in 1782. His relations with
Boswell are of some interest in this place, because they
exhibit Boswell in the *rôle* of son and incidentally
raise an important question. The two never agreed
very well. Was this the fault of the son ? Was he
deliberately unkind, or negligent, or disagreeable ?

There is no reason to suppose that Boswell was
culpable in any such way : indiscretion on the one hand
and intolerance on the other are sufficient to account
for all the friction. Lord Auchinleck had evidently
a very rigid view of the career fitting for his eldest son.
His ideal of progeniture seems to have assumed with a
not uncommon complacency that the ego was worthy
of a second edition. James Boswell must be after
the pattern of his father—a Scotch lawyer, a hard-
headed, practical man of affairs, a wise man of business
successful in his profession.

James, however, was not made like that : and
if he had practical ability he hated the Scotch law
and lawyers far too much ever to use it with success.
He had a taste for extravagant behaviour and
liked to exhibit his high spirits. Johnson might

condone this, though he disapproved of it, and love
Boswell the more, because ' he was a boy longer
than others.' Lord Auchinleck regarded it with
alarm while Boswell was young, and with contempt
when he was of a mature age. Conduct that would
have been regrettable to a milder father, was to
him intolerable.

It is not surprising, then, that Boswell found the
company of his father extremely irksome :

We divaricate so much (he writes to Temple) that
I am often hurt when I dare say he means no harm ;
and he has a method of treating me which makes me
feel like a timid boy, which to me (comprehending
all that my character does in my own imagination, and
in that of a wonderful number of mankind) is intolerable. I have appeared good-humoured ; but it has
cost me drinking a considerable quantity of strong
beer to dull my faculties.

The stern father had undoubtedly some good
reasons for disapproving of the irresponsible James.
Besides the habitual lack of restraint in Boswell's
behaviour, money was a continual source of irritation.
The heir to Auchinleck, it is clear, considered that he
had a sort of natural right to his father's money. He
found an allowance of £300 a year insufficient. He
wrote to Temple in a complaining tone about his
financial difficulties and his father :

He allows me £300 a year. But I find that what I
gain by practice and that sum together will not support

my family.   I have now two sons and three daughters.
I am in hopes that my father will augment my allowance
to £400.

He admits, however, that ' his paying £1000 of my
debt some years ago was a large bounty.' Lord
Auchinleck, no doubt with justice, considered Boswell
to be extravagant ; and he did not approve of his
marriage. ' I understand,' writes Boswell, ' he fancies
that if I had married another woman, I might not only
have had a better portion with her, but might have
been kept from what he thinks idle and extravagant
conduct.'

The indiscretion of Boswell in his correspondence
and conversation with his father must have continually
aggravated the pronounced prejudices and preferences
of the ill-tempered old lawyer.   It was a wanton im-
prudence to express his extreme aversion to his father's
second marriage ; we can hardly doubt that he was
equally imprudent with regard to the Scotch law and
Scotch legal circles.   Boswell intended that his father
should appreciate him for what he was rather than
tolerate him for what he was not.   In 1767 he writes to
Temple :

How unaccountable it is that my father and I
should be so ill together ! He is a man of sense and
a man of worth ; but from some unhappy turn in his
disposition, he is much dissatisfied with a son whom
you know. I write to him with warmth, with an
honest pride, wishing that he should think of me as I

am ; but my letters shock him, and every expression in them is interpreted unfavourably.

Boswell did not understand that the temperaments of his father and himself were in some degree incompatible, and he succeeded in emphasising their points of disagreement rather than cultivating what they had in common. He was very slow to realise how much his father disapproved of his literary friends in London, and of Dr. Johnson in particular : to Temple he exclaims, with horrified surprise, ' he harps on my going over Scotland with a brute (think how shockingly erroneous) and wandering (or some such phrase) to London.' Johnson was actually taken to visit Auchinleck—a most hazardous experiment !

Boswell must certainly be blamed, if blame can be distributed in this sort, for indiscretion, but not for unkindness. From no passage in the ' Letters to Temple ' can it be inferred that he disliked his father, or wished to displease him ; on several occasions he speaks of him with affection. Moreover the obligation to be deliberately kind to one who cannot occupy the position of a friend is based upon a supposed affection on his part. Boswell clearly was not cruel in any positive or malevolent sense ; he can only be condemned as unkind if it be proved that he was inconsiderate to a man who displayed a substantial affection towards him. But Lord Auchlinleck cannot be said to have done this—if we may accept as true the dictum

of Dr. Johnson to Boswell on the occasion of his
father's death : 'His disposition towards you was
undoubtedly that of a kind, though not of a fond
father.' And so we may say that Boswell was a
disappointing, though not a bad son.

. . . . .

In 1782 Boswell, on his father's death, became
Laird of Auchinleck. The new position was a matter
of importance to him. Not only were the duties it
involved such duties as he liked to perform, but it was
a considerable advance in the right direction. He
was the man of property. A part of his dream was
come true ; and he could now invest himself with a
fresh halo of respect and respectability derived from
his new station. Local and public affairs were more
intimately connected in the eighteenth century than
in our own day ; and, when the men of estate had a
monopoly of governing, it was not unnatural for one
who inherited land to cast his eyes beyond the fences
of his patrimony. At the age of forty-two Boswell
was by no means too old to look forward. The event
of inheriting quickened his aspirations, and the prospect
of becoming ' the great man ' seemed nearer.

The ambitions of Boswell were not destined to be
realised in any high degree.

His hopes were of a double nature ; they were
both legal and political. Of his early life at the Bar

we have already spoken, and we must now briefly trace out the course of his legal career to its dismal conclusion.

It was hardly to be expected that a man who disliked and despised so much the whole Scotch atmosphere of his work should persevere with it. Boswell was so discontented with his lot that he began to hope for a change which should bring him into a more congenial situation. In 1775 he entered at the Inner Temple with the intention of being called eventually to the English Bar.

There was much to recommend this plan; for it would enable him to spend far more time in his beloved London. Boswell no doubt considered this a very important reason. In London he was happier and better than elsewhere. ' I own, Sir, the spirits which I have in London make me do everything with more readiness and vigour. I can talk twice as much in London as anywhere else'; and he considered, no doubt with equal justice, that it had some effects of a different nature : ' In reality it is highly improving to me, considering the company which I enjoy'; and he goes on to say, ' I think it is also for my interest, as in time I may get something.'[1]

Ambition was one motive which prompted Boswell to seek a different sphere; he seems to have thought the abilities which were cramped in Scotland and were not appreciated by the Scotch would grow in London

[1] *Letters to Temple*, pp. 146–7.

to their full stature and be handsomely recognised. In 1777 he talked to Johnson upon the subject of the English Bar :

I had long complained to him that I felt myself discontented in Scotland as too narrow a sphere, and that I wished to make my chief residence in London, the great scene of ambition, instruction and amusement : a scene which was to me, comparatively speaking, a heaven upon earth.

There were, however, a number of reasons which prevented Boswell from making his home in London till long after this conversation. The possibility of his father's death, which would probably make him the Laird of Auchinleck, was always present to him, and it would be inconvenient as well as expensive to have a separate establishment in London. It was by no means certain, moreover, as Boswell seems to have realised, that there would be much financial gain by the change, and he could not afford to fail at the English Bar ; his father as well as Johnson opposed the step, a consideration which would probably in itself have prevented it, from interested motives on Boswell's part if from no others.

Boswell, in fact, remained at the Scotch Bar until 1786, when he determined finally, in spite of his position as a Scotch laird, which he had occupied for four years, to try his fortune at Westminster Hall. He had been disappointed of promotion [1] for so long in

[1] *Letters to Temple*, p. 157.

Scotland that it was time to exercise his talents in a
different sphere.

The English lawyers, however, seem to have been
no more congenial than the Scotchmen, for he speaks
of the 'rough scene of the roaring and bantering society
of lawyers,' which he is compelled to be with on the
Northern Circuit.[1] There is an amusing story recounted
by Lord Eldon in his ' Anecdotes ' about Boswell at
the Lancaster Assizes, which belongs to a period
between the years '86 and '88 :

We found Jemmy Boswell lying upon the pavement
—inebriated. We subscribed at supper a guinea for
him and half-a-crown for his clerk, and sent him next
morning a brief with instructions to move for the
writ *Quare adhæsit pavimento*, with observations
calculated to induce him to think that it required great
learning to explain the necessity of granting it. He
sent all round the town to attornies for books, but in
vain. He moved, however, for the writ, making the
best use he could of the observations in the brief. The
judge was astonished and the audience amazed. The
judge said, ' I never heard of such a writ—what can it
be that adheres pavimento ? Are any of you gentlemen at the Bar able to explain this ? ' The Bar
laughed. At last one of them said, ' My Lord, Mr.
Boswell last night *adhæsit pavimento*. There was
no moving him for some time. At last he was carried
to bed, and he has been dreaming about himself and
the pavement.'

Boswell himself pours out to Temple in plaintive

[1] *Letters to Temple*, p. 250.

accents the tangled story of a wig lost at Carlisle in 1789, from which we may suspect, as he did himself, another practical joke. ' I suspected a wanton trick, which some people think witty, but I thought it very ill-timed to one in my situation.'

We might judge from the manner in which he was treated by his fellow-lawyers that Boswell was not wholly successful at the English Bar. No one can have realised this more keenly than himself.

' I am sadly discouraged,' he writes, ' by having no practice, nor probable prospect of it. . . . Yet the delusion of Westminster Hall, of brilliant reputation and splendid fortune as a barrister, still weighs upon my imagination. I must be seen in the courts, and must hope for some happy openings in causes of importance. The Chancellor, as you observe, has not done as I expected ; but why did I expect it ? ' Later in the same year, 1789, he exclaims : ' O Temple ! Temple ! is this realising any of the towering hopes which have so often been the subject of our conversations and letters ? ' It is pathetic to see him clinging still to the old hopes and ideals, when his real title to fame lay near at hand in his Johnsonian stores, so much thought of, and yet so little valued beside the great world of practical affairs.

There were no doubt some special reasons, connected with his attitude towards the law itself, which may account in a large degree for Boswell's failure

at the Bar. We have mentioned already the aversion
which Boswell had for the society of lawyers. This in
itself was likely to be a hindrance in his legal career ;
but it is only the result of the general unfittedness of
Boswell for the Bar. He was not unwilling, when his
plan of being a soldier had been abandoned, to enter
upon a legal career ; it would offer the kind of opportunities for distinction which he wanted. Possibly
he was attracted too by the formalism of the Courts ;
one may suppose that the mere wearing of a wig and
gown would give him pleasure. But the mind of
Boswell was entirely unlegal. He had no capacity for
estimating the value of evidence, and was readily convinced by a plausible story. He applied to his work
rather the common sense of the layman (being actually
advised very often by Johnson, who knew nothing of
Scotch law) than the exact reasoning required by his
profession. And though Boswell could apply himself
at times with continued effort to any work which he
particularly wanted to do, the dislike which he had
for his legal studies made him tire of them so soon
that he never knew very much about any body of
laws. ' Mr. Boswell,' says Malone, ' professed the
Scotch and the English Law ; but had never taken
very great pains on the subject. His father, Lord
Auchinleck, told him one day that it would cost him
more trouble to hide his ignorance in these professions
than to show his knowledge. This Boswell owned

he had found to be true.'[1]   Boswell himself wrote to
Temple on the subject of his chances of success at the
English Bar : ' To confess fairly to you, my friend,
I am afraid that, were I to be tried, I should be
found so deficient in the forms, the *quirks* and
quiddities which early habit acquires, that I should
expose myself.'

Boswell, moreover, had never the reputation which
is suitable for a legal man.   The sober citizen does
not choose either the adventurer or the *littérateur* to
plead his cause before a jury.   His connections with
actors, who were disapproved as a class by the
respectable community, told against Boswell in legal
circles. And worst of all was the tour in the Hebrides
with the avowed enemy of Scotland.

Boswell, besides, acquired a reputation for eccentricity which must have been fatal to the chances
of a barrister.

One habit, that of attending executions, deserves
a closer examination ; by this behaviour Boswell
made himself conspicuous in a wholly unprofessional
attitude, which must have been extremely damaging
to his position as a lawyer.   ' I must confess,' he
writes, ' that I myself am never absent from a public
execution. . . .   When I first attended them I was
shocked to the greatest degree.   I was in a manner
convulsed with pity and terror, and for several days,

[1] *European Magazine*, 1798, p. 376.

but especially nights after, I was in a very dismal situation.' The object in the first place seems then to have been the mere indulgence of morbid sentiment ; but later he continued the habit more out of curiosity and as an inherent part of his whole study of Man.

I can now see one with great composure. I can account for this curiosity in a philosophical manner, when I consider that death is the most awful object before every man who ever directs his thoughts seriously towards futurity. Therefore it is that I feel an irresistible impulse to be present at every execution, as I there behold the various effects of the near approach of death.

In accordance with this practice Boswell accompanied a celebrated criminal, Hackman, in the prison coach to the gibbet ; and he made the acquaintance of the murderess Mrs. Rudd. The latter apparently was an interesting woman. Johnson entirely approved Boswell's conduct, and said he would have done the same himself if he had not been afraid that his presence would be reported in the newspapers. It is interesting to note that Boswell had scruples, and wrote to Temple : ' Perhaps the adventure with Mrs. Rudd is very foolish notwithstanding the approbation of Dr. Johnson.'

On one occasion Boswell persuaded Sir Joshua Reynolds to go with him, and evidently won him over to his view about the question of propriety : ' I am obliged to you,' wrote Sir Joshua, ' for carrying me yesterday to see the execution at Newgate of the five

malefactors. I am convinced it is a vulgar error
in the opinion that it is so terrible a spectacle, or that
it in any way implies a hardness of heart or cruelty
of disposition.'

Sir Walter Scott gives a kinder motive on Boswell's
part than mere curiosity :

He used to visit the prisoners on the day before
execution, with the singular wish to make the condemned wretches laugh by dint of buffoonery, in which
he not infrequently succeeded.

The satisfaction which Boswell had from these
strange interviews was no doubt in part the commend-
able satisfaction of being kind and good ; and his
piety as well as his jesting may have been a comfort
to many of these criminals in their last hours. It was
also a pleasure to Boswell to read his name in the
newspaper on the day following an execution. But
probably this conduct did not earn the praises of the
Scotch lawyers nor inspire the confidence of the
litigating public.

.   .   .   .   .

The failure which attended Boswell's legal career
included also his political schemes.

It is clear that Boswell had an idea of some kind
of Parliamentary career. His ambition was to be a
Minister :

He [Hume] says there will in all probability be a change of the Ministry soon, which he regrets. Oh Temple, while they change so often, how does one feel an ambition to have a share in that great department; but I fear my wish to be a man of consequence in the State is much like some of your ambitious sallies.

Boswell, if he was ambitious in 1775 of some high office in the State, can certainly have had little chance, as he evidently realised, of being immediately satisfied. His financial difficulties alone would have prevented this. But when in 1782 he became the Laird of Auchinleck the increase of his importance seemed to warrant some more definite plan. ' I wish much to be in Parliament, Sir,' he said to Johnson; and though the latter discouraged him he applied himself with energy to his political schemes.

Boswell had two plans by which he hoped to become a member of Parliament. He hoped in the first place that the influence of Lord Lonsdale [1] would procure him a seat. This patron seems to have shown a disposition to be friendly. In the summer of 1786, Boswell received from Bishop Percy, who had formerly been at Carlisle and knew Lord Lonsdale, a most encouraging letter :

You are now connected with a nobleman [Lord Lonsdale] who serves his friends with a zeal and spirit

[1] For an account of Lord Lonsdale v. Sir George Trevelyan's *Life of Fox.*

which I hope will be attended with the happiest consequences to your establishment in England. I also anticipate his bringing you into the House of Commons, as an event no less certain and splendid to your fortunes.

Early in 1788[1] Lord Lonsdale appointed Boswell Recorder of Carlisle. This was not an important post, but it was doubtless a sign of favour. Bishop Percy wrote warm congratulations ; and Boswell was no doubt encouraged to hope for more. Lord Lonsdale, however, would appear to have lost interest in Boswell : he procured no seat in Parliament for his friend, and some years later behaved so insolently that Boswell broke the connection.[2]

Boswell's second plan was to represent his county. Even in Ayrshire he was not altogether independent of Lord Lonsdale, but he relied chiefly upon his own position as head of an old county family. With this project in view, he engaged himself in various activities. The most remarkable of these were his ' Letters to the People of Scotland,' the first dated 1783 and the second 1785. In these two pamphlets Boswell displayed abundantly to his countrymen his ardent patriotism and zealous Tory principles. In 1784 he

[1] Or possibly at the end of 1787—*v.* Nichols' *Illustrations,* vii. 310. The *Dictionary of National Biography* gives 1790, and Dr. Rogers 1789. But Bishop Percy's letter of congratulation (printed in Nichols) was dated 1788. The year is undoubtedly correct, for it refers to a letter of Boswell's dated Feb. 9, 1788, and in this letter Boswell speaks of the forthcoming publication of Johnson's letters to Mrs. Piozzi, which were published actually in 1788.

[2] *Letters to Temple,* pp. 268–9.

took part in a Tory demonstration at York ; and in his county he issued ' An Address to the Real Free-holders of the County of Ayr,' stating his willingness to be their representative, and his qualifications for that position.[1] He also carried an address to his Majesty—'it was most graciously received, and Mr. Boswell had afterwards the honour to kiss his Majesty's hand.'[2] In 1789 he was again very busy electioneering, though he seems to have realised that his chance of success was very small.[3] He carried an address to the Prince of Wales.

I am carrying it up, to be presented by the Earl of Eglintoun, accompanied by such Justices of us as may be in London. This will add something to my ' conspicuousness.' Will that word do ? [4]

The word seems to do very well. Boswell writes later :

The Prince of Wales has received our Address most graciously, and I am to be presented to his Royal Highness, who desired it might be signified that he regretted Mr. Boswell was gone from town.[5]

But this would seem to be the final achievement of Boswell's political career, for he was not successful in the General Election, and we hear no more in the ' Letters ' of political schemes.

Beyond any special reasons which there may be for the failure of Boswell in his legal career, there is a

---

[1] *Life of Johnson*, iv. 265. [2] Fitzgerald's *Life of Boswell*, II, 16.
[3] *Letters to Temple*, p. 244. [4] *Ib.*, p. 244. [5] *Ib.*, p. 249.

more general cause for all his disappointment. We
must remember that Boswell throughout his life was,
like many men in the eighteenth century less gifted
than himself, a thorough-going place-hunter. He
hoped even in his early life for some advantages
through his great patrons, Lord Somerville,[1] Sir
David Dalrymple,[2] Lord Eglintoun,[1] Lord Mount
Stuart,[3] Sir Andrew Mitchell [4] ; he had obtained by
their means a number of introductions. The ardour
with which he pursued the acquaintance of the great
must have been prompted in some degree by an interested expectation, and we may suppose that from
the friendship of Chatham, which he was so eager to
cultivate, he had flattered himself with a hope of
political advancement, a hope of fulfilling the dreams
that he had dreamt, with Temple, in University days,
of their future greatness. They were but vague hopes
in those early years, since he could hardly have expected an immediate recognition of his particular
services. But Boswell when he grew older attached
himself more definitely to particular patrons. There
are a number of names—Lord Pembroke, Lord
Lisburne, Lord Lonsdale, Burke, Dundas.[5] To these
in turn he seems to have pinned his faith and almost
to have expected some promotion to have fallen upon

[1] *Gentleman's Magazine*, June 1795, and Nichols' *Literary
Anecdotes*, ii, pp. 400–2.
[2] *Letters to Temple*, p. 29.   [3] *Ib.*, p. 43.
[4] *Ib.*, p. 190, and *Tour to Corsica*.   [5] *Letters to Temple.*

him. And from all his great acquaintances he was to get but one poor post, the Recordership of Carlisle.

We can hardly be surprised from what we have seen already of Boswell's methods of approaching his patrons that he had no great success in these schemes of advancement. We have quoted already a letter to Chatham, which was designed to impress that Minister with the fact that he was a rising young man, and to solicit his favour. There is another letter of a later date [1] intended to further his acquaintance with Burke. The great orator might have one day at his disposal some Government posts ; his memory must not be allowed to lapse :

Dear Sir,—Upon my honour I began a letter to you some time ago, and did not finish it, because I imagined you were then near your apotheosis—as poor Goldsmith said upon a former occasion, when he thought your party was coming into administration ; and being one of your old barons of Scotland, my pride could not brook the appearance of paying my court to a Minister, amongst the crowd of interested expectants on his accession.

Certainly if one wishes to obtain a post it is better to avoid the ' crowd of interested expectants.' The ' old baron ' too is an excellent card to play to one who is not of the aristocratic circles ; few men are free from the taint of snobbishness, and patronage may be courted by cultivating disinterested friendship.

[1] March 3, 1778.

It is well at the same time to remember *Qui s'excuse s'accuse*. 'At present,' Boswell continues, 'I take it for granted that I need be under no such apprehension, and, therefore, I resume the indulgence of my inclination.' Only one who was really interested and wished to conceal the fact could be so careful. Boswell realises that there is something rather odd about the explanation. It may not after all be entirely wise. It is possible that men rather like it to be thought that they have much patronage, and find some pleasure in being asked for favours. 'This may be, perhaps, a singular method of beginning a correspondence ; and, in one sense may not be very complimentative. But I can sincerely assure you, my dear Sir, that it is a genuine compliment to Mr. Burke himself.' The explanation of how it is a compliment is now to follow, but the desire for self-excuse obtrudes itself again : 'It is generally thought no meanness to solicit the notice and favour of a man in power, and, surely, it is much less a meanness to endeavour, by honest means, to have the honour and pleasure of being on an agreeable footing with a superior man of knowledge, abilities and genius.' A further excuse is furnished by the favours shown to Boswell in the past by Mr. Burke himself :

I have to thank you for the obligation which you have already conferred upon me, by the welcome which I have, upon repeated occasions, experienced under your roof.

When I was last in London, you gave me a general invitation, which I value more than a treasury warrant : an invitation to the ' feast of reason ' ; and what I like still more, the ' flow of the soul,' which you dispense with liberal and elegant abundance, is, in my estimation, a privilege of enjoying certain felicity.

The comparison between the places that come of courting a patron and this sublime ' felicity ' that comes of friendship must still be maintained—' and we know that riches and honour are desirable only as a means of felicity, and that they often fail of the end.'

It is necessary now to give an account of his political opinions, so that Mr. Burke may be assured that Mr. Boswell is his supporter :

Most heartily do I rejoice that our present Ministers have, at last, yielded to conciliation. For amidst all the sanguinary zeal of my countrymen I have professed myself a friend to our fellow-subjects in America, so far as they claim an exemption from being taxed by the representatives of the King's British subjects. I do not perfectly agree with you ; for I deny the Declaratory Act ; and I am a warm Tory, in its true constitutional sense.

It will be noticed that the assertion of independence adds to this declaration a considerable degree of importance. After so careful a preparation the real point of the letter may be disclosed :

I wish I were a Commissioner, or one of the Secretaries of the Commission, for the grand treaty. I am to be in London this spring, and if His Majesty

should ask me what I would choose, my answer will
be, to assist at the compact between Britain and
America.

The letter to Burke is only less absurd than the
letter to Chatham, which was quoted above. What
most surprises us is not the vanity of the young man
who confided to Chatham his hopes and prospects,
nor his impudence in asking a Minister to favour him
with a letter and in bothering Burke with his political
opinions, but the entire ignorance displayed by a man
of intelligence about the kind of impression that letters
such as these would produce upon their recipients.

Boswell indeed as we have said—and it is a sufficient
reason to account for his failure—was a fool.   It is
this ignorance of the minds of others about oneself,
a certain simplicity of character, an unquestioning,
childlike self-confidence, that makes fools of men.
No fool would wish to be thought foolish, and if a fool
were to understand what was thought about him he
would soon alter his behaviour.   His foolishness
depends upon the fact that in this respect he has no
imagination.   The ignorance of Boswell about the
effect of his behaviour is the more remarkable because
he was in many ways intelligent, sagacious, and extremely observant.   It was not a quality which
vanished with maturity, though it was slightly
modified in later years : he was nearly fifty when he
wrote to Temple an account of his attempts to enlist

the patronage of Pitt (the younger), which shows how completely he misunderstood the whole situation :

It is utter folly in Pitt not to reward and attach to his administration a man of my popular and pleasant talents, whose merit he has acknowledged in a letter under his own hand. He did not answer several letters, which I wrote at intervals, requesting to wait upon him ; I lately wrote to him that such behaviour to me was certainly not generous. ' I think it is not just, and (forgive the freedom) I doubt if it be wise. If I do not hear from you in ten days, I shall conclude that you are resolved to have no farther communication with me ; for I assure you, Sir, I am extremely un-willing to give you, or indeed myself, unnecessary trouble.' About two months have elapsed, and he has made no sign.

And it was an ignorance which included even his own father :

I have answered him in my own style : I will be myself. . . . Would you not be pleased to see your son happy in independence, cultivating his little farm and ornamenting his nuptial villa, and filling himself one day, as well as possible, the place of a much greater man ? Temple, would you not like such a son ? Would you not feel a glow of parental joy ? I know you would ; and yet my worthy father writes to me in the manner you see, with that Scots strength of sarcasm which is peculiar to a North Briton. But he is offended with that fire which you and I cherish as the essence of our soul ; and how can I make him happy ? [1]

[1] *Letters to Temple*, p. 88.

But if all fools are alike in so far as they have this common foundation upon which the flimsy fabric of folly is erected, yet they differ widely in the manner of their foolishness. To say that a man is a fool is to say but little of all that is meant by the expression in his individual case. Boswell was a fool in a number of ways which we shall now have to consider.

The extract of Boswell's letter to his father which we have quoted above in his letter to Temple is typical of one phase of all his foolishness. The impulse which made him write in this place about ' cultivating his little farm and ornamenting his nuptial villa ' is one which he frequently had. It is difficult to find a name which exactly fits it. It is the melodramatic instinct applied to real life. The words which he uses in this case contain a sentiment beyond the mere facts they represent ; and it is a false sentiment— false not because he did not feel it, but because there was no occasion for it ; sentiment is wasted. In Boswell there was a sentimental side to the affectation that we have already spoken of as having been partially cured by Johnson. It is not meant, by this expression, that Boswell consciously assumed sentiment which he did not feel : we cannot always tell whether he was conscious or not ; and it does not matter. Affectation implies only the presence of what is unreal ; it is concerned as much with the feeling of what is false as with falsely pretending to feel.

Perhaps the most remarkable of Boswell's extravagant utterances are those to Temple on the subject of their friendship. He idealises this to suit his conception of the most perfect of human relationships, and frequently alludes to it. ' May indulgent Heaven grant a continuance of our friendship ! As our minds improve in knowledge, may the sacred flame still increase, until at last we reach the glorious world above, when we shall never be separated, but enjoy an everlasting society of bliss ! ' He was able to enjoy the ' luxury of philosophy and friendship,' and ' invaluable hours of elegant friendship and classical sociality,' and ' calmly smile ' in consequence ' at the attacks of envy or of malevolence.' Temple, ' whose kind and amiable counsel never failed to soothe my dejected mind,' was told to ' reflect, my friend, that you have sure comfort, you have true friends—you have Nichols and Boswell, whom you may look upon as parts of yourself. Consider this as an exalted comfort which few enjoy, although they have many of the shining gifts of fortune.' He seems at one moment to have suspected that he might grow cold in his affection :

I am a quick fire, but I know not if I last sufficiently, though, surely, my dear Temple, there is always a warm place for you. With many people I have compared myself to a taper, which can light up a great and lasting fire though itself is soon extinguished.

The friendship, indeed, was of the greatest value to Boswell ; as we see, behind his absurd manner of expressing it, it must have been a comfort to him in many disappointments :

When harassed and fretted with Court of Sessions business, when vexed to think myself a coarse labourer in an obscure corner, I get into good humour again by recollecting that I am Temple's most intimate friend.[1]

His friendship with Mrs. Stuart is treated in the same manner :

We talked with unreserved freedom, as we had nothing to fear ; we were philosophical, upon honour, —not deep, but feeling ; we were pious, we drank tea and bid each other adieu as finely as romance paints. She is my wife's dearest friend, so you see how beautiful our intimacy is.[2]

The romantic sphere into which Boswell elevated these friendships contrasts very strangely with his acute analysis to Johnson of his true sentiments : ' The feeling of friendship is like that of being comfortably filled with roast beef.' One would suspect that the feeling of friendship with him was, as he might have expressed it himself, like a balloon, which rises higher and higher as it is more blown out with gas.

In the same fashion he believed that his life was, ' one of the most romantic' he knew of ;[3] that Temple's ' soft admonitions would at any time calm

---

[1] *Letters to Temple*, p. 162.   [2] *Ib.*, p. 158.   [3] *Ib.*, p. 63.

the tempests of his soul,' [1] and that he could 'retire into the calm regions of philosophy' and contemplate the 'heroism' which he was able to see in his conduct towards his father.[2] Philosophy, indeed, had a great attraction for him. It was in the bower of philosophy that many of his best hours were filled with that noble admiration which his disinterested soul was able to enjoy for the character of Lord Chatham. In early years he was Temple's philosophic friend, and Paoli is told that 'with a mind naturally inclined to melancholy and a deep desire of inquiry, I have intensely applied myself to metaphysical researches.'

The affectation or extravagance of Boswell appears also from time to time in his pious and moral remarks.

Being in a frame of mind which I hope, for the felicity of human nature, many experience—in fine weather—at the country house of a friend—consoled and elevated by pious exercises—I expressed myself with an unrestrained fervour to my 'Guide, Philosopher and Friend' : 'My dear Sir, I could fain be a good man ; and I am very good now. I fear God and honour the king, I wish to do no ill, and to be benevolent to all mankind.' [3]

Boswell was very impressionable, by his own account, to good influences. He rose from reading

---

[1] *Letters to Temple*, p. 148.   [2] *Ib.*, p. 4.
[3] *Life of Johnson*, iv, 122.

a dialogue of Hume's 'happier and more disposed to follow virtue.'[1]   Relating how Mr. Edward Dilly repeated on his death-bed a passage from Young's 'Night Thoughts'—'Death, a subterraneous road to bliss,' or some such words—Boswell remarks : 'I am edified here.'[2]   The greatest triumph, one would suppose, of this nature was when, as he says, speaking of his 'moral fences,' 'Reason, that steady builder and overseer, has set them firm.'[3]   Boswell was excellent too at giving moral advice : 'It is certainly true philosophy to submit to the will of Heaven, and to fulfil the amiable duties of morality.'[4] 'Read Epictetus,'[5] he writes to Temple ; on another occasion, 'Read Johnson. Let a manly and firm philosophy brace your mind.'

Boswell, however, though he was continually posing, posed not for others but for himself.   He had an insatiable greed of sensation.   He derived prodigious pleasure from the view of himself in a situation.   'I cannot resist,' he says, 'the serious pleasure of writing to Mr. Johnson from the tomb of Melancthon.   My paper rests upon the tomb of that great and good man.' While he wrote the letter he admired the scene he had arranged.   He admired himself playing every kind of *rôle* ;   he could be the grave author, or the romantic lover, the scholar of 'solid learning' or the elegant

[1] *Letters to Temple*, p. 20.   [2] *Ib.*, p. 195.
[3] *Ib.*, p. 148.   [4] *Ib.*, p. 24.   [5] *Ib.*, p. 127.

man of the world, the sage counsellor or the jolly good
fellow, the enthusiast for liberty who talked heroics
with Paoli and politics with Chatham, explorer and
diplomat, the feudal lord or the humble paterfamilias of
a rustic domesticity ; he could be literary, theological,
pious, philosophical, legal, or political, as occasion
suited, with profound enjoyment of the part he
was acting. He delighted in the solemnity of a vow,
and even had a taste for the solitude of a hermit :
' Sometimes,' he exclaims, ' I have been in the
humour of wishing to retire to a desert.' His gust
for London was the same gust for sensation ; and
his pursuit of distinguished men was partly for the
sake of an added zest and excitement from their
company.

' You can almost see him,' says Lionel Johnson,
' reckoning up, as it were, on his plump fingers, his
eminent acquaintances, the cities and courts he has
visited, his writings and flirtations and experiences
in general : they are his treasures and his triumphs.
The acquisition of Johnson was but the greatest of
them all, his crowning achievement ; all his life
was devoted to social *coups d'état*. To hear service
in an Anglican cathedral, to attend an exceptionally
choice murderer to the gallows ; to contrive a meeting
between Johnson and Wilkes ; . . . to pray among the
ruins of Iona, and to run away for fear of ghosts ;
to turn Roman Catholic, and immediately to run away

with an actress : each and all of these performances were to him sensational, enlivening, vivid.'

Boswell was not unaware of this extravagance in his temperament. He alludes to his ' warm imagination.' In ' Boswelliana,' pleased at having found ' a good image,' he records :

There have been many people who built castles in the air ; but, I believe, I am the first who ever attempted to live in them.

By castles in the air, he means not only glorious plans for the future, but the sensational and emotional in common incidents. A moment during the ' Tour to the Hebrides ' reveals the whole of what he meant :

I can never forget the impression made upon my fancy by some of the ladies' maids tripping about in neat morning dresses. After seeing for a long time little but rusticity, their lively appearance pleased me so much that I thought for a moment I could have been a knight-errant for them.

A knight-errant for a couple of Scotch maids ! A preposterous fancy ! But none the less it is Boswell.

It would be too large a task to deal here with all the recorded affectation or extravagance of Boswell. But we must not omit to mention one particular phase of it. Consciously or unconsciously, Boswell in some degree imitated Dr. Johnson—precisely in what degree it is difficult to determine.

The influence which Johnson had upon his faithful follower has been discussed already. This must be carefully distinguished from the imitation in question now ; for an influence is something acquired from the manner and mind of another, assimilated and repro-duced, not as original but as genuine ; an imitation is, as it were, a garment put on, an adornment of the outward person, reflecting no true sentiment within.

Though Johnson had a real moral influence upon Boswell, some of his remarks, and especially some of the pious exclamations, such as those we have quoted, were of the latter kind. We find passages in the ' Life ' when Boswell makes truly Johnsonian remarks ; as on the occasion when, in a discussion about the freedom of the will, Dr. Mayo alluded to the distinction between moral and physical necessity, and Boswell replied : ' Alas ! Sir, they come both to the same thing. You may be bound as hard by chains when covered by leather, as when the iron appears ' ; or when he said in answer to Dr. Johnson's remark that he had *downed* Dr. Robertson with the King of Prussia, ' Yes, Sir, you threw a *bottle* at his head.'

When actually in his presence, it is clear from Fanny Burney's account that Boswell imitated Dr. Johnson :

He had an odd mock-solemnity of tone and manner that he had acquired imperceptibly from constantly thinking of and imitating Dr. Johnson, whose own solemnity, nevertheless, far from mock, was the result of pensive rumination. There was, also, something slouching in the gait and dress of Mr. Boswell that wore an air, ridiculously enough, of purporting to personify the same model. His clothes were always too large for him ; his hair, or wig, was constantly in a state of negligence ; and he never for a moment sat still or upright upon a chair. Every look and movement displayed either intentional or voluntary imitation. Yet certainly it was not meant for caricature, for his heart, almost even to idolatry, was in his reverence for Dr. Johnson.[1]

It is a curious and striking picture, and we may gather that there was always something odd and laughable, and yet rather lamentable, about Boswell's appearance. The effect of imitation he seems sometimes half-conscious of producing, from the care with which he accentuates in the ' Life ' and the ' Tour ' any point of difference between Dr. Johnson and himself. But it must be remembered that Miss Burney's account is an account of particular circumstances—the company was a large one, and not an inner circle of more intimate friends of Boswell and Johnson. We have no reason to suppose that Boswell's behaviour, particularly his behaviour apart from Dr. Johnson, was greatly affected by this strange homage to his friend.

It is clear in any case that affectation, however

[1] *Diary of Madame D'Arblay*, i, p. 509.

much it may have taken a Johnsonian form, was
fundamental in Boswell's character ; for we can see
it plainly before the date of that eventful meeting.
Johnson indeed had a marked aversion from the kind
of sentimentality which Boswell frequently indulged in,
and there is in it something which could not possibly
have been the effect of imitating Dr. Johnson. How
very far removed from anything which Johnson could
have done is the absurd conduct of Boswell (the best
instance, perhaps, of this kind of affectation in him)
when he visited Mr. Ireland and saw the fraudulent
Shakespeare papers :

On the arrival of Mr. Boswell, the papers were as
usual placed before him, when he commenced his
examination of them ; and being satisfied as to their
antiquity, as far as the external appearance would
attest, he proceeded to examine the style of the
language from the fair transcripts made from the
disguised handwriting. In this research Mr. Boswell
continued for a considerable length of time, constantly
speaking in favour of the internal as well as external
proofs of the validity of the manuscripts. At length,
finding himself rather thirsty, he requested a tumbler
of warm brandy and water ; which having nearly
finished, he then redoubled his praises of the manuscripts ; and at length, arising from his chair, he made
use of the following expression : ' Well, I shall now
die contented, since I have lived to witness the present
day.' Mr. Boswell then, kneeling down before the
volume containing a portion of the papers, continued,
' I now kiss the invaluable relics of our bard : and

o

thanks to God that I have lived to see them ! '   Having
kissed the volume with every token of reverence, Mr.
Boswell shortly after quitted Mr. Ireland's house. [1]

However absurd the behaviour of Boswell in the
rôle of a man of letters may seem to us when we understand the feelings which prompted it, it is doubtful
whether it would have been sufficient alone to give
him the reputation of a fool. Extravagance of this kind
is not very commonly condemned if it is not seen to be
insincere, and though it is easy enough for us who are
in possession of all the records of his life to see the
imposture, it must have been more difficult for those
who knew Boswell to have a real interest in literature,
and to be already a man of letters, to understand that
he was posing as the literary man.   His acquaintance
would more readily have called him a fool on account
of his vanity.

We have all at bottom in some degree the love of
self, and vanity is the expression we apply to it when
it causes us in some way to lose our sense of proportion, to see things, as it were, in a false perspective.
Self-love becomes vanity when we love ourselves
undeservedly, or when it makes necessary to us the
approbation of others.   Usually when it has one
effect it has also the other.

But Boswell was vain, not, like many people, of

[1] *Ireland's Confessions*, pp. 95–6.

qualities which he did not possess, or which, if he did possess them, were no cause for self-congratulation, but because he had an uncontrollable desire that everyone else should know about his success and share his wonder and admiration. It was not so much that he exaggerated his importance, though he did that sometimes, as that he exaggerated the importance to other people of his importance. He not only desired their applause as well as his own, but assumed, with his curious ignorance of the mind of others in matters which concerned himself, that what interested him would naturally interest them.

It was vanity of this kind which, more than anything else, made a fool of Boswell. The insatiable desire to be conspicuous which made him as a young man publish what he must have known to be worthless, appear at the Shakespeare Jubilee as Corsican Boswell, and insert notices of his movements in the papers,[1] did not diminish as one might expect with maturity, but rather grew with his years. There is nothing which he wrote so egotistical and vain as some passages in those most serious documents which he addressed to the ' People of Scotland upon the State of the Nation ' and to which were pinned his hopes of political honour. In the letter of 1783 he says of himself :

' For my own part, I should claim no credit, did I not flatter myself that I practise what I now presume to

---

[1] Prior's *Life of Goldsmith*, i, 449–50.

recommend. I have mentioned former circumstances, perhaps of too much egotism, to show that I am no time server ; and at this moment, friends to whom I am attached by affection, gratitude, and interest, are zealous for the measure which I deem so alarming. Let me add that a dismission of the Portland administration will probably disappoint an object which I have most ardently at heart.

The second letter alludes to the former one as though it had almost created a revolution, and manages in the same sentence to remind his readers that he had the approval of Pitt and was himself descended from an old Scotch family :

I had the happiness to find my letter received not only with indulgence, but with a generous warmth of heart I can never forget, but to the latest moment of my life shall most gratefully remember. The fire of loyalty was kindled. It flew through our counties and our boroughs. The King was addressed : the Constitution was saved. I was proud to have been able thus *ciere viros* ; prouder still than of receiving the applause of the *Minister of the Crown*, which he was pleased to convey to me in a very handsome letter ; upon which, however, I set a high value, considering not only the Minister, but the man ; and accordingly it shall be preserved in the archives of my family.

In the same pamphlet Boswell refers to his wife's aristocratic connections, and intrudes an assertion of his domestic felicity which could have no bearing on the political theme. He wishes to appear as ' the friend of Lord Eglintoun ' :

Amongst those friends I myself am one of the warmest, both as an enthusiast for ancient feudal attachments, and as having the honour and happiness to be married to his Lordship's relation, a true Mont-gomerie, whom I esteem, after fifteen years, as on the day when she gave me her hand.

This declaration satisfied in some strange manner a personal vanity, and was also no doubt intended to enlist the support of his Lordship.

But by far the most remarkable story of Boswell's absurdities is one told by John Taylor, editor of the *Sun*, about his behaviour at a public dinner :

I remember dining with him at Guildhall in 1785, when Alderman Boydell gave his grand civic festival on being raised to the mayoralty. Mr. Pitt honoured the table on that occasion with his presence, and, when the company removed to a room, in a short time Mr. Boswell contrived to be asked to favour the company with a song. He declared his readiness to comply, but first delivered a short preface, in which he observed that it had been his good fortune to be introduced to several of the potentates and most of the great charac-ters of Europe, but with all his endeavours he had never been successful in obtaining an introduction to a gentleman who was an honour to his country, and whose talents he held in the highest esteem and admiration. It was evident to all the company that Mr. Boswell alluded to Mr. Pitt, who sat with all the dignified silence of a marble statue, though, indeed, in such a situation he could not but take the reference to himself. Mr. Boswell then sang a song of his own composition, which was a parody on Dibdin's ' Sweet Little Cherub,' under the title of ' A Grocer of London,' which rendered the reference to Mr. Pitt too evident to be mistaken, as the great minister was then a member of the Grocers' Company. This song Mr. Boswell, partly volunteering and partly pressed by the company, sang at least six times, insomuch that Mr. Pitt was obliged to relax from his gravity and join in the general laugh at the oddity of Mr. Boswell's character.[1]

The value of this tale as evidence of Boswell's behaviour and character depends in some degree upon the extent of his potations. Though he may have had the audacity to do such things when in a normal condition, it must have been easier to do them when tipsy. It may be judged, from the continuation of Dr. Taylor's story, that a part of Boswell's confidence in the presence of Mr. Pitt was due to the festivity of the occasion :

Boswell and I came away together, both in so convivial a mood that we roared out all the way ' The Grocer of London,' till we reached Hatton Garden, where I then resided, to the annoyance of many watchmen whom we roused from their peaceful slumbers, without, however, being taken into custody for disturbing their repose. . . . I met him the next day about twelve o'clock near St. Dunstan's Church, as fresh as a rose.

[1] *Taylor's Records*, vol. i, 89, 90.

Fitzgerald, after quoting this account of the mayoralty dinner, continues :

This ludicrous exhibition was much talked of and laughed at. To heighten the absurdity, his Liberal friends affected to be shocked at his want of principle, in singing praises of the ' Grocer,' whom he had been heard to abuse. They were enchanted to find him rise to the bait, and thus vindicate himself : ' Pray let them know that I am vain of a hasty com-position which has procured me large draughts of the popular applause in which I delight. Let me add that there was certainly no servility on my part, for I publicly declared in Guildhall, between the encores, " that this same Grocer had treated me arrogantly and ungratefully, but that, from his great merit as a minister, I was compelled to support him." The time will come when I shall have a riper opportunity to show, that in one instance, at least, the man has wanted wisdom.'

He goes on to explain that Boswell gained a good deal of notoriety from the escapade, which was alluded to in a popular satirical poem of the time.

It is easy indeed to understand the motives of Boswell. His childish and unrestrained love of merri-ment, his insatiable desire to be the wag and the buffoon, enabled him to give vent in the most mirthful fashion to his passion for self-advertisement, to explain how he had been honoured by the attention of kings and how he intended to have an introduction to the great Minister ; and with all this he retained a certain fundamental honesty about himself, so that he was compelled to exclaim between the encores ' that this same Minister had treated me arrogantly and ungratefully.' He understood so little what was the opinion of the company about him that he seems to have believed that he was recommending himself to a patron, and he was so vain that he was undoubtedly proud of what must have been an absurd compositon.

Boswell indeed was very fond of writing humorous verse.[1] The instinct in him was the natural result of his animal spirits ; the need to be laughing, which he felt so strongly at most times when he was not depressed and melancholy, fixed upon the smallest objects as suitable for his wit, and he was satisfied only by some form of expression. The reason that he collected in his commonplace-book a number of ' good things,' as he would call them, is not so much that he was proud of his own sayings (for those of others are also treasured) or that he wished to preserve them for posterity, though both these feelings were present, as that his huge enjoyment of anything witty must be recorded to be satisfied.

It is remarkable, when we recollect what a large sense of humour he had, that many of his verses and of his jokes should be so dull and colourless. But the faculty for appreciating what is amusing is very different from the capacity for originating it. It is

[1] Fitzgerald's *Life of Boswell*, ii, 73–8.

the difference between humour and wit. The latter
involves the power of expression ; and a man may as
easily be full of humour, without making a joke, as
he may be by nature a poet without ever writing a
line of good poetry. Boswell had some wit, but not
very much—far less than anyone would imagine
merely from reading the ' Life ' or the ' Tour.' His
position perhaps is not unlike that of several poets
who have written some stanzas and stray lines of
a rare beauty, and are none the less poets because
they have written also much that seems quite
unpoetical.

A specimen of Boswell's humorous verse is printed
in the ' Life.' He had dined one evening at Lord
Montrose's and afterwards went to Miss Monckton's,
where ' a great number of persons of the first rank '
were assembled, in a state of improper elevation.
' Next day,' says Boswell, ' I endeavoured to give
what had happened the most ingenious turn I could,
by the following verses :

> Not that with th' excellent Montrose
>   I had the happiness to dine ;
> Not that I late from table rose,
>   From Graham's wit, from generous wine.
>
> It was not these alone which led
>   On sacred manners to encroach ;
> And made me feel what most I dread,
>   Johnson's just frown, and self-reproach.

But when I entered, not abash'd,
  From your bright eyes were shot such rays,
At once intoxication flash'd,
  And all my frame was in a blaze:

But not a brilliant blaze I own,
  Of the dull smoke I'm yet asham'd;
I was a dreary ruin grown,
  And not enlighten'd though enflam'd.

Victim at once to wine and love,
  I hope, Maria, you'll forgive;
While I invoke the powers above,
  That henceforth I may wiser live.

Certainly this is amusing in some degree, and
amusing too in an original way; but much of it is
mere rhyming without any sort of wit. Boswell
could be as banal as anyone. An ode ('Horatian
Ode,' he calls it) to Charles Dilly, which is chiefly
concerned with one Dr. Lettsom, frequently the host
of both Boswell and Dilly, exhibits the author of
humorous verse at his worst; it will be enough to
quote one stanza:

And guests has he in ev'ry degree
  Of decent estimation.
His liberal mind holds all mankind,
  As an extended nation.

Boswell's *mots* are of a common eighteenth-
century type. The turn of phrase admired by both
Johnson and Boswell and most of their contemporaries

was the image. In 'Boswelliana' is a story of
Boswell's introduction to Scotch lawyers: 'Boswell
had a great aversion to the law, but forced
himself to enter upon that laborious profession in
compliance with the anxious desire of his father, for
whom he had the greatest regard. After putting on
the gown he said with great good humour to his brother
advocates, 'Gentlemen, I am prest into the service
here; but I have observed that a prest man, either by
sea or land, after a little time does just as well as a
volunteer.'

That is Boswell at his best.

Here is another specimen of Boswell's wit: 'A
modern man of taste found fault with the avenues
at Auchinleck, and said he wished to see straggling
trees. 'I wish,' said Boswell, 'I could see straggling
fools in this world.'

That is Boswell at his worst.

Why a man who had so much natural humour as
Boswell had should have failed so completely to
discriminate when his own wit was in question must
remain as much a problem to us as is the failure of
many a poet to criticise his own writings—the explanation may be perhaps that it requires some special
effort of the mind which can but rarely be made
and which is impossible after the moment of composition. Boswell certainly seems to have had a
high opinion of his efforts to be witty; his verses to

Miss Monckton are inserted in the ' Life ' with evident pride, and without any excuse of some connection with Johnson such as he usually makes when alluding to his own performances, and he seems frequently to have sung the songs which he composed, obtaining, no doubt, in this way the ' conspicuousness ' which he desired.[1]

The enjoyment which Boswell had in public at Stratford and at the mayoralty dinner and in private, no doubt, on many occasions of which unfortunately we have no account, is perhaps best illustrated and best understood from a single sentence of his own in one of the ' Letters to Temple ' :

I was the great man (as we used to say) at the late Drawing-Room, in a suit of imperial blue lined with rose-coloured silk, and ornamented with rich gold-wrought buttons.

For the eagerness which Boswell had to reveal to others anything about himself which he was proud of, and a sort of inevitable obtrusiveness in him, Johnson with his usual shrewdness found an excellent parallel which is faithfully recounted in the ' Life ' :

Once when checking my boasting too frequently of myself in company, he said to me, ' Boswell, you often vaunt so much as to provoke ridicule. You put me in mind of a man who was standing in the kitchen of an inn with his back to the fire, and thus accosted the person next him, " Do you know, sir,

---

[1] Fitzgerald's *Life of Boswell*, ii, 76.

who I am ? "   " No, sir," said the other, " I have
not that advantage."   " Sir," said he, " I am the *great
Twalmley*, who invented the New Floodgate Iron." '

Endowed with these qualities of unsuspecting
simplicity and open-mouthed vanity, Boswell naturally
became, as we have seen, an object of mirth to his
fellow-lawyers.   When they took away his wig he did
indeed half suspect a trick ; but how confident and
innocent and entirely unsuspicious he is when he
boldly pleads for the writ, ' *Quare adhaesit pavimento*.'
His own story of the storm during the sail to Mull, told
in the ' Tour to the Hebrides,' illustrates perhaps
better than any other the childish confidence of his
conduct.   Boswell, though filled with undisguised
terror, still ardently wished to play the man and be
the hero, and he thought, no doubt, as he stood holding
the rope in expectation of the captain's command, that
the post assigned to him was one of vital importance.

As I saw them all busy doing something, I asked
Col, with much earnestness, what I could do.   He,
with a happy readiness, put into my hand a rope,
which was fixed to the top of one of the masts, and
told me to hold it till he bade me pull.   If I had
considered the matter, I might have seen that this
could not be of the least service ; but his object was
to keep me out of the way of those who were busy
working the vessel, and at the same time to divert my
fear by employing me and making me think that I was
of use.   Thus did I stand firm to my post, while the

wind and rain beat upon me, always expecting a call to pull my rope.'

The vanity and simplicity of Boswell no doubt obtruded themselves very frequently in his behaviour ; and they caused a certain expansiveness and recklessness of conversation which would be interpreted at once as thoughtless and foolish. We have an admirable glimpse into the kind of atmosphere produced by his talk in a story which he tells of a snub he received from Colman :

I was then so impressed with the truth of many of the stories of which I had been told, that I avowed my conviction, saying, ' He is only *willing* to believe ; I *do* believe. The evidence is enough for me, though not for his great mind. What will not fill a quart bottle will fill a pint bottle. I am filled with belief.' ' Are you ? ' said Colman, ' then cork it up.' [1]

' His social propensities,' says Sir J. Prior, ' were well known . . . he opens his mind so freely that we discover much of what is passing there, even when the disclosure is not meant.' [2]   Boswell, indeed, talked very readily even upon the most serious subjects. About morals and religion he was continually questioning Dr. Johnson, and most of all about what to the other was a peculiarly sacred and awful thing, the fear of death. The topics were introduced apparently without any particular reason or fitness, but just as it occurred

[1] *Life of Johnson*, ii, 318.
[2] Prior's *Life of Goldsmith*, i, 452–3.

to Boswell that he might elicit some response from Johnson upon questions about which it was essential to his purpose that he should hear the doctor's views : and they were introduced too not merely in private converse but when a number of people were present.

It seems clear that Boswell was sometimes very tactless in leading Johnson to talk ; he did not understand that not every company nor every occasion is suitable for the discussion of the most serious matters. He had, too, an unfortunate habit of saying things which were extremely injudicious. He did not even understand altogether what was likely to annoy Dr. Johnson—as on the occasion when he referred to him in company by the name ' Gargantua,' which Johnson had spoken of as having been applied to himself, or when he made what must have been an obvious reference to Johnson's curious clothes : ' Would not *you*, sir, be the better for velvet embroidery ? ' These remarks were made, it is evident, without any malevolent intention. It would seem that even when he meant to be rude he did not realise all the harm he was doing : Hume was with some justice annoyed when Boswell quoted the phrase of Temple, ' their infidel pensioner, Hume ; ' [1] and it was introduced just as a child might say in some personal argument, ' I know what someone said of *you* ' ; and Foote can never have felt much friendship for Johnson

[1] *Letters to Temple*, p. 165.

after he heard that the latter had compared his infidelity to that of a dog.[1]   The company in both cases may have been glad to see Boswell defend his friend, but they must have thought him a considerable fool and hardly a harmless one.

Nor was it merely from his disregard of what was appropriate that his conversation might be thought foolish, but rather because a man who is very ready to talk of his most intimate thoughts and feelings is usually supposed to be a fool.

Boswell certainly had far more candour than most men, and he had also a far greater curiosity and interest in mankind, which made him ready to talk like a child of things about which many men prefer to be silent.   But it would seem, too, that though far from incapable of feeling deep emotion he was unaffected where most of us would be touched.   ' He was a boy longer than others,' and this perhaps is the explanation.

[1] *Life of Johnson*, ii, 95.

CHAPTER VII

NOTHING in Boswell's life became him so well as his second important publication, ' The Journal of a Tour to the Hebrides.' The event took place in 1785, not many months after Johnson's death, and less than twelve years after the eventful journey when Johnson was displayed to his biographer's country-men. The ' Tour ' has already been mentioned here as an episode in Boswell's remarkable friendship. It was an episode, besides, in Boswell's life ; it decided his destiny.

In the year 1785 Boswell was in the midst of his political schemes and ambitions. It was exactly in this period of his life that it was most important for him to win respect. Yet the ' Journal ' revealed the whole severity of Johnson's criticisms upon Scotland and the Scotch ; Boswell's position among his country-men was certain to suffer, and did suffer very much by its publication. His candour triumphed by the event. His real self was expressed without com-promise, at the expense of the respectable self which he cherished and cultivated. It matters very little

how much Boswell foresaw the consequence. Probably he was not altogether unsuspicious, for Malone
was at his side, and Malone was a man of the world.[1]
In any case he did publish this amazing book, and he
published it at a critical time. Just when he seemed
to be deserting his genius and drifting into a world
that was never intended for him, the vital truth of
Boswell proved that it was irrepressible and saved
him for Johnson, for himself, and for posterity.

.   .   .   .   .

Johnson and Boswell were typical travellers of the
eighteenth century. They went in no romantic spirit
to see the beauties of Nature in remote corners of the
earth. ' He always said,' reports Boswell of the
Doctor, ' that he was not come to Scotland to see fine
places, of which there were enough in England, but
wild objects, mountains, waterfalls, peculiar manners—
in short, things which he had not seen before. I have
a notion that he at no time has had much taste for
rural beauties. I have myself very little.' This is
a clear statement. They looked at ' wild objects '
because they were unusual, and eschewed almost entirely scenery of a tamer spirit. They were interested
in ' manners.' The Journal bears out this statement.
Observations about the people of the country are part

[1] Malone saw a sheet of the *Tour to the Hebrides* at the printer's
and was so much impressed that he obtained an introduction to
Boswell ; he helped him in the final stage, both of this book
and the *Life*, and was eventually Boswell's first editor.

of the traveller's stock-in-trade, and they seem even
to be one of the *raisons d'être* of Boswell's book.   In
the same way the Journal is filled with archæological
and historical speculations.   Johnson's journey to
the Western Islands is far more so, and seems to have
been written almost entirely from this point of view.
These were the absorbing interests of educated men,
and travel was expected to furnish the occasion for
' an ordered series of learned observations.'   To be
convinced of the paramount importance of these
interests in the eighteenth century one has only to
glance at the periodicals of the time.

But both Johnson and Boswell, especially the
latter, had, though they may have been scarcely
conscious of the fact, a far more important interest
in human nature.   The Tour was admirably arranged
for its gratification.   It consisted for the most part in
visits to the gentlemen of the country :   the travellers
occasionally put up at an inn ;   but for the most part
they took advantage of Highland hospitality.   Their
conversation therefore would naturally be concerned
very much with the qualities of their various hosts.
Now Boswell kept an elaborate and strictly diurnal
diary of which the most important item was
professedly the record of Dr. Johnson's talk.   The
briefest reflection on the Doctor's manner and the
nature of his remarks must therefore reveal at once
the character of Boswell's Journal.

Assuredly it is an amazing fact that this Journal was published within twelve years of the Tour itself ! As we should expect, it is full of observations, many of them condemnatory, about men and women who were still living. ' Nowadays,' says Mr. Percy Fitzgerald, ' we have been regularly trained to personality by what are called the " Society papers," in which the names of private persons as well as their doings are recorded ; still it would cause a commotion if the conversation of some leading personage were reported, in which persons still living were described in such fashion as this : " A—— is a poor creature ; *he has no bottom.*" " B—— is a thorough donkey, talks a good deal of what he *thinks* to be sense," &c.'

One instance will serve to illustrate the tone of Boswell's Journal ; it shows perhaps the ultimate point of indiscretion which he reached, but is a fair indication of his manner. One of the gentlemen who entertained the two travellers was Sir Alexander Macdonald : he had not, it appears, a reputation for generosity.

The penurious gentleman of our acquaintance, formerly alluded to, afforded us a topick of conversation to-night. Dr. Johnson said I ought to write down a recollection of the instances of his narrowness as they almost exceeded belief.

Boswell proceeds to relate a story to the effect that the Highlander gave to an Irish harper a valuable harp-key, because ' he could not find it in his heart to give him any money.' Later, he discovered its value and wished to have it back.

Johnson : ' I like to see how avarice defeats itself ; how when avoiding to part with money the miser gives something more valuable.' Col said the gentleman's relations were angry at his giving away the harp-key, for it had been long in the family. *Johnson :* ' Sir, he values a new guinea more than an old friend.'

One can hardly imagine anything more offensive— unless it were the story which follows it :

Col also told us that the same person having come up with a serjeant and twenty men, working on the high road, he entered into discourse with the serjeant and then gave him sixpence for the men to drink. The serjeant asked, ' Who is this fellow ? ' Upon being informed, he said, ' If I had known who it was I should have thrown it in his face.' *Johnson :* ' . . . he has not learnt to be a miser ; I believe we must take him apprentice.' *Boswell :* ' He would grudge giving half a guinea to be taught.' *Johnson :* ' Nay, sir, you must teach him *gratis*.'

If the ' Tour to the Hebrides ' is uniquely indiscreet, it is only the more typical of Boswell. He loved to be in the public eye and he was now notorious beyond measure. The wags laughed, the injured Scotsmen were angry, and the more respectable parts of the community were profoundly shocked. A sheaf of cartoons did justice to the humour of the situation. Lord Macdonald was represented with uplifted stick,

and the threatened author on his knees before him.[1]
' Johnson's Ghost ' was depicted as appearing to the
terror-stricken Boswell and mournfully reproaching
him. In a series of twenty large caricatures the biographer was represented in twenty absurd situations,
and each sketch had a quotation from his book.
Boswell at all events was the first in the field of all
who intended to write about Johnson, and no doubt
he was glad that all the world was aware of the fact.

But Boswell did not mean to be notorious in this
fashion. He may have expected some ridicule, but not
ill-feeling ; he was too good-humoured himself. Possibly
he satisfied his malice on more than one occasion ;
but as a rule he had no intention of giving pain. The
admirable Dr. Beattie calls him ' a very good-natured
man,' and says he was convinced that Bozzy meant
no harm. Sir William Forbes said that he seemed
sorry for ' some parts,' and Boswell published his own
apology and defence in one of the notes of a later
edition :

Having found, on a revision of the first edition of
this work, that, notwithstanding my best care, a few
observations had escaped me, which arose from the
instant impression, the publication of which might
perhaps be considered as passing the bounds of strict
decorum, I immediately ordered that they should be
omitted in subsequent editions. I was pleased to

[1] Sir Alexander became Lord Macdonald in 1776 (*Boswelliana,*
p. 140).

find that they did not amount in the whole to a page. If any of the same kind are yet left, it is owing to inadvertence alone, no man being more unwilling to give pain to others than I am.

When Boswell says that he is unwilling to give pain we may believe him unreservedly ; there may have been particular cases when he lowered himself to the satisfaction of a grudge, but as a general statement it is true. That Boswell was good-natured is incontestable : it is admitted on all hands. ' Good-nature,' wrote Mr. Courtenay, ' was highly predominant in his character. He appeared to entertain sentiments of benevolence to all mankind, and it does not appear to me that he ever did, or could, injure any human being *intentionally.'* Mr. Malone wrote a letter for the *Gentleman's Magazine* vindicating Boswell's character after his death. ' He had not only an inexhaustible fund of good-humour and good-nature, but was extremely warm in his attachments, and as ready to exert himself for his friends as any man.' His untiring kindness to Johnson might perhaps be refused as evidence that he was ' ready to exert himself for his friends.' Towards Temple and his wife also, from whom he had nothing to gain, ' he always played,' as Mr. Seccombe remarks, ' a very friendly part ' ; ' he made Johnson known to them, for instance ; he took Paoli down to Mamhead, he had Temple up to town and took him and his daughter to Westminster Hall to see the trial of

Warren Hastings. He took them more than once to
Sir Joshua's studio in Leicester Square, he acted
as godfather to one of the sons, and tipped another
who was at Eton.' But the most remarkable testimony that Boswell had, as the French say, *le cœur
bon* is his will. We shall have to pay some attention
to this document in a later chapter : it shows that
Boswell could be remarkably considerate.

Boswell wrote and published the ' Tour ' with a
greedy enjoyment and uncontained expansiveness
entirely typical of him, and in amazing ignorance of
some of the strongest human feelings—of the proprie-
torship that men feel with respect to their own lives
which surrounds them with a sacred halo of privacy, and
of their inordinate desire to appear more virtuous and
more successful than they are. He babbled of himself
as he babbled of others, not unconscious of the folly
that he committed and revealed, but not suspecting
that he would be called a fool for admitting his folly.
Truth, as these pages have already remarked, was of
supreme importance to Boswell, and was not to be
suppressed. He could hardly understand that plain
fact could hurt anyone. A pamphleteer who wished
to make Boswell ridiculous has suggested his attitude
in a picturesque manner : Lord Macdonald is supposed
to be threatening personal violence ; Walcot writes :

> Treat with contempt the menace of this Lord.
> 'Tis Hist'ry's province, Bozzy, to record.

There was fundamentally in Boswell's nature a desire to record observations—a desire which overrode his conventional aims and ambitions and, while decreasing the possibility of his being a successful man, made it certain that he would be a great one.

All that Boswell meant by truth will be examined later in connection with his biographical method. 'The Journal of a Tour to the Hebrides' must be criticised as a book along with the 'Life of Johnson' and not apart from it. It is, in a sense, but a portion of the larger work. The same genius, the same art, has made two incomparable books. The later is more discreet. 'I have been more reserved,' says Boswell. But it is not less vividly life-like : 'I have managed so as to occasion no diminution of the pleasure my book should afford.' The 'Tour,' however—and this is the one important difference—is concerned with Johnson in an extraordinary phase of his life, and one which is not treated in the larger work. Johnson is on a holiday. The journey is called a 'jaunt.' And the atmosphere of the 'jaunt' is reflected on every page of the Journal. The freedom, the expectancy and the high spirits of a travelling holiday to those who very rarely enjoy one, the increased opportunities to Boswell for observation and his unflagging interest and pleasure in his great experiment—all these account, and are sufficient to account, for the different effect we feel in reading the 'Tour to the Hebrides' : and

most of those who perceive this difference will agree
that it is an additional charm.

.   .   .   .   .

During the eight years of Boswell's life between the
ages of forty-two and fifty, several important events
happened beside the publication of the ' Tour to
the Hebrides.'

It is unfortunate that for the greater part of this
period we have no letters from Boswell to Temple.
If there was any correspondence between them, none
has been preserved between the dates November 3rd,
1780, and January 5th, 1787. And so we hear no
private utterances about the death of Boswell's
father, by which he became Laird of Auchinleck, or
about the death of Johnson.

It is not difficult to imagine the feelings of Boswell
about the first event. There can have been no great
sorrow as there had been no great affection ; and there
must have been no little pleasure in becoming the head
of an ancient family and a man of property. It is a
sad thing if the records of this period have indeed been
lost, for they ought to have been peculiarly rich in
extravagant and pompous sayings.

Of Johnson's value to Boswell we have already
spoken. It would be impossible to suppose that
Boswell did not realise his loss. He must have felt
when he visited London, as he continued to do in

spite of his Scotch inheritance, that the central figure was gone, and with it much of the zest of life in his London circle. There was no doubt a yearning sometimes for that rude strength, which had so much of tenderness besides, and a lasting grief.

Of Boswell's sorrows in later life, of his failure to realise those ' towering hopes,' and consequent disappointment, something has been said already in these pages. It was not apparently until the autumn of 1789 that Boswell began to see that he was not destined to succeed in the manner he wished—in politics and in the law. The letters at this time were more frequent than usual, and we are able to see how, earlier in the year, he was quite hopeful about the future, but later became despondent.

A further reason depressed Boswell's spirits at this time : in the summer of 1789 he lost his wife.[1] It is greatly to the credit of Boswell that he was very deeply affected by her death—to his credit, not because as a husband he was able to retain affection for his wife (for affections are not completely under our control), but because he was able to appreciate a woman who from his own accounts must have been a sensible, kind woman, and one who treated him with a patient consideration.

Boswell was not a good husband, because he never became in the ordinary sense domesticated ; his home

[1] *Letters to Temple*, p. 246 *et seq.*

was never to him the predominant interest. During her last illness he seems to have realised that he might have behaved better towards his wife, and to have felt a true remorse :

No man ever had a higher esteem or a warmer love for a wife than I have for her. You will recollect, my Temple, how our marriage was the result of an attachment truly romantic ; yet how painful is it to me to recollect a thousand instances of inconsistent conduct. I can justify my removing to the great sphere of England, upon a principle of laudable ambition ; but the frequent scenes of what I must call dissolute conduct are inexcusable ; and often and often when she was very ill, in London have I been indulging in festivity with Sir Joshua Reynolds, Courtenay, Malone, &c., and have come home late, and disturbed her repose. Nay, when I was last at Auchinleck, on purpose to soothe and console her, I repeatedly went from home ; and both on those occasions, and when neighbours visited me, drank a great deal too much wine.[1]

He was remorseful too after the death of his wife that he had not been present to comfort her at the end. And there was good reason. She, as he remarked, would not have treated him so. But Boswell must not be blamed too severely for this serious omission. His wife was suffering with a disease from which, though it was certain she would not recover, there was no immediate prospect of release. Boswell

[1] *Letters to Temple*, p. 242.

seems to have expected from the medical opinion that her life would linger on longer than actually it did : and, if it was not for pressing duties that he left his wife, it was not for pleasure, but for the kind of activity incident to the career he had chosen.

Boswell was not unlike many people inasmuch as he found out rather late in life the true value of his wife, and was more sorry than could have been expected when he no longer had her help and companionship ; he found perhaps that he had rated too highly by comparison the greater intellectual stimulus of his literary circle. His sorrow in any case, at her death, whatever the proportion of remorse to the sense of loss, is pleasant to see. There was so much affectation in his character, that whenever he shows that he had simple, genuine feelings—and he had them more often than might be supposed—we must have some regard for them, however commonplace they may be.

Boswell was evidently quite miserable at his loss ; he was unrestrained in grief as he was in enjoyment, and the tale of his woe was poured out to Temple in the same fervid manner as the love affairs of earlier years :

I am amazed when I look back. Though I often and often dreaded this loss, I had no conception how distressing it would be. May God have mercy on me ! I am quite restless and feeble and desponding. . . . I have an avidity for death ; I eagerly wish to be laid by my dear wife ; years of life seem insupportable.

I cannot express to you, Temple [he writes in a later letter], ' what I suffer from the loss of my valuable wife and the mother of my children. While she lived, I had no occasion to think concerning my family ; every particular was thought of by her, better than I could. I am the most helpless of human beings ; I am in a state very much that of one in despair.'

It must not be thought that Boswell faced the world in the sad and sometimes complaining vein in which he wrote to Temple. There was no whining self-pity, and no pride of the grievance, as might perhaps have been expected, in his public attitude. ' It is astonishing what force I have put upon myself since her death, how I have entertained company, &c., &c.' [1] He no doubt tried to be cheerful in company, and probably he succeeded.

The weakness of Boswell was shown in a different way, by an increase of those vices which he had been encouraged to resist by Johnson, and also, we may suppose, by his wife. Johnson had said, long before the bereavement : ' In losing her you would lose your sheet-anchor, and be tost, without stability, by the waves of life.' This prediction was fulfilled.

Boswell had always been a self-indulgent man. Before his marriage he was, as may be seen from the letters, sexually self-indulgent. Whether he was so in later years, or in what degree, it is difficult to determine ;

[1] *Letters to Temple*, p. 253.

he may have been alluding to this when he talks of
' little fondnesses,' and of being ' dissipated '; [1] and
the fact that he says on one occasion that he had no
' confessions ' to make rather suggests the possibility
that this may not always have been the case, though
he never actually confesses.

But the particular form of his self-indulgence was
drunkenness. Besides frequent references to his habit
of drinking, there are, altogether, some half-dozen recorded instances of Boswell being drunk or intoxicated,
and as they are referred to only because they had some
curious results they suggest that this was far from
being unusual. In the letters, Boswell records on
several occasions that he has been drinking too much
lately, or that he was becoming a drunkard.

His mode of resisting what he quite well saw to
be an evil habit was to take a series of vows. It is
a method which seems to have had a curious appeal
for Boswell's nature. There was something to his
mind rather romantic about a vow: something heroic
in taking that great resolve, made so quickly to endure
for so long, something of the saintly penance ; and
there was something of the martyr about one who had
bound himself in this way. In Boswell's drunkenness,
however, there was nothing romantic ; it was rather
sordid ; and he was neither saint, nor hero, nor martyr,
for the vows, even if they could have made him all

---

[1] *Letters to Temple*, p. 231.

these, were too frequently broken.   There was no doubt some serious effort on Boswell's part ; but the impulse of the moment was always too strong for him, and the efforts which lasted too short a time were apparently followed by grave relapses.

Boswell's drinking habits had ill effects.   Johnson, when reminded of the headache which his companion was wont to feel after sitting up with him, exclaimed :   ' Nay, Sir, it was not the *wine* that made your head ache, but the sense that I put into it.'   But though the nature of Johnson's sense and of Boswell's head may fortify the explanation, it was not the common case ;   excess of alcohol was injurious to Boswell's health.

It has been pointed out with justice that Boswell's melancholy was to some extent the result of this excess.   How much of it was affectation we cannot easily tell.   When Boswell first made his appearance to the world as the young *littérateur*, he may have hoped to increase the appearance of genius by assuming hereditary hypochondria.   But it must be remarked that he seems, as far as we can judge, to have given very little impression of ever being morose ; it is on the contrary his gaiety and good spirits that are always emphasised.   And we may at least suppose when, as has been mentioned above, he entirely denies, in a number of the ' Hypochondriack,' that genius and melancholy have any particular connection, that he

had by that time outgrown any affectation there may
originally have been. That one of Boswell's great
vivacity should sometimes be dejected, is really very
natural, and when we add to this his self-indulgent
habits, it is not hard to account for occasional
attacks of low spirits. Sir Walter Scott remarks :

There was a variation of spirits about James Boswell which indicated some slight touch of insanity.
His melancholy which he so often complained of to
Johnson was not affected but constitutional, though
doubtless he thought it a mark of high distinction to
be afflicted with hypochondria like his moral patron.

Malone too denies altogether ' that he caught from
Johnson a portion of his constitutional melancholy.'
' This was not the fact,' writes Malone. ' He had a
considerable share of melancholy in his own temperament ; and though the general tenour of his life was
gay and active, he frequently experienced an unaccountable depression of spirits.' [1] It was natural
that Boswell's malady of depression should have
become worse towards the end of his life ; not only

---

[1] ' In a subsequent number of the *Gentleman's Magazine*,' says
Dr. Rogers in his *Memoir of J. B.*, ' Mr. Temple, under the signature
of " Biographicus," denied a statement by Mr. Malone that Boswell
was of a melancholy temperament ; he maintained that he was
quite otherwise prior to his attachment to Dr. Johnson.' It may
be remarked, however, that Boswell might have a constitutional
melancholy without showing many signs of it before the age of
twenty-three ; and that Temple after 1763 saw Boswell very
seldom. Malone's view, therefore, based upon an intimate connection with Boswell for some years at the end of his life, apart
from the fact that it was likely to be a wiser view, should carry
more weight than that of Temple.

because habits of excess take their revenge upon the constitution, but because these too are likely to grow with the disease. The result of Boswell's sorrows when his wife had died and his ambitions were being thwarted was that he was driven still more to drink.

I have drunk too much wine for some time past. I fly to every mode of agitation. [1]

With grief continually at my heart, I have been endeavouring to seek relief in dissipation and in wine, so that my life for some time past has been unworthy of myself, of you, and of all that is valuable in my character and connections.[2]

It is a pitiable picture this, of a man's decay ; grief and self-indulgence reacted upon each other, each of them adding something to the causes of disappointment.

[1] *Letters to Temple*, p. 255.   [2] *Ib.*, p. 257.

CHAPTER VIII

THERE is one redeeming feature, the most important feature of all, in the last years of Boswell's life.

The biographer had gradually during the life of Johnson relaxed his efforts in collecting material for the *magnum opus* ; we can see in the ' Life ' how he grew less industrious in recording conversations ; for though even in the later part many are preserved at great length, he neglected to write up his journal more often than in the early years of the friendship. This was due no doubt in part to his drinking habits. Conviviality of that kind has a curious effect upon the memory. But Boswell had still very firmly the purpose of writing the ' Life,' after Johnson had died, though he was not the person chosen to do so by the literary executors.[1]

The ' Life of Johnson ' was published about six years later than the ' Tour to the Hebrides,' in the spring of 1791. The latter, it is clear from its nature, re- quired far less labour from the author than his *magnum opus* : the whole scope of the book is infinitely smaller,

[1] Sir John Hawkins wrote the official life.

and there was none of the endless trouble of collecting
and verifying the materials of others as in the great
biography ; for the ' Tour ' deals only with Johnson
as observed by Boswell himself during their journey
in the Hebrides.   Boswell, moreover, had wanted to
publish his journal during Johnson's lifetime, and we
cannot doubt that he had written up a good deal.   It
would be quite unjust therefore to say that the biographer became more idle, as he was more dissipated,
after 1785.   The reverse is nearer the truth.   It is
remarkable and it is praiseworthy that Boswell, in
spite of his political schemes, the depression which
followed the death of his wife, and the illness which
was the consequence of his unhealthy habits of life
and in particular the habit of drink, should still
have worked hard at the ' Life.'   He may have
become less regular, but he retained the energy of
earlier years.

There was, in fact, in him the need to satisfy somehow those better qualities.   His intense belief in the
merit of his work and the almost endless trouble he
took to verify the accuracy of the smallest fact and to
discover the minutest information about Johnson—
to satisfy, in a word, his ' sacred love of truth'—are
the expression of this need within him.   Sometimes,
indeed, he is despondent about his book : ' Many a
time have I thought of giving it up.'   ' I am in such
bad spirits that I have every fear concerning it.'

Sometimes he feels the immensity of the labour without the enthusiasm which has urged him on : ' Though I am now in woeful indifference, I trust that before it is finished a taste or relish shall return.' The vastness of the task seems almost to weigh him down. In November 1789 he writes to Temple explaining that he cannot pay him a visit because he must stay in London to receive Malone's help, Malone who is ' Johnsonianissimus,' in revising the ' Life ' :

You cannot imagine what labour, what perplexity, what vexation I have endured in arranging a prodigious multiplicity of materials, in supplying omissions, in searching for papers, buried in different masses, and all this besides the exertion of composing and polishing : many a time have I thought of giving it up.

And yet he has the firmest conviction that the book will be a masterpiece ; it will be an unparalleled history of a man ; and for that reason of supreme importance to the world :

However, though I shall be uneasily sensible of its many deficiencies, it will certainly be to the world a very valuable and peculiar volume of biography, full of literary and characteristical anecdotes *told with authenticity and in a lively manner*. Would that it were in the booksellers' shops ! Methinks if I had this *magnum opus* launched, the public has no further claim upon me ; for I have promised no more, and I may die in peace, or retire into dull obscurity, *reddarque tenebris*.

It is a curious mixture, this, of weariness and optimism ; it shows that there was something in Boswell which drove him on, in spite of a good many difficulties, though he himself (as we see in the last sentence) understood little of its nature. ' The " Life of Johnson," ' he says in another place, ' still keeps me up ; I must bring that forth.' [1]

At times his enthusiasm breaks out and he expresses his real conviction of the supreme merit of his work :

The next [day] I am in Malone's study revising my ' Life of Johnson,' of which I have the highest expectations both as to fame and profit. I surely have the art of writing agreeably. The Lord Chancellor told me he had read every word of my Hebridean Journal ; he could not help it ; adding, ' Could you give a rule how to write a book that a man *must read* ? I believe Longinus could not.' [2]

Boswell understood the scale and interest of his book :

In truth it is a view of much of the literature, and many of the literary men, of Great Britain for more than half a century.[3]

' I think,' he says, in the same letter to Temple, ' it will be without exception the most entertaining book you ever read.' To Mr. Dempster he

---

[1] *Letters to Temple*, p. 252.   [2] *Ib.*, p. 267.
[3] *Ib.*, p. 265.

said : ' I really think it will be the most entertaining collection that has appeared in this age.' [1]

Boswell's belief in his own work was based not so much upon his literary powers as upon his conception of biography :

Mason's ' Life of Gray ' is excellent, because it is interspersed with letters which show us the *man*. His ' Life of Whitehead ' is not a life at all, because there is neither a letter nor a saying from first to last. I am absolutely certain that my mode of biography, which gives not only a *history* of Johnson's *visible* progress through the world, and of his publications, but a *view* of his mind in his letters and conversations, is the most perfect that can be conceived, and will be more of a Life than any work that has ever yet appeared.[2]

To Bishop Percy he writes in February 1788 :

I do it chronologically, giving year by year his publications, if there were any ; his letters, his conversations, and everything else that I can collect. It appears to me that mine is the best plan of biography that can be conceived ; for my readers will, as near as may be, accompany Johnson in his progress, and as it were see each scene as it happened.[3]

The conviction that Boswell had that his was the best possible conception of biography seems never to have been in doubt, though he might be sometimes depressed or indifferent, and exactly the same

---

[1] *Letters to Temple*, p. 338.   [2] *Ib.*, p. 218.
[3] Nichols' *Illustrations*, vii, 309.

conception as that which we have seen in his letters to Temple and Bishop Percy was expressed more fully later in the ' Life ' itself.

Instead of melting down my materials into one mass, and constantly speaking in my own person, by which I might have appeared to have more merit in the execution of the work, I have resolved to adopt and enlarge upon the excellent plan of Mr. Mason, in his Memoirs of Gray. Wherever narrative is necessary to explain, connect, and supply, I furnish it to the best of my abilities ; but in the chronological series of Johnson's life, which I trace as distinctly as I can, year by year, I produce, wherever it is in my power, his own minutes, letters, or conversation, being convinced that this mode is more lively, and will make my readers better acquainted with him, than even most of those were, who actually knew him, but could know him only partially ; whereas there is here an accumulation of intelligence from various points, by which his character is more fully understood and illustrated.

Indeed I cannot conceive a more perfect mode of writing any man's life, than not only relating all the most important events of it in their order, but interweaving what he privately wrote, and said, and thought, by which mankind are enabled as it were to see him live, and to ' live o'er each scene ' with him, as he actually advanced through the several stages of his life. Had his other friends been as diligent and ardent as I was, he might have been almost entirely preserved. As it is, I will venture to say that he will be seen in this work more completely than any man who has ever yet lived.

And he will be seen as he really was ; for I profess

to write not his panegyrick, which must be all praise, but his Life ; which, great and good as he was, must not be supposed to be entirely perfect. To be as he was, is indeed subject of panegyrick enough to any man in this state of being ; but in every picture there should be shade as well as light, and when I delineate him without reserve, I do what he himself recommended, both by his precept and his example.[1]

The ' Life ' then is, as Boswell intended, a complete picture of Johnson ; complete, inasmuch as it gives a picture of Johnson in every phase of his living, as the writer, the talker, the correspondent, and most of all simply as a man in his dealings with other men, and in all these gives a living picture : complete especially in this, that it gives not merely what there is to praise in Johnson, but every little detail as it occurred, the shade as well as the light.

But Boswell had something further in his mind as he wrote the ' Life.' He was, as we have said before, essentially the moralist. He seems to have had a purpose as he wrote, not only of not doing moral harm, but of doing moral good. When he talks of the faults of Dr. Johnson he does so with a kind of apology and explanation, with quotations from the great moralist himself, to show that to mention the vices of a famous man may as well do good as harm :

When I objected [evidently for the sake of argument] to the danger of telling that Parnell drank

[1] *Life of Johnson*, i, 29–30.

to excess, he said, that ' it would produce an instructive caution to avoid drinking, when it was seen that even the learning and genius of Parnell could be debased by it.' And in the Hebrides he maintained, as appears from my journal, that a man's intimate friend should mention his faults, if he writes his life.

After saying that ' it must not be concealed, that like many other good and pious men, among whom we may place the Apostle Paul upon his own authority, Johnson was not free from propensities which were ever " warring against the law of his mind," and that in his combat with them, he was sometimes overcome,' he gives a moral lecture to his readers :

But let no man encourage or soothe himself in ' presumptuous sin,' from knowing that Johnson was sometimes hurried into indulgences which he thought criminal. I have exhibited this circumstance as a shade in so great a character, both from my sacred love of truth, and to shew that he was not so weakly scrupulous as he has been represented by those who imagine that the sins, of which a deep sense was on his mind, were merely such little venial trifles as pouring milk into his tea on Good Friday.

In the ' Advertisement to the Second Edition,' Boswell seems to go further :

His strong, clear, and animated enforcement of religion, morality, loyalty, and subordination, while it delights and improves the wise and the good, will, I trust, prove an effectual antidote to that detestable sophistry which has been lately imported from France,

under the false name of *Philosophy*, and with a malignant industry has been employed against the peace,
good order, and happiness of society, in our free and
prosperous country ; but thanks be to God, without
producing the pernicious effects which were hoped for
by its propagators.

This history of the deeds and words and thoughts
of his hero is compared by Boswell to the Odyssey.
He seems almost to think that the merit of Homer's
epic lies in the good behaviour of Ulysses, just as he
conceives that the value of his own work is in the
excellence of Johnson :—

> ——Quid virtus et quid sapientia possit,
> Utile proposuit nobis exemplar Ulyssen.

It is not perhaps remarkable in itself that Boswell
should have had this attitude towards his work ; it
is the attitude in some degree of most biographers,
the attitude especially of the age in which he lived, and
the attitude of Johnson himself. Boswell's principles
as a biographer are indeed the same as Johnson's.
We cannot suppose, when he has revealed so clearly his
supreme faculty for biography, that there was anything
of this which was not entirely his own.   But he took the
trouble to find out on several occasions the opinions
of his great friend, to ask him about particular doubts
which troubled him from time to time, and obtain his
approval.   He had a profound respect for Johnson's
manner of estimating character.   Mr. Pennant, ' a

traveller in Scotland,' is censured in the 'Life' for a book of travel which is compared to Johnson's 'Journey to the Western Islands' and then quoted on the subject of Johnson ; the quotation speaks of ' the numerous weaknesses and prejudices which his friends have kindly taken care to draw from their dread abode.' Boswell's note is :

This is the common cant against faithful biography. Does the worthy gentleman mean that I, who was taught discrimination of character by Johnson, should have omitted his frailties, and in short, have *bedaubed* him, as the worthy gentleman has bedaubed Scotland ?

It was also due in some degree to the influence of Johnson that Boswell himself was so much a moralist : it was something of the same influence, it was in part the honest ruggedness which exalted that morality, by denuding it of excessive and affected sentiment, that enabled Boswell to be a moralist without being (in the Johnsonian phraseology) a canting moralist. Boswell, indeed, became a moralist because he wanted to be respectable ; but he was not entirely respectable because he succeeded in being a moralist. A man who is a moralist to the extent that Boswell and Johnson were moralists may be too respectable to be an honest biographer. It does not become the stainless respectability of the moralist to bring to light the blemishes of a man in a book ; in

conversation that may be done ; there is no harm in
a few people knowing ; but it would be dangerous and
improper to reveal them in print to the public gaze ;
and so it was not respectable in Boswell to say anything
about the sexual temptations of Johnson, and Miss
Burney and Hannah More would no doubt be shocked.
But the love of truth which Johnson nourished was
fundamental in Boswell, and it was irrepressible ; we
know Johnson, chiefly for this reason, better than any
other man whose life has been recorded.

It is remarkable for other reasons besides this—
that he was a moralist—that Boswell produced an
impartial biography. He was by no means free from
personal animosities. Sir John Hawkins had written
the official life at the request of Johnson's literary
executors, and Boswell, naturally, was jealous of him
on this account. A matter for greater irritation was
that Boswell himself had been almost entirely ignored,[1]
the one slighting mention of his name being worse than
no mention of his connection with Johnson. And
Mrs. Thrale also, who had published her 'Anecdotes,'
had alluded to Boswell only in one contemptuous
passage. Boswell therefore had the deliberate intention of showing up the faults of these two rivals ; a
long paragraph is introduced as early as possible,
explaining fully why the 'Life' by Sir John Hawkins
is a bad book, and ending thus :

[1] *Memoirs of Sir J. Hawkins*, i, 235.

There is throughout the whole of it a dark uncharitable cast, by which the most unfavourable construction is put upon almost every circumstance in the character and conduct of my illustrious friend ; who, I trust, will, by a true and fair delineation, be vindicated both from the injurious misrepresentations of this author, and from the slighter aspersions of a lady who once lived in great intimacy with him.[1]

The same lady was alluded to afterwards in a note of peculiar malice :

I am obliged in so many instances to notice Mrs. Piozzi's incorrectness of relation, that I gladly seize this opportunity of acknowledging that, however often, she is not always inaccurate.

It was not only for his personal grievances that Boswell was anxious to contradict Sir John Hawkins and Mrs. Piozzi, but also because he had a different conception of Johnson, a far more loving appreciation and veneration, which was a reason in itself that he should write the life of his friend ; to vindicate his character and express his admiration would be some tribute to their long friendship. Boswell, indeed, always retained something of the ' mysterious veneration ' of his early years. Johnson to him was always the hero ; he was the ' literary Colossus,' the ' Rambler,' the ' awful and majestick Philosopher.' The thought

[1] *Life of Johnson*, i, 28.

that he might lose his reverence was a source of anxiety to Boswell :

In my interview with Dr. Johnson this evening, I was quite easy, quite as his companion ; upon which I find in my journal the following reflection : ' So ready is my mind to suggest matter for dissatisfaction that I felt a sort of regret that I was so easy. I missed that awful reverence with which I used to contemplate Mr. Samuel Johnson, in the complex magnitude of his literary, moral, and religious character. I have a wonderful superstitious love of mystery.'

Boswell, as a matter of fact, as we may see from the ' Life,' preserved his ' reverence,' and his view of Johnson as the solemn and wise writer and moralist has tinged the biography. He records a jovial mood of Johnson's as a most extraordinary moment in a man of his dignified character :

I have known him at times exceedingly diverted at what seemed to others a very small sport. He now laughed immoderately, without any reason that we could perceive, at our friend's making his will ; called him the *testator,* and added, ' I daresay, he thinks he has done a mighty thing.' . . . In this playful manner did he run on, exulting in his own pleasantry, which certainly was not such as might be expected from the authour of The Rambler, but which is here preserved, that my readers may be acquainted even with the slightest occasional characteristicks of so eminent a man.

He goes on to tell how Dr. Johnson ' could not stop

his merriment, but continued it all the way till he got without the Temple Gate. He then burst into such a fit of laughter that he appeared to be almost in a convulsion ; and, in order to support himself, laid hold of one of the posts at the side of the foot pavement, and sent forth peals so loud, that in the silence of the night his voice seemed to resound from Temple Bar to Fleetditch.' Boswell talks of the episode as ' this most ludicrous exhibition of the awful, melancholy, and venerable Johnson.'

CHAPTER IX

It is remarkable, as we have observed, in view of his personal animosities, and of his determination to prove Dr. Johnson to be both a greater and a better man than would appear from previous accounts, and to be an extremely dignified man as fitted his own conception of him, that Boswell should have presented a complete picture of Johnson—that he should have mentioned all the incidents from which he might appear both a less important and a less pleasant man—all the circumstances that might detract from his dignity.

The explanation which seems so simple and involves, when we come to understand all that it means, not only the exact shades of what the author said, but many things that he refrained from saying, is that Boswell in this particular sphere, the sphere of the biographer, was entirely truthful. And truth meant far more than that he did not distort the facts and did not suppress them ; it involved in him the capacity for creating, the essential quality of his genius. Boswell had in fact the scientific spirit and applied it to the greatest of all subjects, to human nature. He was, in the first place, extremely accurate both in observing and recording ; he watched attentively and often ; and he described patiently what he had seen and heard. The biographer's own pen has given us a short account of his qualifications, as they appeared to him, for the task of writing the life of Johnson :

As I had the honour and happiness of enjoying his friendship for upwards of twenty years ; as I had the scheme of writing his life constantly in view ; as he was well apprised of this circumstance, and from time to time obligingly satisfied my inquiries, by communicating to me the incidents of his early years ; as I acquired a facility in recollecting and was very assiduous in recording his conversation, of which the extraordinary vigour and vivacity constituted one of the first features of his character ; and as I have spared no pains in obtaining materials concerning him, from every quarter where I could discover that they were to be found, and have been favoured with the most liberal communications by his friends ; I flatter myself that few biographers have entered upon such a work as this, with more advantages ; independent of literary abilities, in which I am not vain enough to compare myself with some great names who have gone before me in this kind of writing.' [1]

With this statement we may heartily agree ; but all that it really says is that Boswell had opportunities, and acquired a faculty, for *recording*. He had, besides, a quite remarkable faculty of acute observation.

[1] *Life of Johnson*, i, 25–6.

All that he says of Johnson's appearance, his clothes, his walk, that truly horrible paragraph about his nails and knuckles, is admirable, because he tells us in a few words exactly what is most characteristic. The event of his first visit to Dr. Johnson was naturally an occasion for Boswell to describe his hero :

His brown suit of clothes looked very rusty ; he had on a little old shrivelled unpowdered wig, which was too small for his head ; his shirt-neck and knees of his breeches were loose ; his black worsted stockings ill drawn up ; and he had a pair of unbuckled shoes by way of slippers.

That is all ! And what more or what less could anyone want ? In the ' Tour to the Hebrides ' it is recorded that

He wore . . . a very wide brown cloth great-coat, with pockets which might have almost held the two volumes of his folio ' Dictionary ' ; and he carried in his hand a large English oak stick.

What a difference it makes to our knowledge of Johnson that we know these details ! Boswell compels us to see Johnson. Plenty of men would have noticed what he noticed, but few would have presented it so vividly. Boswell's superiority depends upon his powers as an observer ; he saw things clear and strong, and so they are clear and strong for his readers.

And Boswell excelled not only in painting the mere exterior ; he often alludes to the spirit that it expresses with the same dexterity. 'Generally,' he says, speaking of Johnson in the course of a dispute, ' when he had finished a period, by which time he was a good deal exhausted by violence and vociferation, he used to blow out his breath like a whale. This I suppose was a relief to his lungs ; and seemed in him to be a contemptuous mode of expression, as if he had made the arguments of his opponents fly like chaff before the wind.' We are told the physical details, but so much more ! The whole attitude of Johnson is described. Similarly all the little touches, as when Johnson ' sprung away with a kind of pathetick briskness,' reveal his feelings with startling fidelity. Perhaps most remarkable of all is the account of Johnson's behaviour to his cat :

I never shall forget the indulgence with which he treated Hodge, his cat : for whom he himself used to go out and buy oysters, lest the servants having that trouble should take a dislike to the poor creature. . . . I recollect him one day scrambling up Dr. Johnson's breast, apparently with much satisfaction, while my friend, smiling and half-whistling, rubbed down his back, and pulled him by the tail ; and when I observed he was a fine cat, saying, ' Why yes, Sir, but I have had cats whom I liked better than this ' ; and then as if perceiving Hodge to be out of countenance, adding, ' but he is a very fine cat, a very fine cat indeed.'

We are pleased to find that Boswell has preserved for us the motive of Johnson, ' lest the servants having

that trouble should take a dislike to the poor creature.'[1]
This is characteristic and interesting. But how
deeply satisfying it is to discover that poor Hodge, as
it appeared to Johnson, was ' out of countenance.'

It is not, however, only because he observed so
accurately what was obviously relevant, as the appearance of Johnson, or that he saw exactly what his
motives were, that Boswell was a good observer ; the
range of his observation is equally remarkable. He
observed everything ; no detail was too insignificant
for his attention. It was of vital importance for him
to record (in the ' Tour to the Hebrides ') ' I slept in
the same room with Dr. Johnson. Each had a neat
bed, with Tartan curtains, in an upper chamber,' and
it is well that he did so ; it is highly agreeable to
imagine Johnson and Boswell in this situation. It is
also interesting to know that Boswell, on the following
morning, found upon the table in their room a slip of
paper, on which Dr. Johnson had written these words :
' *Quantum cedat virtutibus aurum* ' ; and that when
Johnson turned his cup at Aberbrothick, where they
drank tea, he muttered ' *Claudite jam rivos pueri.*' And
what an invaluable devotion it was that has preserved
for us so small a fact as this—that the book which
Johnson presented to a Highland lass was ' Cocker's
Arithmetic ' !

These details are ours not by the fortune of a

[1] So also Mrs. Piozzi.

naturally endowed memory, but by the labour and patience and attention that trained a mind to a point of excellence. Miss Burney has left us an admirable account of Boswell's deportment when in the act of ' memorandising ' Dr. Johnson's conversation, and from this we may see something of what it cost him to observe and record and remember :

In truth, when he met with Dr. Johnson, he commonly forbore even answering anything that was said, or attending to anything that went forward, lest he should miss the smallest sound from that voice to which he paid such exclusive, though merited, homage. But the moment that voice burst forth, the attention which it excited in Mr. Boswell amounted almost to pain. His eyes goggled with eagerness ; he leant his ear almost on the shoulder of the Doctor ; and his mouth dropped open to catch every syllable that might be uttered ; nay, he seemed not only to dread losing a word, but to be anxious not to miss a breathing, as if hoping from it, latently or mystically, some information.

Miss Burney had no admiration for Boswell, and the effect of this description is merely grotesque. It is probable that Boswell was not so wholly unconscious of self in this performance as Miss Burney seems to have thought. His behaviour appears to have been absurd, in a degree unnecessary alike to his curious character and his extraordinary task. It is possible that Boswell, aware that his minute attention to Dr. Johnson was a rather laughable affair, tried by a sort of buffoonery to avoid the natural consequence. Boswell, when he imitates Dr. Johnson in his presence, and when his eyes goggle with eagerness, was perhaps attempting to divert the company by caricaturing what was already ridiculous.

But however that may be, Miss Burney's account is no doubt faithful enough as regards the original motive of the biographer's behaviour ; his eyes goggled with a genuine eagerness. That exclusive attention was the attention of one who had a difficult task to perform and was extremely anxious to perform it.

Boswell's infinite capacity for concentration in observing and recording, and for patience in collecting and preserving the smallest facts, is indeed an essential part of his genius ; for genius, whenever it achieves anything, implies devotion, implies the relentless pursuit of its object, however small the actual result of the moment may seem when compared to the trouble which has been expended upon it. And this capacity for concentration enabled Boswell not merely to observe and record what he saw and heard, but to seek continually for any information, however it was to be obtained, which might be of value to him.

It is easy to see from many passages in the early portion of the ' Life '—the portion, that is, which deals with Johnson before Boswell made his acquaintance, and which naturally required the greatest labour, in collecting and investigating material, on the part of the biographer—how much trouble Boswell took. In order to obtain a copy of the famous letter to Lord Chesterfield he tells us :

I for many years solicited Johnson to favour me with a copy of it, that so excellent a composition might not be lost to posterity. He delayed from time to time to give it me ; till at last, in 1781, when we were on a visit at Mr. Dilly's, at Southill in Bedfordshire, he was pleased to dictate it to me from memory. He afterwards found among his papers a copy of it, which he had dictated to Mr. Baretti, with its title and corrections in his own handwriting. This he gave to Mr. Langton ; adding that if it were to come into print, he wished it to be from that copy. By Mr. Langton's kindness, I am enabled to enrich my work with a perfect transcript of what the world has so eagerly desired to see.

It appears that, though he had at last succeeded in obtaining a copy from Johnson, he was willing to take the further trouble of getting Mr. Langton's copy, which was more likely to be absolutely accurate. Still more remarkable is the manner in which he discovered the facts about Johnson's pension :

Lord Bute told me[1] that Mr. Wedderburne, now Lord Loughborough, was the person who first mentioned this subject to him. *Lord Loughborough told me* that the pension was granted solely as a reward of his literary merit. . . . *Mr. Thomas Sheridan and Mr.*

[1] The italics throughout are of course mine.

Murphy, who then lived a good deal both with him and Mr. Wedderburne, *told me*, that they previously talked with Johnson on this matter. . . . *Sir Joshua Reynolds told me* that Johnson called on him.

The mere number of names consulted is sufficiently imposing. Boswell in fact was collecting evidence for a case. He must examine all the witnesses : also he must examine them in such a way that the truth might be discovered.

Mr. Murphy and the late Mr. Sheridan severally contended for the distinction of having been the first who mentioned to Mr. Wedderburne that Johnson ought to have a pension. *When I spoke of this to Lord Loughborough*, wishing to know if he recollected the prime mover in the business, *he said* : ' All his friends assisted,' and when I told him that Mr. Sheridan strenuously asserted his claim to it, his Lordship said : ' He rang the bell.' And it is but just to add, that *Mr. Sheridan told me* that when he communicated to Dr. Johnson that a pension was to be granted him he replied in a fervour of gratitude. . . . *When I repeated this to Dr. Johnson he did not contradict it.*

The profusion of information about this particular point may seem to us unnecessary—it is of course controversial, and the controversy has lost much of its interest. But it shows in any case not only the great number of questions Boswell was willing to ask in order to find out exactly what had taken place and the scale upon which his investigations were

conducted, but also the minute and detailed care with
which he preserved the truth.

Boswell has himself said something of the labour it
cost him to compile the ' Life ' :

> The labour and anxious attention with which I
> have collected and arranged the materials of which
> these volumes are composed, will hardly be conceived
> by those who read them with careless facility. The
> stretch of mind and prompt assiduity by which so
> many conversations were preserved, I myself, at some
> distance of time, contemplate with wonder ; and I
> must be allowed to suggest, that the nature of the
> work in other respects, as it consists of innumerable
> detached particulars, all of which, even the most
> minute, I have spared no pains to ascertain with a
> scrupulous authenticity, has occasioned a degree of
> trouble far beyond that of any other species of com-
> position. Were I to detail the books which I have
> consulted, and the inquiries which I have found it
> necessary to make by various channels, I should
> probably be thought ridiculously ostentatious. Let
> me only observe, as a specimen of my trouble, that I
> have sometimes been obliged to run half over London
> in order to fix a date correctly. [1]

Something of all that Boswell meant by this can
be seen more nearly in Dr. Birkbeck Hill's essay upon
Boswell's Proof-sheets :

> A delay was sometimes caused by his desire to
> ' ascertain particulars with scrupulous authenticity.'
> ' Sheet 777,' he wrote, ' is with Mr. Wilkes to look at
> a note.' . . . A short delay is caused in ascertaining

[1] *Life of Johnson*, Advertisement to First Edition.

the number of years the Rev. Mr. Vilette had been Ordinary of Newgate. A blank had been left in the text. On the margin Boswell wrote : ' Send my note to Mr. Vilette in the morning and open the answer. Or inquire of Mr. Akerman (the keeper of Newgate) for the number of years. Get it somehow.' . . . On page 505 of the second volume Boswell writes : ' I could wish that the forme in which page 512 is were not thrown off till I have an answer from Mr. Stone, the gentleman mentioned in the note, to tell me his Christian name, that I may call him Esq.' . . . In the margin of the passage in which he quotes the inscription on a gold snuff-box given to Reynolds by Catherine II., he writes, ' Pray be very careful in printing the words of the Empress of *all the Russias*.' . . . Opposite the long note where he quotes the anonymous editor of ' Tracts by Warburton and a Warburtonian,' he writes in the margin : ' *This page* must not be laid on till I hear from Dr. Parr whether his name may be mentioned.' Accordingly he wrote to him requesting ' to have by return of post if I may say or guess that Dr. Parr is the editor.'

The success of these inquiries was far from certain. Dr. Parr's name does not appear.

Boswell was more fortunate in obtaining a name for another entry, which had originally stood : ' He was in this like . . . who, Mr. Daines Barrington told me, used to say : ' I hate a *cui bono* man ! ' In the margin he filled up the blank with ' a respectable person ' ; but before the sheet was ' laid on,' he learnt this respectable person's name. In the published text he figures as ' Dr. Shaw, the great traveller.' [1]

[1] *Johnson Club Papers*, pp. 58–60. The proof-sheets were in 1893 possessed by Mr. R. B. Adam, Barnstaple, Cape Cod.

The proof-sheets which Dr. Birkbeck Hill was so fortunate as to see were not the first sheets, but only ' revises ' : in the earlier stages there must have been many more minute facts for Boswell to find out. But they are undoubtedly documents of great interest, and the point which stands out most clearly from the essay we have quoted is the extraordinary minuteness of Boswell's care and attention.

.   .   .   .   .

The devotion of Boswell to his biographical work is illustrated not so much by the prodigious toil it cost him—for many men have this power of sustained labour when they have found the right object for it—as by the reckless disregard of conventions and people to which it led him.

The admirable account in the ' Memoirs of Thomas Holcroft '[1] of how Boswell obtained from Mr. Lowe a copy of one of Johnson's letters shows how attentive he could be even to a man whom, it would seem, he rather despised, when there was a chance of acquiring any document or information which might be of use to him. Lowe had requested Johnson to write him a letter, which Johnson did, and Boswell came in while it was writing ; his attention was immediately fixed. Lowe took the letter, retired, and was followed by Boswell.

[1] Quoted in the introduction to Mr. Birrell's edition of the *Life*.

'Nothing,' said Lowe, 'could surprise me more. Till that moment he had so entirely overlooked me that I did not imagine he knew there was such a creature in existence, and he now accosted me with the most overstrained and insinuating compliments possible. "How do you do, Mr. Lowe? I hope you are well, Mr. Lowe? Pardon my freedom, Mr. Lowe, but I think I saw my dear friend Dr. Johnson writing a letter for you." "Yes, sir." "I hope you will not think me rude, but if it would not be too great a favour, you would infinitely oblige me if you would just let me have a sight of it; everything from that hand, you know, is so inestimable." "Sir, it is on my own private affairs, but——." "I would not pry into a person's affairs, my dear Mr. Lowe, by any means. I am sure you would not accuse me of such a thing, only, if it were no particular secret——" "Sir, you are welcome to read the letter." "I thank you, my dear Mr. Lowe, you are very obliging. I take it exceedingly kind." . . . (Having read): "It is nothing I believe, Mr. Lowe, that you would be ashamed of——" "Certainly not." "Why, then, my dear sir, if you would do me another favour you would make the obligation eternal. If you would but step to Peele's coffee-house with me and just suffer me to take a copy of it I would do anything in my power to oblige you." 'I was so overcome,' said Lowe, 'by this sudden familiarity and condescension, accompanied with bows and grimaces, I had no power to refuse. We went to the coffee-house. My letter was presently transcribed, and as soon as he had put his document in his pocket Mr. Boswell walked away as erect and as proud as half an hour before. I ever after was unnoticed. Nay, I am not certain,' added he sarcastically, 'whether the

Scotchman did not leave me, poor as he knew I was, to pay for my own dish of coffee.' [1]

Miss Burney also gives an amusing account of how she was pressed to give her recollections of Johnson.

Boswell met her at the gate of St. George's chapel, and since the lady relates ' Mr. Turbulent brought him to me,' it would seem that the anxious biographer sought the mediation of a friend so as to have a better reception. Miss Burney, however, found the occasion unsuitable ; she was on the way to the ' Queen's Lodge ' ; a Queen's lady has to reflect the aloofness of royalty, and a conversation with Mr. Boswell would not add to her dignity. Her assistance is sought in most eloquent terms :

Yes, madam ; you must give me some of your choice little notes of the Doctor's ; we have seen him long enough upon stilts ; I want to show him in a new light. Grave Sam, and great Sam, and solemn Sam, and learned Sam—all these he has appeared over and over. Now I want to entwine a wreath of the graces across his brow ; I want to show him as gay Sam, agreeable Sam, pleasant Sam ; so you must help me with some of his beautiful billets to yourself.

Miss Burney apparently had no wish that her ' choice little notes ' should appear in the ' Life.' Boswell did his best in vain. ' I evaded this by de- claring I had not any stores at hand. He proposed a

[1] *Memoirs of Thomas Holcroft*, iii, 29–31.

thousand curious expedients to get at them, but I
was invincible. . . .'

But Boswell was not easily to be dismissed ; he
must glean what he may from Miss Burney ; she must,
at least, give judgment on the style of the work.

He then told me his ' Life of Dr. Johnson ' was
nearly printed, and took a proof-sheet out of his pocket
to show me, with crowds passing and repassing, knowing
me well, and staring well at him : for we were now at
the iron rails of the Queen's Lodge.

I stopped ; I could not ask him in : I saw he expected it, and was reduced to apologise, and tell him
I must attend the Queen immediately. . . .

But finding he had no chance for entering, he
stopped me again at the gate, and said he would read
me a part of his work.

There was no refusing this : and he began, with a
letter of Dr. Johnson's to himself. He read it in
strong imitation of the Doctor's manner, very well,
and not caricature. But Mrs. Schwellenberg was at
her window, a crowd was gathering to stand round the
rails, and the King and Queen and Royal Family now
approached from the Terrace.

It is a delightful scene—the enthusiastic Boswell
oblivious of Royalty as he declaims the sonorous
words of the Doctor, and Miss Burney anxious only to
effect an escape. The whole account shows how im-
portunate Boswell could become in the cause of his
art and for his ' sacred love of truth.'

CHAPTER X

THERE is an even more remarkable feature of Boswell's work—the scientific manner in which he deliberately made experiments. Here again we shall see his uncompromising attitude.

Dr. Johnson has been considered, and very properly considered, a great talker. Not the least of our reasons for reading the ' Life ' is that we are interested to know what Johnson had to say ; and we find there the expressed thoughts of Johnson upon a great number of subjects. That Boswell should have preserved so much—that, though the same topics may more than once be discussed, yet every conversation gives a distinct and separate impression, and each one is valuable— tells us not only that Boswell himself must have had a high order of intelligence to apprehend and preserve the point of Johnson's discourse upon so many occasions, but, what is important for our purpose at the moment, tells us (when we remember how little time altogether he spent with Johnson and that the time most fruitful in records, during the famous tour in the Hebrides, is not included in the ' Life ') that he himself must have had some part in finding out the Doctor's opinion. For Johnson was not exactly what is called an expansive person ; it was an effort to him to talk seriously, and it was usually necessary to engage him gradually in conversation before he talked his best. Boswell has told us, ' he very often sat quite silent for a long time.' He said of himself : ' Tom Tyers described me the best. He once said to me, " Sir, you are like a ghost. You never speak until you are spoken to." '

It is remarkable that Boswell should have had so much to record. The explanation is that he made Johnson talk ; he did it not by accident but quite deliberately ; this is a substantial part of his whole biographical method. ' I also,' he says in the ' Tour to the Hebrides,' ' may be allowed to claim some merit in leading the conversation. I do not mean leading as in an orchestra, by playing the first fiddle ; but leading as one does in examining a witness—starting topics and making him pursue them.' And he did not find this part of his task particularly easy :

He appears to me like a great mill, into which a subject is thrown to be ground. It requires, indeed, fertile minds to furnish subjects for this mill—I regret when I see it unemployed ; but sometimes I feel myself quite barren, and have nothing to throw in.

On most occasions, however, Boswell's mind was sufficiently fertile, and it enabled him to say some

s

very odd things ; his ingenuity was exercised in asking
Johnson the most absurd questions, and he did this
very often in the hope of some good retort.   ' If, Sir,'
he once demanded irrelevantly, ' you were shut up in a
castle and a new-born child with you, what would you
do ? '   Johnson is said to have related that one question
was, ' Pray, Sir, can you tell why an apple is round and
a pear pointed. ? '[1] On one occasion Boswell, apparently
without reference to anything which had previously
been said, asked ' if he had ever been accustomed to
wear a night-cap.'   And such questions were apt to
produce an amusing discussion.

But Boswell's spirit of investigation did not lead
him merely to ask questions like these ; it was frequently both serious and subtle—indeed there are so
many instances in the ' Life ' of his leading Johnson
to talk that it is difficult to choose one for illustration.
Perhaps the most characteristic kind of method employed is where Boswell , evidently having thought of
his subject beforehand, brings in at a convenient
moment a quotation, which furnishes an excuse for
starting a discussion ; as when he relates :

Talking of divorces, I asked if Othello's doctrine
were not plausible—

He that is robbed, not wanting what is stolen,
Let him not know 't, and he 's not robbed at all.[2]

---

[1] *Autobiography, Letters, &c., of Mrs. Piozzi*, ii, 125.
[2] *Life of Johnson*, iii, 347.

Then follows a discussion about divorce, in which Boswell takes a prominent part.

A few pages later we find Boswell re-starting a topic upon which Johnson, on a former occasion, has no doubt exhibited some warmth of feeling, and, having thought out his own line of argument, is able to lead him on to one of those moments of thunder which he loves to see.

After Mrs. Thrale was gone to bed, Johnson and I sat up late. We resumed Sir Joshua Reynolds' argument on the preceding Sunday, that a man would be virtuous though he had no other motive than to preserve his character. [1]

In the course of the argument Johnson exclaims (' very angry ') :

Nay, sir, what stuff is this ! You had no more this opinion after Robertson said it than before. I know nothing more offensive than repeating what one knows to be foolish things, by way of continuing a dispute, to see what a man will answer—to make him your butt ! (angrier still).

The scenes which illustrate perhaps better than any others Boswell's minute interest in his friend and experimenting attitude have already been quoted. In the account of the breakfast at Lochbuy (when Johnson was offered the cold sheep's head) we see how great was his passion for experiment and what a depth of

---

[1] *Life of Johnson*, iii, 349.

S 2

enjoyment he had from it : 'I sat quietly by and enjoyed my success'—that is the point of view. The manner in which he arranged the meeting with Wilkes shows the trouble he could take to form his plans for creating a situation and his ingenuity in carrying them out. This is not the only occasion when he made arrangements for his observation of Johnson ; the whole of the tour in the Hebrides was in a sense a great series of experiments, and we feel as we read it that the circumstances of Johnson's riding bespurred upon a Highland pony, of his sitting majestically in the stern of the little boat, of his dinner with the Duke of Argyle, of his visit to Auchinleck, are consciously arranged, in some way, for effect by Boswell.

No less a person than Walter Scott, who knew much at first hand from the contemporaries of Johnson and Boswell, and could remember distinctly the tour in Scotland and the discussion it provoked, held this view of the biographer :

[1]After all, Bozzy, though submitting to Johnson in everything, had his means of indemnification. Like the jackanapes mounted on the bear's back he con- trived now and then to play the more powerful animal a trick by getting him into situations like the meeting with Wilkes merely to see how he would look. The voyage to the Hebrides exhibited some tricks of that kind, the weather being so stormy at that late season that everyone thought they must have been drowned.

[1] *Croker Papers*, iii, 33.

Undoubtedly Bozzy wanted to see how the Doctor would look in a storm.

Boswell himself explains the visit to Lord Monboddo : ' I knew Lord Monboddo and Dr. Johnson did not love each other ; yet . . . I was curious to see them together.' It could hardly be supposed that Boswell adopted this attitude without encountering some opposition from Dr. Johnson. The latter evidently wished that a good life of him should be written, and was pleased with Boswell's journal and glad to tell him from time to time about his early life ; but there were limits to his endurance. ' I will not be put to the *question*. Don't you consider, Sir, that these are not the manners of a gentleman ? I will not be baited with *what* and *why* ; what is this ? what is that ? why is a cow's tail long ? why is a fox's tail bushy ? ' ' Sir,' he said on one occasion, ' you have but two topicks, yourself and me. I am sick of both.' Boswell indeed was continually taking risks ; he compares himself to ' the man who has put his head into the lion's mouth a great many times : ' his ordinary method of conversing with Johnson was to push his inquiries to the furthest possible point. His courage in this respect must have been notorious. ' I won a small bet,' he relates on one occasion, ' from Lady Diana Beauclerk, by asking him as to one of his particularities, which her Ladyship said I durst not do. It seems he had been frequently observed at the Club to put into his pocket the Seville oranges, after he had squeezed the juice of them into the drink which he had made for himself. Beauclerk and Garrick talked of it to me, and seemed to think he had a strange unwillingness to be discovered. We could not divine what he did with them ; and this was the bold question to be put.' Boswell on this occasion was not successful in his inquiries ; but it is to be observed that Boswell was deputed to inquire, and that he asked the question, and won his bet.

Occasionally Boswell remarks that Johnson was not in a good humour for talking. He must have wondered at such times how long it would take before his irritation would break forth, and he would make some typical utterance. ' But I wonder, Sir,' &c., was a sort of Boswellian formula to be met sooner or later with : ' Sir, you *may* wonder,' or some similar retort.

But what irritated Johnson perhaps more than the endless questions was to be made a ' butt ' as he termed it. ' On Monday, September 22, when at breakfast, I unguardedly said to Dr. Johnson, " I wish I saw you and Mrs. Macaulay together ! " He grew very angry, and, after a pause, while a cloud gathered on his brow, he burst out : " No, Sir, you would not see us quarrel to make you sport." ' Boswell eventually owns that he had wished to see a contest between Mrs. Macaulay and Johnson.

It is not to be supposed that Boswell's provocations

were always intentional, though there are many occasions upon which they clearly were so. Sometimes he
was ' out of countenance,' and when Johnson ' carried
the company with him,' his discomfiture perhaps
was greater than he would have wished. Not infrequently he made mistakes. On one occasion when
Johnson began : ' If I kept a seraglio,' Boswell was
so much amused that he failed to keep his countenance
and was overwhelmed with ' a variety of degrading
images ' ! Yet he was well aware of the general
tendency of his behaviour to provoke the ridicule of
Johnson, and though there may have been moments
when he did not intend it to do so, we may say that
he consciously led to his own humiliation, or consciously
at least ran the risk of it.

How much humiliation Boswell was able to support may be seen from Miss Burney's account of
a party at Streatham. Boswell, finding that there was
no place at the side of Dr. Johnson, had taken up a
seat immediately behind and between Dr. Johnson and
Miss Burney. It was not very polite, and the discovery
of his position by Dr. Johnson was disastrous :

The Doctor turned angrily round upon him, and,
clapping his hand rather loudly upon his knee, said,
in a tone of displeasure, ' What do you do there,
Sir ? Go to the table, Sir ! '
Mr. Boswell instantly, and with an air of affright,
obeyed ; and there was something so unusual in such
humble submission to so imperious a command that

another smile gleamed its way across every mouth
except that of the Doctor and of Mr. Boswell, who now,
very unwillingly, took a distant seat.

Anything more ignominious could hardly be imagined, and that Boswell was sensitive to a rebuke from
the Doctor we cannot doubt.   And yet, within a few
minutes, he was to run the risk of a second.   For some
reason or other he wished to leave the room while the
ceremony still demanded his presence at the table.
The Doctor, calling after him authoritatively, said :
' What are you thinking of, Sir ?   Why do you get
up before the cloth is removed ?   Come back to your
place, Sir ! '   ' Again,' Miss Burney continues, ' and with
equal obsequiousness, Mr. Boswell did as he was bid.'

Boswell's behaviour, indeed, on this particular
occasion was not heroic.   His position near Dr.
Johnson cannot have been essential to his purpose of
taking notes ;   he was unwilling to abandon it out
of a childish feeling of dignity ; he considered it his
natural right to sit near the doctor, and was obstinate
about it.   And it was no experiment of his to leave
the room unceremoniously with the purpose of hearing
what Dr. Johnson might have to say.   But it was
heroic of Boswell to put himself continually, and often
intentionally, in the way of such rebuffs ; for this he
undoubtedly did.   It was heroic because he had a
noble purpose.   Boswell was a man of science, and his
science was concerned with nothing less than the mind

and soul of Man. He was none the less scientific
because he did not deal in generalities; he was
concerned with detail rather than with deduction and
with one man rather than with all men. Science
may not have been the only motive for enduring.
Boswell may have supported the harsh sayings of Dr.
Johnson and suffered for the sake of his friendship,
for its honour as well as for its value; but when we
consider the humiliation of those rebukes we know
at least that he suffered not a little; and inasmuch
as he courted them, and courted them deliberately,
friendship offers no explanation. Here we are compelled to accept the scientific motive. Boswell must
be allowed the credit of having suffered as a man of
science for the sake of Biography.

Miss Burney, though she neither understood nor
appreciated Boswell, and even disliked him, has no
doubt given a truthful picture. It is clear that Boswell
suffered from the rebuffs which he received from
Johnson. If he endured them on the whole willingly,
yet he endured them not without feeling some pain. He
could not carry it off; Boswell had no natural dignity;
he had a 'jovial bluntness' and a comical air about
him, but these could not help him on such occasions,
and he was obliged as it were to lose prestige, to appear
in fact mean-spirited and servile.

Miss Burney tells us also that Johnson generally
treated him as a schoolboy. The difference in their

ages was more than thirty years ; but even so the expression is remarkable, and shows as does the whole account how complete was the submission of Boswell.

His behaviour, however, was not merely un-dignified and grotesque, it was rude. His whole attitude towards Johnson was a rude one. Curiosity indulged as he indulged it cannot be polite. Johnson told him more than once that he had no manners. Langton said : ' Boswell's conversation consists en-tirely in asking questions, and is extremely offensive.' Boswell, in fact, as the biographer, was rude not only to Johnson but to the whole company ; concerned entirely with his own purpose, he ignored the social obligation. It seems to have been his common habit to sit down, note-book in hand, to record the conversa-tion. Mr. Barclay said that he had seen Boswell lay down his knife and fork, and take out his tablets, in order to register a good anecdote. Mrs. Thrale refers to his ' reporting ' as a usual and obnoxious practice.

A trick which I have seen played on common occasions, of sitting steadily down at the other end of the room to write at the moment what should be said in company, either *by* Dr. Johnson or *to* him, I never practised myself, nor approved of in another. There is something so ill-bred, and so inclining to treachery in this conduct, that were it commonly adopted, all confidence would soon be exiled from society, and a conversation assembly-room would become tremendous as a court of justice.

CHAPTER XI

THE habit which annoyed Mrs. Thrale was necessary to Boswell's conception of his task ; it involved what he spoke of as his ' authenticity.'

To understand what he meant by this, an attitude perhaps not only towards himself, but to the public also, since he wished very much that those who read his book should feel that it was true in every detail, we must examine more nearly Boswell's method of carrying out his biographical plan.

It is remarkable that Boswell should have begun his system of recording when quite a young man. A man of forty is more easily forgiven some eccentricity than one of two-and-twenty. Yet we find Boswell, during his travels on the Continent, tablets in hand on his first visit to Paoli, who gives an amusing account of him :

He came to my country and he fetched me some letter of recommending him : but I was of the belief he might be an impostor, and I supposed in my minte, he was an espy ; for I look away from him and in a moment I look to him again, and I behold his tablets. Oh ! he was to the work of writing down all I say !

Indeed I was angry. But soon I discover he was no impostor and no espy ; and I only find I was myself the monster he had come to discover. Oh—he is a very good man, I love him indeed ; so cheerful ! so gay ! so pleasant ! but at the first, oh ! indeed I was angry.[1]

Boswell's method of recording conversations was not completed in these memoranda taken down at the moment. He had, besides these, his journal. It has been remarked already that he began to keep this regularly as early as 1758 during his tour on the Northern Circuit in the company of his father and Lord Hailes, and he tells us something of it at the time of his journey to Greenwich with Johnson in 1763 :

I was the more sensible of it (the cold) from having sat up all the night before *recollecting and writing* in my journal what I thought worthy of preservation ; an exertion which, during the first part of my acquaintance with Johnson, I frequently made. I remember having sat up four nights in one week, without being much incommoded in the daytime.

In the 'Tour to Corsica,' also, he tells us:

From my first setting out on this tour, I wrote down every night what I had observed during the day, throwing together a great deal, that I might afterwards select at leisure.[2]

We have then two processes mentioned by which Boswell recorded conversation : the notes taken down

[1] *Miss Burney's Diary*, ii, 100.   [2] *Tour to Corsica*, p. 297.

at the moment, and the journal written up at night. The relation of these two—the function which each of them performed—is not difficult to conjecture.

Boswell's object was to get his records written up as soon as possible after the events or conversations which he was describing :

I found, from experience, that to collect my friend's conversation so as to exhibit it with any degree of its original flavour, it was necessary to write it down without delay. To record his sayings, after some distance of time, was like preserving or pickling long-kept or faded fruits, or other vegetables, which, when in that state, have little or nothing of their taste when fresh.[1]

It was upon the fact that he trusted, not to his memory, but to 'exact transcript of conversations,' that Boswell based his claim to authenticity.[2] He was so absolutely truthful himself, that it never occurred to him to think that the truth of what was actually written down at the time could be doubted, and it was to him an entire refutation of any adversary to confront him with his method.

If this book should again be reprinted, I shall with the utmost readiness correct any errours I may have committed, in stating conversations, provided it can be clearly shown to me that I have been inaccurate. But I am slow to believe (as I have elsewhere observed) that any man's memory, at the distance of several

[1] *Life of Johnson*, iii, 183.
[2] *Tour to the Hebrides*, p. 434 (Dr. Hill's edition).

years, can preserve facts or sayings with such fidelity as may be done by writing them down when they are recent : and I beg it may be remembered, that it is not upon *memory*, but upon what was *written at the time*, that the authenticity of my ' Journal ' rests.[1]

But it is clear enough that the notes which Boswell made at the time must have been very unlike the final form in which he wrote the dialogue. In the course of conversations in which he himself took part, it would have been impossible without shorthand to make so full a record. The kind of notes which Boswell took may be gathered from the following passage :

I this evening boasted, that though I did not write what is called stenography, or short-hand, in appropriated characters devised for the purpose, I had a method of my own of writing half words, and leaving out some altogether, so as yet to keep the substance and language of any discourses which I had heard so much in view, that I could give it very completely soon after I had taken it down.[2]

It would seem then that what was written down during a conversation was far from including every word which was spoken ; it was rather an aid, though a very substantial aid, to memory. We may conjecture that the most important expressions were recorded, and the course of the argument indicated, so as to be intelligible to Boswell, but not even to him, perhaps, after a long

[1] *Tour to the Hebrides*, Appendix 1.   [2] *Life of Johnson*, iii, 270.

interval. He was able to 'keep in view' the 'substance and language.'

To give a full and permanent form to these rough drafts must therefore have been a work of considerable labour; and it is this no doubt that the journal accomplished.

We may see in the 'Life' the traces of two kinds of record. For we have sometimes the actual words of the speakers, but at others only the purport of their remarks. What we should naturally suppose—if this theory of the respective functions of the notes and the journal is correct—that the former came from the journal and the latter from the notes taken down at the moment, or sometimes perhaps shortly afterwards—is confirmed by the fact that, when we have only the less complete account, Boswell very often regrets the neglect of his journal, and talks of presenting such scraps as he has; and on one occasion says:

I kept very imperfect notes of his conversation, which had I according to my usual custom *written out at large soon after the time*, much might have been preserved.[1]

He was obliged in consequence of his neglect to write the text directly from notes; with their aid he filled in what he could remember; but he dispensed with the intermediate assistance of the journal, and the account is therefore far less full.

[1] *Life of Johnson*, ii, 372.

The rough notes of the moment and the elaborate journal made by writing them out at large ' soon after the time '—these, then, form the basis of Boswell's method for preserving Johnson's talk. It is not to be supposed that Boswell strictly adhered to this method on every occasion. He was too much an experimentalist for that ; and sometimes it must have been very difficult to take notes. We cannot imagine that when Boswell was alone with Johnson he pulled out ' tablets ' in the course of an argument. More probably he seized an opportunity, as soon afterwards as possible, when Johnson was not talking, to put down the more striking phrases and record the point of the discussion. But there must have been some occasions when opportunities did not occur. Johnson, no doubt, became accustomed to his companion's habits and was often willing to help him by telling him details about his early life or dictating the text of a letter for Boswell to write down there and then. But sometimes he was in the mood to resent memoranda ; and sometimes the talk was too continuous for Boswell's task to be an easy one. At such times Boswell may have written the journal as well as he could without the notes, and as soon afterwards as possible. At Ashbourne, for instance, in 1777, he may have done this : he was alone with Johnson more than usual, and several discussions made Johnson very angry ; he may well have waited to record anything until he wrote the journal, for he had no lack of time to devote to this purpose while staying in the quiet country town, and in point of fact he actually kept the journal more fully at this time than at any other. He mentions that he has ' acquired a facility in recollecting his conversation.'[1] This may refer to the effort of memory required in recalling altogether what had been said, as well as to the effort of reconstructing the talk from what he had written down at the moment. In the early part of the ' Life ' Boswell says :

> In progress of time, when my mind was, as it were, *strongly impregnated with the Johnsonian æther*, I could, with much more facility and exactness, *carry in my memory and commit to paper* the exuberant variety of his wisdom and wit.[2]

Here again he may well have had in mind a process of writing the journal with no notes to help him.

All the original documents from which Boswell compiled the ' Life ' are concealed from this generation. There are, however—or at least there were—in existence two of Boswell's note-books. Mr. Fitzgerald relates that in Mr. Pocock's ' Johnsonian Catalogue ' there was

a note-book in which Boswell jotted down from day to day the actual sayings and doings of the eminent lexicographer. This volume contains literary opinions and aphorisms peculiar to this great man, and of which many have never been published. He gives a specific

---

[1] *Life of Johnson*, i, 26.   [2] *Ib.*, i, 421.

account of the manner in which he compiled the
'Dictionary,' and relates other matters of interest,
bearing on his long literary career and contemporaries.

This manuscript, if it were to be seen, might reveal
more definitely what Boswell's method was. The description of it can do nothing but emphasise the use of the
'tablets'; but its value as evidence depends upon
its accuracy with regard to the sequence of the notes:
if they were really 'jotted down from day to day,'
then they are the 'tablets' without a doubt.

The other note-book is 'Boswelliana'; and it is
of a different kind.

Boswell kept in a portfolio a quantity of loose
quarto sheets, inscribed on each page *Boswelliana*. In
certain of these sheets the pages are denoted by
numerals in the ordinary fashion; another portion is
numbered by the folios; while a further portion
consists of loose leaves and letter-backs. The greater
part of the entries are made so carefully as to justify
the belief that the author intended to embody the
whole in a volume of literary anecdotes.[1]

Emphatically this collection was not 'tablets.' It
was probably intended for a particular purpose. Boswell
may have had several collections of a similar kind.
But it is clear that the purpose of 'Boswelliana' has no
connection with the 'Life of Johnson.' [2]   Stories of

[1] *Boswelliana*, Grampian Club, 1874. Preface.
[2] Boswell on one occasion told a lady that her joke should be
included in *Boswelliana*.

Johnson it does indeed contain; but they are few, and are unconnected by any chronological arrangement. They form only a small part of the whole.

The journal itself was kept in quarto and octavo volumes,[1] and Boswell on one occasion showed it to Sir William Forbes.[2] It seems that his object in doing this was to get an opinion which might encourage him to publish; he quotes with great pleasure in the 'Life' the praise which this gentleman had bestowed upon it. One would suppose that the journal displayed in this way gave the Johnsonian conversations and anecdotes in words almost identical with the text of the 'Life.' In the preface to the 'Corsican Journal' Boswell says of the Paoli memoirs:

As I have related his remarkable sayings, I declare upon my honour, that I have neither added nor diminished; nay, so scrupulous have I been, that I would not make the smallest variation even when my friends thought it would be an improvement. I know with how much pleasure we read what is perfectly authentick.[3]

One might easily expect that the same words would equally well apply to the 'Life.' But this is not the case.

It is reasonable to suppose that the Johnsonian stories in 'Boswelliana' are not less polished than

[1] *Life of Johnson*, iv, 83.   [2] *Ib.*, iii, 308.   [3] p. xiii.

T 2

those in the journal ; they are themselves in a definite form ; and since the journal itself is only the second stage of Boswell's method, these stories must be in a state at the least no less advanced. And yet the verbal differences between these stories and those in the ' Life ' are often considerable and sometimes large. The truth is that Boswell's method must have developed very much in one direction from the account he gave of it in the ' Tour to Corsica.' As Dr. Birkbeck Hill has clearly proved, he made changes in the way of ' touching up ' the conversations and stories.

One or two instances of these variations will illustrate Boswell's treatment of his materials ; the stories are given below in double columns for purpose of comparison.

Boswelliana.

1. Boswell asked Mr. Samuel Johnson what was best to teach a gentleman's children first. ' Why, Sir,' said he, ' there is no matter what you teach them first. It matters no more than which leg you put first into your bretches [*sic*]. Sir, you may stand disputing which leg you

Life

We talked of the education of children ; and I asked him what he thought was best to teach them first. *Johnson*: ' Sir, it is no matter what you shall teach them first, any more than what leg you shall put in your breeches first. Sir, you may stand disputing which leg you shall put in first, but in shall put in first, but in the meantime your legs are bare. No matter which you put in first so that you put 'em both in, and then you have your bretches on. Sir, while you think which of two things to teach a child first, another boy, in the common course has learnt both.'

I was present.

the meantime your breech is bare. Sir, while you are considering which of two things you shall teach your child first, another boy has learnt them both.

Boswelliana

2. Boswell told Mr. Samuel Johnson that a gentleman of their acquaintance maintained in public company that he could see no distinction between virtue and vice. ' Sir,' said Mr. Johnson, ' does he intend that we should believe that he is lying, or that he is in earnest ? If we think him a lyar, that is not honouring him very much. But if we think him in earnest, when he leaves our houses let us count our spoons.'

Life

The same gentleman maintained that there was no distinction between virtue and vice. *Johnson :* ' Why, Sir, if the fellow does not think as he speaks, he is lying ; and I see not what honour he can propose to himself from having the character of a liar. But if he does really think that there is no distinction between virtue and vice, why, Sir, when he leaves our houses let us count our spoons.'

A comparison of the two versions of No. 1 reveals at once the brevity of the final form. It is evident, as Mr. Fitzgerald remarks, that the text itself could not have represented the talk as it came from Johnson's lips. 'The whole is too deliberate, too close, too well winnowed, as it were.' Conversation is more discursive. Boswell's method as we see it here is in the first place to compress—to give not the whole of Johnson's words, but only the essence of them. In the result the story in its last state preserves the most important expressions and is more pointed for being shorter.

The second story in the table has not been cut down in the same fashion. It illustrates very well another process. It is the process, one may say, of Johnsonising. Not only has the argument, as in the former case, been made clearer and more concise, but the words themselves have been considerably altered. The result indicates the reason of these changes. The version in the ' Life ' is stronger and more convincing ; it has more of the energy of human tongues. The assertion 'he is lying' has more force than the corresponding question : the ' why, Sir,' introduced before the climax gives the proper snort of war before the culminating triumph of the dilemma. Boswell made these changes that he might retain the spirit of Johnson's talk and the atmosphere of the moment as the listeners felt it. He succeeded whenever he added force and directness ; one may easily be convinced of this by recalling the uncouth figure with its suggestion of abnormal strength which uttered slowly in a very loud voice, occasionally shaking the head, ' as if to promote the fermentation of his wit.'

A most remarkable instance of the two processes—of compressing and Johnsonising—is furnished by two stories in ' Boswelliana ' which become one story in the ' Life.'

Boswelliana

Mr. Sheridan, though a man of knowledge and parts, was a little fanciful in his projects for establishing oratory and altering the mode of British education. ' Mr. Samuel Johnson,' said Sherry, ' cannot abide me, for I always ask him, Pray, Sir, what do you propose to do ? '

From Mr. Johnson : Boswell was talking to Mr. Samuel Johnson of Mr. Sheridan's enthusiasm for the advancement of eloquence. ' Sir,' said Mr. Johnson, ' it won't do. He cannot carry through his scheme. He is like a man attempting to stride

Life

He now added, ' Sheridan cannot bear me. I bring his declamation to a point. I ask him a plain question, What do you mean to teach ? Besides, Sir, what influence can Mr. Sheridan have upon the language of this great country by his narrow exertions ? Sir, it is burning a farthing candle at Dover to show light at Calais ! '

the English Channel. Sir,
the cause bears no proportion to the effect.   It
is setting up a candle at
Whitechapel to give light
at Westminster.'

The compression and alteration are of the same
character as in the two previous stories.   The argument
is closer and the point clearer ;   and the effect of the
whole is stronger.   One verbal change is very striking.
One might expect that the image with which Johnson
summarises his views would be wholly inviolate.
Yet here we see Dover and Calais substituted for
Whitechapel and Westminster :   probably the reason
is that Boswell regrets the phrase he has omitted,
' He is like a man attempting to stride across the
English Channel,' and tries to combine the two
images.

It must not be forgotten that the stories in ' Boswelliana ' were probably not used by Boswell in writing
the ' Life.'   If they were to be written down in full
once only, then why not in the proper Johnsonian
stores ?   Or why should this peculiar collection of
' Boswelliana ' take precedence ?   Some of the stories,
indeed, must have been in the journal ;   the record in
' Boswelliana,' for instance, of Johnson's retort about
Scotland—the first remark he made to Boswell—cannot be the only record of the famous meeting in Tom
Davies' back parlour ;   clearly Boswell must have

kept a more elaborate account. But though the 'Boswelliana' manuscripts were not used, as seems most likely, it may fairly be argued that the difference between the versions given there and the final forms in the 'Life' are a proper indication of Boswell's method of adapting his material. There is no reason to suppose that Boswell was less accurate in the 'Boswelliana' than in his journal and other Johnsonian stores; or indeed, that there was a great difference between 'Boswelliana' versions and any others in an unfinished state. And it is clear that two versions of a story, both in an unfinished state, must differ from the final form more or less, perhaps, but with the same species of difference.

It is contended, therefore, that Boswell altered his written Johnsoniana in a way which could account for the differences we have observed between the versions of stories in 'Boswelliana' and those in the 'Life.' This proposition, however, casts no reflection upon his reputation for accuracy. He preserved the 'substance and language'; and if he changed some words he preserved the colouring and made the whole a better representation of Johnson.

Boswell himself gives some suggestion of his method when he presents a series of Johnsoniana for which he was indebted to Mr. Langton:

Very few articles in this collection were committed to writing by himself, he not having that habit. . . .

The authenticity of every article is unquestionable. For the expressions, I, who wrote them down, am partly answerable.

By ' unquestionable authenticity ' it was meant, no doubt, that the purport of what Johnson said had been correctly reported.   In ' Boswelliana ' a story told by Mr. Langton is written out with suggestions for its improvement.   It may be quoted as a final example of the manner in which Boswell was partly answerable for the expressions :

Johnson had a sovereign contempt for Wilkes and his party, whom he looked upon as a mere rabble. ' Sir,' said he, ' had Wilkes's mob prevailed against Government, this nation would have died of *phthiriasis* ! Mr. Langton told me this.   The expression *morbus pediculosus*, as being better known, would strike more. *Lousy disease* may be put in a parenthesis.'

CHAPTER XII

THE method we have been examining has revealed, in a sense, a second aspect of Boswell as the biographer, the natural complement of that scientific spirit which inspired the acute observation, the delicate experiments, the methodical accuracy; for he brought to the work of recording not merely the faculty for stating truthfully what he had seen, but the power of expressing his feelings; and it was particularly this feeling—an interest at the same time full-blooded, comprehensive and minute—that insisted upon expression.

The emotion which compels a man to bind himself to an ideal, and, having determined that something must be done under certain conditions, compels the doing of it without capitulation, is one which enters into many kinds of work and is to be found no doubt very often among scientists; but it is in a peculiar degree the possession of the artist. To him indeed it seems to be essential; for his value depends certainly not more on the quality of what he has to express than on the completeness with which he expresses it. And so perhaps we ought to connect the consistency, the truth, the faith of Boswell, and his disregard for obstacles, with his artistic rather than with his scientific qualities ; so we ought to interpret Boswell's love of his labour and his conviction that it was good, and so to understand all the trouble that it cost to his mind and to the more sensitive part of him. The refusal to depart from his ideal which he made to Hannah More (' I would not cut off his claws, nor make my tiger a cat, to please anybody '),[1] and again to Bishop Percy when he declined, for the sake of ' authenticity,' to suppress the bishop's name,[2] is an indication of the need he had to express himself as an artist.[3]

But how was it that he came so to express himself ? And what is it that he succeeded in expressing ?

Of the impulse to expression and what it meant in Boswell's case something has been said already in these pages. We cannot understand the engine if we forget the power that drives it, and we must emphasise once again the force that Boswell obeyed. His passion for truth was not comprehensive : and it was for the truth of the realist, not the truth of the idealist. It did not include the whole of life ; it did not attempt to view the entire scene in correct perspective ; and

[1] *Autobiography, Letters, &c., of Mrs. Piozzi*, ii, 403.
[2] Nichols' *Illustrations*, vii, 313.
[3] Henley, in *Views and Reviews*, speaks of Boswell as an artist.

Boswell was decidedly not a philosopher. He did not greatly need explanations of the universe; he tended to accept such as seemed convenient. He had no logic about abstract theories, and only a very limited power of criticising evidence. One who cares for truth with respect to every fact and deduction is inclined to reject his first impressions, because experience has taught him that 'all men are liars.' The face of things is so often false ! But Boswell was content to look no further ; he sometimes deliberately disregarded the facts of existence ; he lived one half his life in a glitter of his own creation. Nevertheless, the passion for truth was vivid and vital. It lived apart to work out its own consummation ; and it was all the more vehement for being confined. It is perhaps for this reason—that the truth inherent in Boswell was confined within such strict limits—that it required expression. In these circumstances Boswell's buoyant nature had need of a safety-valve. Truth for him was concerned entirely with an external view of people. He was rarely analytical ; he did not care for subtle states of mind and the feelings that composed them ; he looked directly at actions and their primary motives. The vision was so clear and strong that Boswell by its very insistence was obliged to create an imperishable image.

The reasons that made it certain from the beginning that Johnson would become the vehicle for this expression extend beyond those qualities which made Boswell prefer and admire him above all other men; they depend upon Boswell's attitude towards mankind. We have seen that he apologises and justifies himself for relating the weaknesses and absurdities of Johnson. And yet he sometimes seems to have a peculiar delight in them. These shades in Johnson's character are dealt with not as an unpleasant but necessary task, to be despatched with a light touch as though it ill became him to speak of them, but with a full flavour of rich and lasting enjoyment.

They were in fact to Boswell the most striking and salient qualities of his great hero, and it was necessary therefore that they should be well and completely related. But in the story as we read it, we do not merely observe that the rude victories and uneven justice of Johnson were supremely significant in the eyes of the author. To Boswell the whole personality of Johnson was a source of the keenest pleasure. He took an insatiable delight in it. He loved to imitate the curious gestures and manner of the Doctor. He became, to use his own word, ' Johnsonised ' ; and no doubt he reached that state which he desired his readers to attain, and both ' talked and thought ' Johnson. He was ' strongly impregnated with the Johnsonian æther ' ; and when he had drunk his fill and it had all soaked in, it was

reproduced with a relish of the joyous moments it
had given him. The picture of Johnson, as he saw it,
was a source of deep and satisfying enjoyment to
Boswell : he overflowed with mere pleasure in the
contemplation of a man, and expressed himself, as an
artist, out of the abundance of this sympathy, in
terms of ' Johnson.'

And the enjoyment, one may say, depending as
it did very largely upon a certain dramatic quality
of that curious figure, was concerned necessarily very
much with the oddities and weaknesses of the man, and
particularly with that greatest weakness of all, the
abuse of strength.

When it is said that Boswell is an artist, it is not
meant that the whole of the ' Life of Johnson ' was
treated artistically. It exhibits, no doubt, a certain
elegance of proportion ; it is a good composition, well
arranged, well spaced ; and in as far as it has those
qualities we may consider that it belongs to art.
But it is not chiefly because, having recorded what
happened in a perfectly straightforward manner, he
then fitted together the fragments to make as it were
a complete model of a man—it is not for the design—
that we call Boswell an artist. It is because he did
not very often, as we have seen, relate the facts quite
simply, but related them in such a manner that the
whole atmosphere of the scene, all that is most human
and most humorous, strikes upon us. It is in what

have been called his comedy scenes that we see the supreme art of Boswell.

A characteristic passage relates an attempt to make fun of Johnson by inquiring if he took dancing lessons :

I ventured to mention a ludicrous passage in the newspapers, that Dr. Johnson was learning to dance of Vestris. Lord Charlemont, wishing to excite him to talk, proposed in a whisper, that he should be asked whether it was true. ' Shall I ask him ? ' said his Lordship. We were by a great majority clear for the experiment.

In these few words Boswell has recalled the spirit of the scene. We have a vision of Johnson sitting terrible in the midst, and his hearers feeling and behaving like schoolboys in the presence of some bearish pedagogue. Some one proposes an audacious jest, and all await with eagerness the crucial moment. You may sit upon the edge of a volcano, or you may fire the train which shall explode a planet, but no expectancy is so keen as this.

His Lordship very gravely and with a courteous air said, ' Pray, sir, is it true that you are taking lessons of Vestris ? ' . . . This was risking a good deal, and required the boldness of a General of Irish Volunteers to make the attempt.

The explosion unerringly follows, but the rumble dies away in rippling laughter :

Johnson was at first startled and in some heat answered, ' How can your Lordship ask so simple a question ? ' But immediately recovering himself, whether from unwillingness to be deceived or to appear deceived, or whether from real good-humour, he kept up the joke. . . .

Johnson in these scenes of comedy is always the dictator ; the elements of the ridiculous are constantly present when someone who behaves with a pompous manner is rarely willing to be laughed at, and Boswell's sense of what was incongruous was near the surface and ready to make merry.

The company on one occasion were greatly tickled by a word applied in Johnson's most majestic manner to a rather laughable female character, and the incident furnishes Boswell with material for one of his best descriptions of this kind. Johnson had re-marked ' The woman had a bottom of good sense.'

The word *bottom* [says Boswell] thus introduced, was so ludicrous when contrasted with his gravity, that most of us could not forbear tittering and laughing ; though I recollect that the Bishop of Killaloe kept his countenance with perfect steadiness, while Miss Hannah More slyly hid her face behind a lady's back who sat on the same settee with her. His pride could not bear that any expression of his should excite ridicule, when he did not intend it ; he therefore resolved to assume and exercise despotick power, glanced sternly around, and called out in a strong tone, ' Where's the merriment ? ' Then collecting himself, and looking aweful, to make us feel how he could impose restraint,

U

and as it were searching his mind for a still more ludicrous word, he slowly pronounced, ' I say the *woman* was *fundamentally* sensible ; ' as if he had said, ' Hear this now, and laugh if you dare.' We all sat composed as at a funeral.

This, like the other scene, is extremely dramatic. Neither would have been so had not the writer himself realised the full humour of the situation. Perhaps the most remarkable quality of the description is the amount left out.[1] The few details which Boswell gives us are sufficient to reveal the secret of everybody's feelings, and then Johnson strikes in with the characteristic remark. It is difficult to appreciate to the full the merit of these scenes without comparing them with those supplied by less talented pens ; when we read the accounts of Mrs. Piozzi and Sir John Hawkins, and even of Miss Burney, we realise the immeasurable superiority of Boswell's. They have the elusive quality of all impressionist [2] art ; they might be ranked with the nocturnes of Whistler : if they were produced, as it almost seems they were, with as little apparent care, they were produced, however, only by the experience of a lifetime. By continually thinking ' Johnson,' Boswell was able to give the few necessary touches which expressed the inward vision.

[1] Fitzgerald and Birkbeck Hill both say something of this.

[2] I use this term not in a particular technical sense (as applied to a school of French painters) but in a general sense, of all art that neglects details for the sake of general effect.

In the two passages we have quoted, Boswell has revealed the humour of a situation ; those supreme moments of Johnson's dictatorship were to him a never-failing treasure-house of priceless mirth ; and he has given us a key which enables us to hear with him the magic thunder, to see each bright flash of the lightning, and with him to laugh the rich mellow laughter because it is so absurd, and yet so inevitable, and so good, that men should have been fashioned so.

Boswell delights in showing us the mind of Johnson, how he was prompted like the rest of us by all the little motives of men. He enjoys Johnson's humanity. Sometimes he is more solemn. One great subject is Johnson's tenderness—as in an account of an argument with Sir Joshua about drinking :

Johnson (who from drinking only water supposed everybody who drank wine to be elevated) : ' I won't argue any more with you, Sir. You are too far gone.' *Sir Joshua :* ' I should have thought so indeed, Sir, had I made such a speech as you have now done.' *Johnson* (drawing himself in, and I really thought blushing) : ' Nay, don't be angry. I did not mean to offend you.'

The best instance perhaps of Johnson's compunction after rudeness is on the occasion of Dr. Percy's defence of Dr. Mounsey :

Mr. Davies, who sat next to Dr. Percy, having after this had some conversation aside with him, made a discovery which, in his zeal to pay court to Dr.

Johnson, he eagerly proclaimed aloud from the foot of the table : ' O, Sir, I have found out a very good reason why Dr. Percy never heard Mounsey swear or talk bawdy ; for he tells me, he never saw him but at the Duke of Northumberland's table.' ' And so, Sir (said Johnson loudly, to Dr. Percy), you would shield this man from the charge of swearing and talking bawdy, because he did not do so at the Duke of Northumberland's table. . . .' Dr. Percy seemed to be displeased, and soon afterwards left the company.

Later, in the course of conversation, Johnson denied any merit to Swift for writing ' The Conduct of the Allies ' ; then

recollecting that Mr. Davies, by acting as an informer, had been the occasion of his talking somewhat too harshly to his friend Dr. Percy, for which, probably, when the first ebullition was over, he felt some compunction,[1] he took an opportunity to give him a hit ; so added, with a preparatory laugh, ' Why, Sir, Tom Davies might have written " The Conduct of the Allies." ' Poor Tom being thus suddenly dragged into ludicrous notice in presence of the Scottish doctors, to whom he was ambitious of appearing to advantage, was grievously mortified.

The compunction, however, on this occasion seems to have had a short duration, for Boswell goes on to say :

When I called upon Dr. Johnson next morning, I found him highly satisfied with his colloquial prowess the preceding evening : ' Well (said he), we had good talk.' *Boswell :* ' Yes, Sir, you tossed and gored several persons.'

---

[1] The italics are mine.

Boswell seems to have had the power of picking out all that was characteristic and important, of ruthlessly discarding unnecessary details and presenting only the salient points, of seeing a scene as a whole, with its more vivid colours flashing out as it were from a dull background, so that the whole impression is complete and clear. The smallest conversations, as we saw, were dealt with in this way. And as he ' Johnsonised ' the talk which he had himself taken down, and ' Johnsonised ' the stories given to him by Mr. Langton, he ' Johnsonised ' in the same way these larger scenes. While retaining most of the words used by Johnson himself, Boswell seems to have added here and there a characteristic expression to make the whole more pointed, and to have compressed it all till it preserved nothing but the true Johnsonian flavour.

.   .   .   .   .

In all this, the artistic part of his work, Boswell was expressing his own conception of Johnson. But it has been doubted by some whether this is a true view of him, or whether the whole is not overdrawn. Dr. Birkbeck Hill says that Johnson was drawn by Boswell as ' too awful.' [1]

It is indeed, as has been said before, the awfulness of Johnson which Boswell had in mind when he wrote

[1] *Life of Johnson*, ii. 262, n. 2.

his ' comedy scenes,' and even in relating less pungent moments. The humour of it all depended so much upon that !

It must be remarked, at the outset, that several individuals may have quite different impressions of one man. Not only do the observers emphasise different qualities, so that the same person might be described by one as kind and affectionate, and by another as sentimental and stupid, without either account being untrue, except in so far as it is incomplete, but a man's behaviour often varies with the company. The truth of Boswell, since he expressed quite truthfully his own impressions, would be in nowise confounded if it were discovered that the majority did not share his view of Johnson ; still less if he had seen what they saw, while they had not seen what he revealed.

But the fact is that Boswell's conception of Johnson as being 'awful' was the common one. The idea that he was not so is probably derived from Miss Burney's ' Diary.' It will be remembered, however, that Johnson's behaviour to Miss Burney was quite unlike his behaviour to the great majority of people : she was chosen to be the special object of his gallantry. It was extremely pleasant for her ; she was naturally pleased to be continually the recipient of the most charming compliments ; and her ' Diary ' tells us all about it. Boswell was well aware that to her

more than to anybody else Johnson showed the gayer
side of his character, and he was anxious, as we have
seen, to make use of her ' stores ' :

I want to show him as gay Sam, agreeable Sam,
pleasant Sam ; so you must help me with some of
his beautiful billets to yourself.

Miss Burney indeed can hardly be excused for not
giving her assistance to Boswell, since she afterwards
talks of vindicating Johnson to his King and Queen,[1]
which she would hardly have found necessary had she
contributed largely herself to Boswell's ' Life.'   And
even Miss Burney alludes to the fear in which Johnson
was held by his contemporaries, and reports a terrible,
if deserved, rebuke to Hannah More, when Johnson,
after politely bearing the lady's adulation for some
little time, exclaimed, ' Madam, before you flatter a
man so grossly to his face, you should consider whether
or not your flattery is worth his having.' [2]   Mrs. Piozzi,
too, in whose house it was that she met Dr. Johnson,
has, in her own account of him, emphasised very
much the other side of the picture.

It must also be remembered that Boswell, though
he loves to relate the roughness of Johnson and his
imperiousness, is always at pains to show that he was
a really kind and considerate man, and even seems
to make allowance for the possibility that he has made
the harshness too prominent, and takes care to explain
that it was not so common as might be supposed:

[1] *Miss Burney's Diary*, iv, 478.   [2] *Ib.*, i, 100.

How very false is the notion which has gone round the world of the rough, and passionate, and harsh manners of this great and good man. That he had occasional sallies of heat of temper, and that he was sometimes, perhaps, too ' easily provoked ' by absurdity and folly, and sometimes too desirous of triumph in colloquial contest, must be allowed. The quickness both of his perception and sensibility disposed him to sudden explosions of satire ; to which his extraordinary readiness of wit was a strong and almost irresistible incitement. I admit that the beadle within him was often so eager to apply the lash, that the judge had not time to consider the case with sufficient deliberation.[1]

Boswell is prepared to admit, as he is obliged to do, the dogmatist and the fighter in Johnson, but not that he was in the ordinary way disagreeable.

That he was occasionally remarkable for violence of temper may be granted : but let us ascertain the degree, and not let it be supposed that he was in a perpetual rage, and never without a club in his hand, to knock down everyone who approached him. On the contrary, the truth is, that by much the greatest part of his time he was civil, obliging, nay, polite in the true sense of the word ; so much so, that many gentlemen, who were long acquainted with him, never received, or even heard a strong expression from him.

It will be seen from his lengthy defence of Johnson against what he considered a common accusation and an unjust one, and it may be seen also from other

[1] *Life of Johnson*, iii, 80–1.

passages, that Boswell regards his own life of Johnson as likely to weaken the prevalent opinions about Johnson's rough behaviour. Mrs. Piozzi is violently attacked by him for having exaggerated and maliciously enlarged upon this part of his character.[1]

It is not to be supposed that the conception of Johnson's 'awfulness' depended entirely upon his capacity for giving rude blows to his antagonists in conversation. There is a certain gravity of demeanour, amounting almost to pompousness, which Boswell loves to depict. It may seem that the Doctor is not sufficiently good-humoured. No doubt it was Boswell's particular delight to represent the majesty of the great man of letters, and the many occasions on which Johnson is jovial and pleasant are, for him perhaps, the exceptions to a rule. But how many there are ! The ' Tour to the Hebrides ' especially (and in considering Boswell's presentation of Johnson we must consider always the ' Tour ' with the ' Life ') is full of instances of this kind of behaviour. It was indeed a serious departure from Boswell's ideal that the Rambler should take upon his knee a Highland lady, but it would be difficult to count the number of times that Johnson is reported quite naturally to have laughed and to have been good-humoured. He is even reported to have perverted a line of Shakespeare, with the spontaneous merrymaking of a schoolboy, to

[1] *Life of Johnson*, iv, 340 *et seq.*

suit his companion.   Surely it could be said by no one
that his impression of Johnson after reading Boswell's
' Life ' and the ' Tour to the Hebrides ' was that of a
cross and grave old man.

Boswell perhaps does not give the picture of
affability and even gaiety which Miss Burney gives ;
but her account too is qualified.   ' Dr. Johnson,' she
says, ' has more fun and comical humour, and love
of nonsense about him, than almost anybody I ever
saw : I mean when with those he likes ; for otherwise
he can be as severe and as bitter as report relates him.' [1]
On another occasion she speaks of ' a formality that
accompanies whatever he says,' which conveys exactly
the impression of ' awfulness ' that we get so often from
Boswell.[2]

The criticism which could perhaps be made with
most justice of the Johnson whom we know from
Boswell is that he is not playful enough.   Miss Burney's
Johnson may seem a jollier man.   She alludes to his
' love of nonsense ' and ' a turn for burlesque humour.' [3]
But it must be remembered that behaviour of this
kind is mentioned very seldom—only four or five
times at the most, even in Miss Burney's ' Diary.'   And
it would be not unnatural (from the circumstances
mentioned before) that Miss Burney would see more
of this side of his character than other people.

Boswell, in the preface to the second edition of

[1] *Miss Burney's Diary*, i, 211.   [2] *Ib.*, i, 231.   [3] *Ib.*, i, 102.

the ' Life,' tells us that the book had been received with favour, that he had obtained a great deal of spontaneous praise, and that Sir Joshua Reynolds lived to give the strongest testimony to its fidelity. These are expressions which he could not use, had they been untrue, in that place ; for they would invite a damaging attack from the reviewers. But a book which upset the popular conception of a figure like Johnson, or even one which merely overdrew the ' shades ' in his character, would hardly have been received like that. And Boswell in fact was never attacked in print for these faults, which, considering what a number of enemies he had, and the disputes in which he was engaged after the publication of the ' Life,' is almost conclusive evidence that his accounts of Johnson's ' awfulness ' corresponded with the observations of other people. Courtenay was a good judge when he wrote the following lines about the ' Tour to the Hebrides ' :

> With Reynolds' pencil, vivid, bold, and true,
> So fervent Boswell gives him to our view :
> In every trait we see his mind expand ;
> The master rises by the pupil's hand.
> We love the writer, praise his happy vein,
> Grac'd with the *naiveté* of the sage Montaigne.
> Hence not alone are brighter parts display'd,
> But e'en the specks of character pourtray'd :
> We *see* the Rambler with fastidious smile . . ."[1]

[1] *Life of Johnson*, ii, 268.

CHAPTER XIII

FOUR years of life remained to Boswell after the publication of the great biography. His death came at
the due moment ; he was not cut off in the midst of
a great undertaking or in the course of an important
development. It is inconceivable that, had he lived,
he would have produced another biography which
should be comparable to the ' Life of Johnson.' An
autobiography he might indeed have written, but
there is no sign that he was engaged upon such a work
in the closing years, or that the idea had taken definite
shape in his mind ; his nature was rather that of the
casual autobiographer, such as we find him in the
' Life ' from time to time, and particularly in the
' Letters to Temple ' ; and it is doubtful whether his
autobiography, if ever it had been written, would have
added much to letters and diaries which were no doubt
in existence, though not preserved for our eyes.[1] The

[1] Boswell's literary executors were Temple, Malone, and Sir
William Forbes. ' The three persons,' says Dr. Rogers, ' nominated
as literary executors did not meet, and the entire business of the
trust was administered by Sir William Forbes, Bart., who appointed
as his law-agent Robert Boswell, Writer to the Signet, cousin-german
of the deceased. By that gentleman's advice Boswell's manuscripts

great labour of his life had been accomplished : and he was allowed a little time longer to see that it was approved by his own generation.

Several questions naturally present themselves when we consider the end of a man's life. Has he been successful ? What is his position in the world ? Do men respect him ? Do they love him ?

Boswell, we had occasion to remark before, had not been, in the ordinary sense, successful. He had always been ambitious ; he had wanted to be 'the great man' ; he had coveted the world's honours ; he would have liked to be busy with the affairs of a nation, or, at the least, to have been reputed a leading barrister. But the glory which fell to the lot of those who governed this country was withheld from Boswell ; in the legal and political spheres he failed. The one post which he obtained, as Recorder of Carlisle—and it was one of no importance—he resigned in 1790, because he could no longer brook the overbearing behaviour of an insolent patron.

Certainly Boswell was far from attaining such fame as he desired ; but at the same time he had a very remarkable success. What then was Boswell's reputation among his contemporaries ?

were left to the disposal of his family, and it is believed that the whole were immediately destroyed. The Commonplace-book escaped, having been accidentally sold among the printed books.'

I believe there is still at Auchinleck the manuscript of a diary and some letters, but I have not been permitted to see them. Undoubtedly Boswell must have left far more than these.

The literary world had welcomed the ' Tour to the Hebrides ' ; men of discrimination had seen that it was a very remarkable book. And yet Boswell's talents won little respect from this performance. It was amazingly indiscreet ; and censure was more readily bestowed upon the author's indiscretion than praise upon his art. It was easy to account for the interest of the book, as Gray and Walpole had accounted for the charm of the ' Tour in Corsica,' by the peculiarities of the writer ; and though to many so shallow an explanation must have been unsatisfactory, it detracted from Boswell's reputation as a man of letters. Moreover, the caricaturists were always busy with Boswell's oddities : the ' Tour to the Hebrides ' provided ample store for the exercise of their wit, and the persistency of their ridicule no doubt hindered the recognition of Boswell's talents. When the ' Life of Johnson ' was published, the subject of Boswell and Johnson had been somewhat played out. A number of ' Lives ' of Johnson had already appeared ; besides Hawkins, Mrs. Thrale, and Murphy, several less known pens had made use of so promising a subject. The public interest in Johnson had begun to wane. The sale of Boswell's ' Life ' was actually rather less rapid than was expected. This was, on the whole, an advantage. The work obtained a less hasty and more serious consideration. Some who would have bought the book five years before, when the subject was fresh, and the expectation to be amused by Boswell was still keen, probably now refrained. Those who bought Boswell's ' Life ' bought it, one may surmise, as the best book about Johnson ; and, to anyone who read it, Boswell's work must have profited by comparison with those who had published before him. No doubt another reason for the graver attitude of the public towards the ' Life ' was that it was less indiscreet than the ' Tour ' ; it provided less capital for those whose trade it was to amuse, and—by comparison—provoked very little ridicule.

Boswell's reputation as a serious writer certainly gained enormously from the ' Life of Johnson.' It gained, in fact, disproportionately. The plan and scope of the ' Life ' are larger than that of the ' Tour ' ; but the earlier book exhibits in their maturity, and equally well, all the qualities for which we most value Boswell.

It was the later work, however, that brought honour to Boswell. The publication of the *magnum opus* in April 1791 led to a distinction which he can hardly have expected. ' In July 1791,' we read in Taylor's ' Life of Reynolds,' ' Boswell to his great delight was appointed Secretary for Foreign Correspondence to the Academy in lieu of Baretti. The newspapers abounded in squibs at his appointment, for Bozzy's weaknesses were favourite game with the small wits.' The announcement, with its double import of respect and ridicule, gives a fair indication of Boswell's reputation among his contemporaries.

It was easy not to respect Boswell ; it was difficult not to love him. He was a 'truly social' man. 'His conversation talents were always pleasing and often fascinating.'[1]   Boswell, in his best form, must have been irresistible. His spirits were tremendous and they were constantly bubbling over. Such spirits are infectious and intoxicating. They are like 'tone' in a violin ; the full resonance, the very robustness of the sound, carries one away. Boswell, it may be said, had 'tone.' His gaiety and good humour were not self-contained, but expanded to others. The mainspring, or whatever it be that works the human being, was particularly powerful and active in his case ; and his companions must have felt it.

The testimony as to his radiating good humour is unanimous. Dr. Rogers in describing his personal appearance says 'his well-set features beamed with perpetual good humour,' and certainly the portraits bear him out. 'It was impossible,' remarked a contemporary, 'to look upon his face without being moved by the comicality which always reigned upon it.'[2]   'It is no wonder,' says his friend John Taylor,

---

[1] The quotation is from a letter, quoted before in these pages, which appeared in the *Gentleman's Magazine* for June 1795 ; it is clearly written by one of Boswell's friends, and the signature 'C.' suggests Courtenay.   Dr. Rogers accepts it as by him.

[2] Quoted in Dr. Rogers's *Memoir* with reference to *Traditions of Edinburgh*, 1869, p. 74.   I have not verified.

' that Mr. Boswell was universally well received. He was full of anecdote, well acquainted with the most distinguished characters, good-humoured, and ready at repartee. There was a kind of jovial bluntness in his manner, which threw off all restraint even with strangers, and immediately kindled a social familiarity.'[1]

Malone, replying to a detractor of Boswell, wrote :

The most important misrepresentation is, that Mr. Boswell was convivial without being *social or friendly* ; a falsehood, which all who knew him intimately, can peremptorily contradict. He had not only an in-exhaustible fund of good-humour and good-nature, but was extremely warm in his attachments, and as ready to exert himself for his friends as any man.

It would be tedious to discuss Boswell's character with reference to his popularity, explaining the various qualities which were or were not attractive in him. A good-natured and affectionate disposition, supported by high spirits, gives the key to many hearts ; and Boswell's lack of dignity, and even his weaknesses, may have endeared him still more, when it was considered that there was nothing low or mean about him.

Popular he certainly was ; he had many acquaint-ances and also a number of very good friends. Boswell, though he was volatile enough in some of his relations with the opposite sex, was very constant in his real

[1] *Records of my Life*, by John Taylor, Esq., 1832, i, 214.

affections. Temple was still his greatest friend at the end of his life. His fidelity to Johnson was remarkable, and surprised his contemporaries ; and he was no less faithful to his other hero, Paoli. The General, indeed, was always very kind to Boswell, especially when he came to live in London after the death of his wife, and Boswell more than once stayed in his house.[1] Reynolds, the most distinguished among Boswell's friends of the Johnsonian circle, is mentioned by Malone as having had ' a very warm regard ' for Boswell.[2] He left him £200 to buy a picture, to be kept for his sake.[3] Charles Dilly was Boswell's friend only for a less time than was Temple ; and Boswell, it appears, was a second host in Dilly's house :

If ever the strict rule of decorum was by chance infringed on, it was on those occasional days when, inevitable business preventing the master of the house from sitting so long with his guests as he could wish, the pleasure of entertaining them was deputed to his kind-hearted and pleasant friend, James Boswell.[4]

Courtenay, Dempster and Sir William Forbes were all old friends, and friends to the last. Forbes was Boswell's literary executor in company with Malone and Temple. Malone's acquaintance with Boswell was

[1] Nichols' *Literary History*, vii, 303–13.
[2] *Gentleman's Magazine*, June, 1795.
[3] *Life of Reynolds*, ii, 636.
[4] Nichols' *Literary Anecdotes*, iii, 192.

more recent ; but his friendship does Boswell more
credit almost than any other. Its ten years began by
Malone correcting the proof-sheets of the ' Tour to the
Hebrides,' and ended by his preparing the third edition
of the ' Life.' His affection for Boswell not only
survived these labours, but grew up with them.[1] Shortly
after Boswell's death he wrote a handsome defence of
Boswell, who had been attacked by a journalist in the
Gentleman's Magazine. Some parts of it have already
been quoted here. Malone knew Boswell at the end
of his life better perhaps than anyone, and the letter
is authoritative as coming from his pen ; it not only
bears testimony to his friendship, but also gives a
valuable estimate of Boswell.

He was ' extremely warm in his attachments,'
Malone tells us. He also pays a striking tribute to
his devotion to Dr. Johnson and his intellectual
abilities :

His fervent attachment to Dr. Johnson at the early
age of three-and-twenty, when the dissipation and
amusements of London hold out to men of such lively
parts as he possessed irresistible attraction, reflects
great credit on his memory. His veneration and
esteem for his friend induced him, at a subsequent
period, to go through the laborious task of arranging
and digesting the immense mass of materials with
which his own diligence and the kindness of his friends
had furnished him ; and of forming his history of the

---

[1] See Nichols' *Literary History*, v, 456–7.

life of that excellent and extraordinary man ; one of the most instructive and entertaining books in the English language. . . . Mr. Boswell undoubtedly possessed considerable intellectual powers, for which he has not had sufficient credit ; many supposing him to be a mere relator of the sayings of others : but it is manifest to every reader of any discernment that he never could have collected such a mass of information and just observation on human life as his very valuable work contains, without great strength of mind and much various knowledge ; as he never could have displayed his collections in so lively a manner as he has done, had he not possessed a very picturesque imagination, or, in other words, had he not had a very happy turn for poetry as well as for humour and for wit.

Mr. Malone ends his letter by paying a final tribute to the affection of Boswell's friends :

He will long be regretted by a wide circle of friends, to whom his good qualities and social talents always made his company a valuable accession ; and by none more sincerely than the present vindicator of his fame.

.   .   .   .   .

Life is commonly somewhat of a battle. Blows are given and received. Flags are lost and won. Positions are captured and surrendered. Limbs are crushed and amputated. There are many ugly wounds ; some bleed and fester ; some are healed. It is natural to look back on life, as the general surveys the battle-field and the hospitals, to count the score. At the end of all the struggle and the horror, the strange joys and the fantastic dreams, what has happened ?   What view does the fighter take himself ?   Was the cause worth struggling for, after all is done ?   Would he fight on the same side if he could start again ?   Would he refrain from fighting ?   Or would he fight with a different object ?   Is the essential man the same ?   Or have his ambitions and desires and the vital force of the man been modified ?   And if so how much ?   Can they be recognised as the same equipment with which he set forth, or has the consuming fire burnt out, and the bright flame grown pale and dim ?

Boswell was not an old man when he died ; and apart from the prostration caused by ill-health—for he was frequently ill towards the close of his life—his robust vigour seems hardly to have diminished. In July 1790, a year after Mrs. Boswell's death, he seems already to entertain some matrimonial scheme.[1] This apparently was the first of a fresh suite.   In the spring of 1791 he is looking forward to the pleasure of meeting a certain Miss Bagnal, ' who may probably have six or seven hundred a year.'   ' Here then I am, my Temple,' exclaims Boswell, ' my flattering self ! A scheme, an adventure, seizes upon my fancy.' Assuredly this is the old Boswell.

In his whole outlook upon life Boswell, in fact, changed very little.   He had failed in the main battle ;

---

[1] *Letters to Temple*, p. 272.

the ambitious dreams which pleased him most had
not come to pass. Neither as politician nor as barrister
had he won the smallest degree of fame. He was, and
is, famous in a rarer sort : yet he had esteemed literary
fame at a much lower rate. And at the end of his life
he still measured distinction by the same old standards.
He felt that the struggle had gone against him : but
he never doubted of the cause for which he was fighting.
As late as August 1791, some months after the 'Life of
Johnson' appeared, he wrote to Temple as though he
were on the eve of a legal career :

I have gone the full round of the Home Circuit,
to which I have returned, finding it much more pleasant,
and, though I did not get a single brief, do not repent
of the expense, as I am showing myself desirous of
business and imbibing legal knowledge.

He still was building castles in the air of the old
type ; still, sometimes, he took an opportunity to be
' conspicuous ' and made conscious efforts to 'be the
great man.' Almost simultaneously with the ' Life,'
he published a political poem, ' No Abolition of Slavery,
or The Universal Empire of Love.' It was of a semi-
frivolous nature, the argument being drawn from a
premise that slavery is the most agreeable of ' goods,'
when it is enforced by the chains of loving devotion.
The name of Miss Bagnal is introduced, and it is
difficult to tell whether the whole may not be an
elaborate attempt to bring off a marriage with that

lady. But it is evident from a remark to Temple, that the main purpose is political :

I am thinking to curtail my poem on the Slave Trade, and throw it into the world just before the great question comes on next Wednesday.

A rumour of war with Russia also rouses the public spirit of Boswell to seek distinction, and he hesitates

whether I should not write one of my characteristical pamphlets on this crisis—An Appeal to the People upon the threatened project of involving this country in a war with Russia, in order to assist the Turks.

At the end of his life Boswell had not deserted his ambition, and, as far as we can tell, he had not forgotten his disappointment. There are few ' Letters to Temple ' during these last few years, and it is difficult to form an exact idea of Boswell's state of mind. For the year 1792 we have only one note of a few lines : it begins, ' Still I cannot write a long letter.' These words suggest, though they do not prove, that Boswell had been in low spirits ; for such a condition was frequently a reason for neglecting to write. For the following year there are three letters. In the first, Boswell refers to the pain it gives him to visit Auchinleck ; in the second, he discusses with remorse his habit of indulgence in wine ; in the third, he says ' My spirits are somewhat better, but by no means right yet.' It is probable that Boswell wrote more regularly in 1794, but only one letter to Temple exists. This, the last letter written in his own hand, is much more cheerful in tone, and concerned more with Temple than with himself. But this alone is no evidence to prove that Boswell at the end of his life was contented with his lot and satisfied with the measure of success he had attained. The reverse is far more likely to be the case. As late as 1791 he had time, in the very throes of publishing the *magnum opus*, to brood over ' the disappointment of my hopes in life.' He clearly suffered from low spirits during the next two years, and it can hardly be supposed that his disappointment, though only one of several causes, had nothing to do with it.

The old standards had not changed. The same weights and measures, which were adopted early in life, still at the end of it were used to determine the deeds of men and fix their value. And yet a change had come. In the ' Letters to Temple ' a certain difference of tone may be distinguished after Boswell lost his wife. It was partly that he began fully to realise the failure of his ambitious plans ; and it was still more a different attitude which that realisation involved. When a man discovers that he cannot get what he wants, he is apt to pay more attention to what he already has.

Though literature did not supply for Boswell the wine of life, it had always attracted him very strongly. He had a taste for books and a very keen desire for learning ; above all, he had literary ambition. He made a number of literary plans besides that of writing Johnson's ' Life.' [1] He was not merely, in his own conception, the biographer of Johnson, but the man of letters in a most extended fashion, and something of a scholar. And it was towards the end of his life, though then concerned almost exclusively with Johnson, that Boswell was most industrious in the literary field. Not only did he publish the *magnum opus* four years before his death, but he continued diligently to collect fresh material. The second edition appeared two years later, in July 1793. The third edition was being prepared, with Malone's valuable help, when Boswell died. The biographer evidently did not consider his labours ended when the ' Life of Johnson ' was at last published. Its favourable reception ' has excited,' he says in the Advertisement to the Second Edition, ' my best exertions to render my Book more perfect ; and in this endeavour I have had the assistance not only of some of my particular friends, but of many other learned and ingenious men, by which I have been able to rectify some mistakes, and to enrich the Work with many valuable additions.'

The scale of Boswell's literary efforts towards the end of his life is the measure of his satisfaction in the performance, and this satisfaction, though it did not

[1] *James Boswell*, by W. K. Leask, p. 155.

take the place of the magnificent pleasure he had imagined in being ' the great man,' and did not cure his
disappointment, must have frequently consoled, and,
in some moods, keenly delighted Boswell. In the
' Life ' he expresses, with a note of triumph, his
satisfaction in the fate of the ' Tour to the Hebrides ' :

To please the true, candid, warm admirers of
Johnson, and in any degree increase the splendour of
his reputation, I bid defiance to the shafts of ridicule,
or even of malignity. Showers of them have been
discharged at my ' Journal of a Tour to the Hebrides ' ;
yet it still sails unhurt along the stream of time, and,
as attendant upon Johnson,

Pursues the triumph, and partakes the gale.

Boswell is equally triumphant about the ' Life ' :

That I was anxious for the success of a Work which
had employed much of my time and labour, I do not
wish to conceal : but whatever doubts I at any time
entertained, have been entirely removed by the
very favourable reception with which it has been
honoured.

It was not merely literary fame that so much
delighted Boswell : it was literary fame of the best
sort. The most respected of Johnson's friends and
the best critics had praised his book. Boswell could
now feel secure in his own conviction that his ' Life '
was beyond comparison as a portrait of a man and as
a portrait of Johnson :

In reflecting that the illustrious subject of this Work, by being more extensively and more intimately known, however elevated before, has risen in the veneration and love of mankind, I feel a satisfaction beyond what fame can afford. . . . It seems to me, in my moments of self-complacency, that this extensive biographical work, however inferior in its nature, may in one respect be assimilated to the Odyssey.

Boswell goes on to explain that the ' Hero,' like Ulysses, ' in the whole course of the History, is exhibited by the authour for the best advantage of his readers.' So certain is he of the merits of his book that he tells his readers, in so many words, that, if they do not like it, their own bad temper is to blame.

Should there be any cold-blooded morose mortals who really dislike this Book, I will give them a story to apply. When the great Duke of Marlborough, accompanied by Lord Cadogan, was one day reconnoitering the army in Flanders, a heavy rain came on and they both called for their cloaks. Lord Cadogan's servant, a good-humoured, alert lad, brought his Lordship's in a minute. The Duke's servant, a lazy sulky dog, was so sluggish, that his Grace being wet to the skin, reproved him, and had for answer, with a grunt, ' I came as fast as I could,' upon which the Duke calmly said, ' Cadogan, I would not for a thousand pounds have that fellow's temper.'

Boswell's satisfaction with his literary labours was certainly well-founded. It is fair to remind those who may condemn this attitude that he allowed an unduly large share of the book's merits to Dr. Johnson.

Interesting and lovable as Johnson was, he had little
to do with Boswell's execution. The biographer was
fortunate—peculiarly fortunate—in his subject : so
much must be allowed and no more. Boswell's pride
did not exceed his deserts. But his 'moments of self-
complacency' must have provided a considerable
compensation for despondent moods when he regretted
failure in other spheres. His 'satisfaction' reached a
very high pitch when he could calmly say to an un-
appreciative reader—for that is what it amounts to—
that he would be sorry to have a temper like that.

It is not remarkable for an author to feel as self-
satisfied as Boswell. Many authors tell their readers,
though not so frankly, that they ought to be interested
in a book, and few give so good reasons as Boswell gave.
The point has been laboured here in order to illustrate
the final stage in his paradoxical development ; to
show in what degree Boswell, while realising failure
in all his magnificent dreams, was satisfied with the
fame he had of another sort. Assuredly he was pleased
with what he had ; the degree may be judged from
this final extract from the Advertisement to the
Second Edition :

There are some men, I believe, who have, or think
they have, a very small share of vanity. Such may
speak of their literary fame in a decorous style of
diffidence. But I confess, that I am so formed by
nature, and by habit, that to restrain the effusion of

delight, on having obtained such fame, to me would be truly painful. Why then should I suppress it ? Why ' out of the abundance of the heart ' should I not speak ? Let me then mention with a warm, but no insolent exultation, that I have been regaled with spontaneous praise of my work by many and various persons eminent for their rank, learning, talents and accomplishments ; much of which praise I have under their hands to be reposited in my archives at Auchinleck. An honourable and reverend friend, speaking of the favourable reception of my volumes, even in the circles of fashion and elegance, said to me, ' You have made them all talk Johnson.'—Yes, I may add, I have *Johnsonised* the land ; and I trust they will not only *talk* but *think* Johnson.

Boswell, after all, had changed very little since the publication of the ' Tour in Corsica ' in his desire for literary fame, but he must have had a very different view of what it meant. In early life this literary ambition was but one aspect of the prevailing idea, to be ' the great man ' ; and he intended to win respect through literature as a wise and honoured ' citizen of the world.' He cannot have retained this delusion after publishing the ' Tour to the Hebrides.' It was in the very month when the ' Life ' appeared that he spoke of ' the disappointment of my hopes of success in life.' There was no thought that the ' Life ' would redeem these hopes. It was to win praise and bring esteem : but not in the same sphere with these ' hopes of success.' Boswell's literary fame compensated his disappointment in some degree, but by no means banished it. His triumphant satisfaction was founded, as is the case with many literary men, upon the merits of literary work and the applause of competent judges.

.   .   .   .   .

Such changes as may be observed in Boswell towards the end of his life arose, it must be repeated, from the failure of his political and legal ambitions. When he ceased to pursue the adventures suggested by his wild imagination, he paid more attention to the natural interests of his position. He was a landlord and a father ; and his children had now no mother. Boswell not only accepted his responsibilities, but performed something more than his duty.

When Boswell had left Auchinleck and came to live in London, his opportunities for interesting himself in the welfare of his tenants and dependants were naturally curtailed. With the strict view of a land-lord's obligations which is commonly held in this age, we may be inclined to condemn Boswell simply on the ground that he did not live upon his estate. But, though Ayrshire is a far cry from London, the Laird of Auchinleck did not forget his position. He was willing to travel to Scotland ' to transact business with my tenants.' On one occasion, in 1793, he undertook the journey in order to see that the parish was provided

with a suitable parson : ' The choice of a minister
to a worthy parish is a matter of importance, and I
cannot be sure of the real wishes of the people without
being present.' He went to Auchinleck not because he
enjoyed going, but because he thought he ought to go :
' though the journey will no doubt be uncomfortable
(probably because Boswell was in bad health), and my
being alone in that house where once I was so happy,
be dreary in a woeful degree, the consciousness of duty,
and being busy, will I hope support me.' In Boswell's
will special provisions were made for his tenants and
servants :

As there are upon the estate of Auchinleck several
tenants whose families have possessed their farms
for many generations, I do by these presents grant
leases for nineteen years and their respective lifetimes
of their present farms to John Templeton etc. . . .
And I do beseech all the succeeding heirs of entail to
be kind to the Tenants and not turn out old possessors
to get a little more rent.

' Seldom,' exclaims Dr. Rogers, 'has Scottish land-
lord evinced greater consideration for his tenantry and
domestics.'

As a father, Boswell was no less kind. He had
had six children altogether, three sons and three
daughters ; [1] one of the sons had died early in 1777.
His interest in his children no doubt increased very

[1] For an account of Boswell's family, see Dr. Rogers in *Boswelliana*, pp. 192–7.

much after their mother's death. Frequently in the 'Letters to Temple' after that event (June, 1789) one or other of them is mentioned, and Boswell shows anxiety both for their present happiness and for their future welfare. Malone, in answering a detractor of Boswell's, says :

This writer acknowledges that he was an affectionate father ; he was more ; he was extremely liberal and indulgent to his children, having, for some years past, expended out of his moderate income, £300 a year to educate his two sons, one at Eton and the other at Westminster, and one of his daughters at a boarding-school : to effect which he confined his own personal expenses within the narrowest bounds.

That Boswell could stint himself in this way for his children shows a larger degree of self-sacrifice than might be expected from one of his extravagant tastes. It shows also a development in his character. The old passion for being conspicuous could now be put aside for the sake of his children.

Boswell, in fact, became less extravagant and affected towards the end of life. He was less often carried away by his 'warm imagination.' He lived less in his 'castles in the air,' and nearer the solid earth.

.   .   .   .   .

The next cause of this development is not far to seek. It lies in the result of the main struggle in Boswell's life. Truth had won the day. The irrepressible quality of Boswell's genius had triumphed in spite of his commonplace aims and the conventionality of his beliefs and standards ; and it had found its expression in biography. The nature of that triumph reacted inevitably upon Boswell. The highest of his qualifications for writing the ' Life of Johnson ' was simply honesty. He was honest about human nature. He had related without omission and without perversion the story of a man as he had witnessed it. All his powers of observing and of judging character had been brought to bear upon the great work of his life. His own character had developed in the process. It is impossible for a man to concentrate all his mind upon the effort to understand the human being, without involving himself in his investigations ; and Boswell was no exception. He had always been interested in his own character, though in a rather uncritical fashion ; and no doubt, as often happens, his knowledge of others began with himself. He was himself both the primer of psychology and the standard for comparison, upon which his whole view of individuals was based ; and it is often clear, when he is discussing some moral question, that he has his own case in mind. The ' Life of Johnson ' was necessarily concerned with Boswell in some degree ; and so it was that the author, when he came to record his observations of Johnson and his friends and acquaintances, found that the process which he applied to others was being applied to himself.

Y

Nothing in Boswell's 'Life of Johnson' is more remarkable, as nothing is more charming, than the author's candour when his own person is concerned. He does not obtrude himself upon the reader's notice ; he relates the events quite naturally as they occurred. And though Boswell was not a little vain, he was able to relate what was not to his credit. Most of the stories of Boswell's folly we know from himself. He has recorded the sledge-hammer blows of Johnson provoked by his own absurdity ; he has told us of occasions when he lacked in manners, even when, more than once, he was drunk in a lady's drawing-room ; he has described at length, in the 'Tour to the Hebrides,' the story of a carouse at Corrichatachin, and has not failed to mention how very ill he felt next morning, and how much he dreaded Johnson's rebuke ; it is in his own account that we read of the ridiculous figure he cut in a storm at sea ; it is from his own correspondence with Johnson that we learn of all the weaknesses that earned the Doctor's reproof.

Boswell was perfectly conscious of his folly when he allowed us to see the absurdity of his behaviour. He was sometimes conscious, at the moment, of provoking ridicule. Occasionally, as he takes care to explain, he deliberately planned his own discomfiture :

Desirous of calling Johnson forth to talk and exercise his wit, though I should myself be the object of it, I resolutely ventured . . .

This was a common attitude.   It has been discussed
before in these pages with reference to Boswell's biographical method.   Boswell even mentions once that
he spoke ' with an assumed air of ignorance, to incite
him to talk, for which it was often necessary to employ
some address.'   He realised well enough that he made
the best possible foil to Johnson.   And if he was able
to understand his position in these undignified moments,
still more must he have been conscious of it when he
allowed his records to be printed many years afterwards in the ' Life.'   He tells us as much himself
in the Dedication to Sir Joshua Reynolds :

In one respect, this Work will, in some passages,
be different from the former.   In my ' Tour,' I was
almost unboundedly open in my communications, and
from my eagerness to display the wonderful fertility
and readiness of Johnson's wit, freely shewed to the
world its dexterity, even when I was myself the object
of it.   I trusted that I should be liberally understood,
as knowing very well what I was about, and by no
means as simply unconscious of the pointed effects of
the satire.   I own, indeed, that I was arrogant enough
to suppose that the tenour of the rest of the book
would sufficiently guard me against such a strange im-
putation.   But it seems I judged too well of the world ;
for, though I could scarcely believe it, I have been
undoubtedly informed, that many persons, especially in
distant quarters, not penetrating enough into Johnson's
character, so as to understand his mode of treating his
friends, have arraigned my judgement, instead of seeing
that I was sensible of all that they could observe.

It is related of the great Dr. Clarke, that when in one of his leisure hours he was unbending himself with a few friends in the most playful and frolicksome manner, he observed Beau Nash approaching ; upon which he suddenly stopped.   ' My boys (said he) let us be grave : here comes a fool.'   The world, my friend, I have found to be a great fool, as to that particular, on which it has become necessary to speak very plainly.   I have, therefore, in this Work been more reserved ; and though I tell nothing but the truth, I have still kept in my mind that the whole truth is not always to be exposed.   This, however, I have managed so as to occasion no diminution of the pleasure which my Book should afford ; though malignity may sometimes be disappointed of its gratifications.

Boswell's statement speaks for itself.   He realised as well as anyone his own vanity and affectation.   It had been necessary when writing Johnson's ' Life ' to apply the searching light of truth indiscriminately. Boswell had not flinched from applying it to himself : on the contrary it amused him to do so.   He enjoyed his own absurdities as he enjoyed those of Johnson himself and of every other figure portrayed with good-humoured ridicule in the course of his great book. Boswell, we may be sure, laughed wherever his readers may laugh : indeed his readers laugh at all only because he himself laughed so whole-heartedly.

Assuredly the laughter which comes when the searching light is turned inwards is not without a lasting effect.   The desire for dignity in some measure

is with most men almost an instinct. It is rare for a
man to perceive that he has been ridiculous without a
blush, even though he smile ; and the result of such
perception is almost invariably preventive ; the
absurdity must not be repeated. Boswell was able
to laugh at himself more whole-heartedly than the
majority. But the mere fact of looking inwards
with the seeing glance was certain to arrest him in
moments of absurdity ; and the necessity, as it
appeared to him, of writing out an account of
himself in the most undignified situations made his
realisation more vivid and the inevitable tendency
more sure.

And so, in the end, the truth of Boswell, his innate
and unquenchable candour, not only won a victory, but
spoiled the enemy. We may observe, if we care to,
that the natural development has taken place. Much
of the old affectation has disappeared. Boswell, to
the last, is still tempted to give rein to that ' warm
imagination ' ; but now as a rule the impulse is checked
with a smile by a moment of self-consciousness.
The development is clearly to be seen in the ' Letters
to Temple,' and one instance will suffice to illustrate
his attitude. Boswell, when telling of his intention
of visiting Auchinleck, for the purpose related before in
these pages of choosing a minister for the parish, cannot
refrain from exclaiming in the old manner, ' Only think,
Temple, how serious a duty I am about to discharge ! '

But then comes the inward glance and Boswell laughs :

I, James Boswell, Esq.—you know what vanity that name includes !—I have promised to come down on purpose, and his Honour's goodness is gratefully acknowledged.

Boswell was not systematic in his self-examination ; but he came to know himself with a truer judgment than most men have where self is concerned. His principles had been ill carried out ; his ideals had not been comprehensive. He had neglected the personal discipline which we look to see in men of power and in men who have accomplished important matters ; he had neglected to train his mind to deal with all the problems of life. His grasp upon the whole scheme of things was feeble, as his control of himself was limited. And yet this knowledge of self with the good-humoured laugh—and it was not unaccompanied by fervent regret for his weakness, and anxious piety— this knowledge, which is the key to all right knowing, was a fitting achievement for one whose predominant interest was Human Nature, and whose prevailing passion was Truth.

INDEX

PRINTED BY
SPOTTISWOODE AND CO. LTD., COLCHESTER
LONDON AND ETON

Z

Biography

Biography

NEW SUPPLEMENT (1901-1911)
of
The Dictionary of National Biography

Edited by Sir SIDNEY LEE, Litt.D., &c.

SECOND SUPPLEMENT, IN THREE VOLUMES.

1,650 Memoirs by 290 Contributors.

Roy. 8vo. 15s. net each volume, in brown or blue cloth ; or in half-morocco, 20s. net.

VOL. I.   ABBEY—EYRE.
VOL. II. FAED—MUYBRIDGE.
VOL. III. NAPIER—YOUNG.

This second Supplement of the Dictionary supplies biographies of all noteworthy persons who died between the day of Queen Victoria's death, 22nd January, 1901 (the limit of the First Supplement) and 31st December, 1911.

SOME PRESS OPINIONS.

Times.—' The remarkable biography of King Edward VII. shows qualities of careful preparation and of judgment.'

Daily Telegraph.—' The biography of the late King written by the Editor reviews the life from every standpoint, and makes a closer personal study of the man and the King than has hitherto been attempted.'

Morning Post.—' The Editor is to be heartily congratulated on the conscientious execution of a delicate but most interesting task.'

Standard.—' A most valuable contribution to the political and constitutional history of the period that lies immediately behind us.'

Manchester Guardian.—' The appearance of the first volume of the Second Supplement is an event of more than usual importance.'

Daily Chronicle.—' The first real, intimate, authoritative account of King Edward.'

London : Smith, Elder & Co., 15 Waterloo Place, S.W.